Y0-CJH-602

¶ Of the *Shrewsbury Edition* of the Works of Samuel Butler seven hundred and fifty numbered sets only have been printed for sale. Of these, numbers one to three hundred and seventy-five are reserved for the British Empire, and numbers three hundred and seventy-six to seven hundred and fifty are reserved for the United States of America.

¶ Set number ~~598.~~ 683

THE SHREWSBURY EDITION OF THE WORKS OF SAMUEL BUTLER. EDITED BY HENRY FESTING JONES AND A. T. BARTHOLOMEW. IN TWENTY VOLUMES. VOLUME NINETEEN: COLLECTED ESSAYS, VOL. II

There I oft great Handel live, imperious still,
Unseen & all impalpable as air,
Yet holding one's living bodies so his will
Effectually as though his fiesh were there.
He who have eyes & ears & sound or sound
All thought or thing in earth or heaven above
From fine & lasterers running along the frame
To Salatan grieving for her love;
From land of piped angel trumpet ringing
To shepherds watching o'er their flocks by night
From the nine muses round Jove Saturn's singing
To youths & maidens dancing for delight.
He'll meet with Jones & me, & clap on him us
Vicariously for having writ Narcissus—

That's the best I can do at present. If you are out with or
coming (which I haven't [illeg.]) you can to post it, as I dare say I
shall so friendly. Love to the Larken ye S.B.

FACSIMILE OF POSTCARD TO H. F. JONES

2nd September 1898

COLLECTED ESSAYS

by

SAMUEL BUTLER

VOL. II

LONDON: JONATHAN CAPE
NEW YORK: E. P. DUTTON & COMPANY
MCMXXV

MADE AND PRINTED IN GREAT BRITAIN AT THE CHISWICK
PRESS BY CHARLES WHITTINGHAM & GRIGGS
(PRINTERS), LTD. AT TOOKS COURT
LONDON   MCMXXV

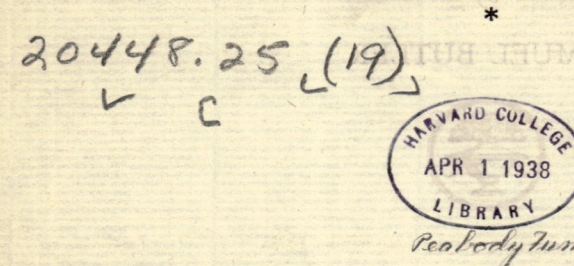

Contents of Vol. II

*THE DEADLOCK IN DARWINISM	1
*THOUGHT AND LANGUAGE	59
*HOW TO MAKE THE BEST OF LIFE	91

*

*QUIS DESIDERIO . . . ?	103
*THE AUNT, THE NIECES, AND THE DOG	115
*RAMBLINGS IN CHEAPSIDE	131

*

PORTRAITS OF GENTILE AND GIOVANNI BELLINI	149
*THE SANCTUARY OF MONTRIGONE	157
L'AFFAIRE HOLBEIN-RIPPEL	171
*A MEDIEVAL GIRL SCHOOL (OROPA)	197
*ART IN THE VALLEY OF SAAS	217

*

*THE HUMOUR OF HOMER	237
WAS THE ODYSSEY WRITTEN BY A WOMAN?	273
THE "WORKS AND DAYS" OF HESIOD TRANSLATED	307

Note. The pieces marked with an asterisk have already appeared in one or both of the collections of Butler's essays brought out by R. A. Streatfeild in 1904 and 1913.

Illustrations

FACSIMILE OF A POST-CARD FROM BUTLER TO JONES
Frontispiece
THE "BELLINI HEADS." FROM THE PAINTING IN THE
LOUVRE *to face p.* 151
THE SANCTUARY OF MONTRIGONE:
  ST. ANNE (CHAPEL OF THE BIRTH OF THE VIRGIN)
to face p. 160
  THE VIRGIN'S GRANDMOTHER (CHAPEL OF THE
BIRTH OF THE VIRGIN) *to face p.* 162
  THE PROPHETESS ANNA (CIRCUMCISION AND PURIFI-
CATION CHAPEL) *to face p.* 166
L'AFFAIRE HOLBEIN-RIPPEL:
  DESIGN BY HOLBEIN FOR PART OF HIS "HAUS ZUM
TANZ," NOW IN THE BERLIN GALLERY *to face p.* 173
  DETAIL FROM THE SAME DESIGN } *between pp.* 174
  THE LEFT-HAND FIGURES OF A DRAWING *and* 175
  IN THE BASLE MUSEUM
  TRACING FROM PHOTOGRAPH OF A FIGURE IN THE
BASLE DRAWING *p.* 175
  TRACING FROM PHOTOGRAPH OF A FIGURE IN THE
BERLIN DRAWING *p.* 175
  INSCRIPTION ON THE BASLE DRAWING (HIS) *p.* 182
  INSCRIPTION ON THE BASLE DRAWING (BURCKHARDT)
p. 182
  DETAILS FROM HOLBEIN'S PASSION SERIES AND FAMILY
OF SIR THOMAS MORE *p.* 189
A MEDIEVAL GIRL SCHOOL (OROPA):
  THE CONVERSATION ROOM (DIMORA CHAPEL) *to face p.* 199
  THE VIRGIN AND HER NURSE (CHAPEL OF THE BIRTH
OF THE VIRGIN) *to face p.* 202
  THE BISHOP'S MITRE (DIMORA CHAPEL) *to face p.* 206
  CENTRAL VIEW OF THE DIMORA CHAPEL *to face p.* 208

THE DEADLOCK IN DARWINISM

NOTE

THESE three articles appeared in 1890 in the April, May, and June issues of *The Universal Review*, and constitute a sort of postscript to Butler's four books on Evolution, viz., *Life and Habit* (1878); *Evolution, Old and New* (1879); *Unconscious Memory* (1880); and *Luck, or Cunning?* (1887). They were reprinted in the two collections of essays edited by R. A. Streatfeild in 1904 and 1913 to which reference has already been made. See also H. F. Jones's *Memoir*, ii, 95-98 and 131-2.

A.T.B.

The Deadlock in Darwinism

PART I[1]

IT WILL BE READILY ADMITTED THAT OF ALL living writers Mr. Alfred Russel Wallace is the one the peculiar turn of whose mind best fits him to write on the subject of natural selection, or the accumulation of fortunate but accidental variations through descent and the struggle for existence. His mind in all its more essential characteristics closely resembles that of the late Mr. Charles Darwin himself, and it is no doubt due to this fact that he and Mr. Darwin elaborated their famous theory at the same time, and independently of one another. I shall have occasion in the course of the following article to show how misled and misleading both these distinguished men have been, in spite of their unquestionable familiarity with the whole range of animal and vegetable phenomena. I believe it will be more respectful to both of them to do this in the most outspoken way. I believe their work to have been as mischievous as it has been valuable, and as valuable as it has been mischievous; and higher, whether praise or blame, I know not how to give. Nevertheless I would in the outset, and with the utmost sincerity, admit concerning Messrs. Wallace and Darwin that neither can be held as the more profound and conscientious thinker; neither can be put forward as the more ready to acknowledge obligation to the great writers on evolution who had preceded him, or to place his own developments in closer and more conspicuous historical connection with earlier thought upon the subject; neither is the more ready to welcome criticism and to state his opponent's case in the most pointed and telling way in which it can be put; neither is the more quick to encourage new truth; neither is the more genial, generous adversary, or has the profounder horror of anything even approaching literary or scientific want of candour; both display the same inimitable power of putting

[1] From *The Universal Review*, April 1890.

their opinions forward in the way that shall best ensure their acceptance; both are equally unrivalled in the tact that tells them when silence will be golden, and when on the other hand a whole volume of facts may be advantageously brought forward. Less than the foregoing tribute both to Messrs. Darwin and Wallace I will not, and more I cannot, pay.

Let us now turn to the most authoritative exponent of latter-day evolution—I mean to Mr. Wallace, whose work, entitled *Darwinism*, though it should have been entitled *Wallaceism*, is still so far Darwinistic that it develops the teaching of Mr. Darwin in the direction given to it by Mr. Darwin himself—so far, indeed, as this can be ascertained at all—and not in that of Lamarck. Mr. Wallace tells us, on the first page of his preface, that he has no intention of dealing even in outline with the vast subject of evolution in general, and has only tried to give such an account of the theory of natural selection as may facilitate a clear conception of Darwin's work. How far he has succeeded is a point on which opinion will probably be divided. Those who find Mr. Darwin's works clear will also find no difficulty in understanding Mr. Wallace; those, on the other hand, who find Mr. Darwin puzzling are little likely to be less puzzled by Mr. Wallace. He continues:

"The objections now made to Darwin's theory apply solely to the particular means by which the change of species has been brought about, not to the fact of that change."

But "Darwin's theory"—as Mr. Wallace has elsewhere proved that he understands—has no reference "to the fact of that change"—that is to say, to the fact that species have been modified in course of descent from other species. This is no more Mr. Darwin's theory than it is the reader's or my own. Darwin's theory is concerned only with "the particular means by which the change of species has been brought about"; his contention being that this is mainly due to the natural survival of those individuals that have happened by some accident to be born most favourably adapted to their surroundings, or, in other words, through accumulation in

The Deadlock in Darwinism

the common course of nature of the more lucky variations that chance occasionally purveys. Mr. Wallace's words, then, in reality amount to this, that the objections now made to Darwin's theory apply solely to Darwin's theory, which is all very well as far as it goes, but might have been more easily apprehended if he had simply said, " There are several objections now made to Mr. Darwin's theory."

It must be remembered that the passage quoted above occurs on the first page of a preface dated March 1889, when the writer had completed his task, and was most fully conversant with his subject. Nevertheless, it seems indisputable either that he is still confusing evolution with Mr. Darwin's theory, or that he does not know when his sentences have point and when they have none.

I should perhaps explain to some readers that Mr. Darwin did not modify the main theory put forward, first by Buffon, to whom it indisputably belongs, and adopted from him by Erasmus Darwin, Lamarck, and many other writers in the latter half of the eighteenth century and the earlier years of the nineteenth. The early evolutionists maintained that all existing forms of animal and vegetable life, including man, were derived in course of descent with modification from forms resembling the lowest now known.

Mr. Darwin went as far as this, and farther no one can go. The point at issue between him and his predecessors involves neither the main fact of evolution, nor yet the geometrical ratio of increase, and the struggle for existence consequent thereon. Messrs. Darwin and Wallace have each thrown invaluable light upon these last two points, but Buffon, as early as 1756, had made them the keystone of his system. " The movement of nature," he then wrote, " turns on two immovable pivots: one, the illimitable fecundity which she has given to all species: the other, the innumerable difficulties which reduce the results of that fecundity." Erasmus Darwin and Lamarck followed in the same sense. They thus admit the survival of the fittest as fully as Mr. Darwin himself, though they do not make use of this particular expression. The dispute turns not upon natural selection, which is common to all writers on evolution, but upon the nature and causes of the variations that are supposed to be selected from and thus accumulated. Are these mainly attributable to the inherited effects of use and disuse, supplemented by occasional sports and happy accidents? Or are they mainly due to sports and happy accidents, supplemented by occasional inherited effects of use and disuse?

The Lamarckian system has all along been maintained by Mr. Herbert Spencer, who, in his *Principles of Biology*, published in 1865, showed how impossible it was that accidental variations should accumulate at all. I am not sure how far Mr. Spencer would consent to being called a Lamarckian pure and simple, nor yet how far it is strictly accurate to call him one; nevertheless, I can see no important difference in the main positions taken by him and by Lamarck.

The question at issue between the Lamarckians, supported by Mr. Spencer and a growing band of those who have risen in rebellion against the Charles-Darwinian system on the one hand, and Messrs. Darwin and Wallace with the greater number of our more prominent biologists on the other, involves the very existence of evolution as a workable theory. For it is plain that what Nature can be supposed able to do by way of choice must depend on the supply of the variations from which she is supposed to choose. She cannot take what is not offered to her; and so again she cannot be supposed able to accumulate unless what is gained in one direction in one generation, or series of generations, is little likely to be lost in those that presently succeed. Now variations ascribed mainly to use and disuse can be supposed capable of being accumulated, for use and disuse are fairly constant for long periods among the individuals of the same species, and often over large areas; moreover, conditions of existence involving changes of habit, and thus of organization, come for the most part gradually; so that time is given during which the organism can endeavour to adapt itself in the requisite respects, instead of being shocked out of

The Deadlock in Darwinism

existence by too sudden change. Variations, on the other hand, that are ascribed to mere chance cannot be supposed as likely to be accumulated, for chance is notoriously inconstant, and would not purvey the variations in sufficiently unbroken succession, or in a sufficient number of individuals, modified similarly in all the necessary correlations at the same time and place to admit of their being accumulated. It is vital therefore to the theory of evolution, as was early pointed out by the late Professor Fleeming Jenkin and by Mr. Herbert Spencer, that variations should be supposed to have a definite and persistent principle underlying them, which shall tend to engender similar and simultaneous modification, however small, in the vast majority of individuals composing any species. The existence of such a principle and its permanence is the only thing that can be supposed capable of acting as rudder and compass to the accumulation of variations, and of making it hold steadily on one course for each species, till eventually many havens, far remote from one another, are safely reached.

It is obvious that the having fatally impaired the theory of his predecessors could not warrant Mr. Darwin in claiming, as he most fatuously did, the theory of evolution. That he is still generally believed to have been the originator of this theory is due to the fact that he claimed it, and that a powerful literary backing at once came forward to support him. It seems at first sight improbable that those who too zealously urged his claims were unaware that so much had been written on the subject, but when we find even Mr. Wallace himself as profoundly ignorant on this subject as he still either is, or affects to be, there is no limit assignable to the ignorance or affected ignorance of the kind of biologists who would write reviews in leading journals thirty years ago. Mr. Wallace writes:

"A few great naturalists, struck by the very slight difference between many of these species, and the numerous links that exist between the most different forms of animals and plants, and also observing that a great many species do vary considerably in their forms, colours and habits, conceived the idea that they might be all produced one from the other. The most eminent of these writers was a great French naturalist, Lamarck, who published an elaborate work, the *Philosophie Zoologique*, in which he endeavoured to prove that all animals whatever are descended from other species of animals. He attributed the change of species chiefly to the effect of changes in the conditions of life—such as climate, food, etc.; and especially to the desires and efforts of the animals themselves to improve their condition, leading to a modification of form or size in certain parts, owing to the well-known physiological law that all organs are strengthened by constant use, while they are weakened or even completely lost by disuse. . . .

" The only other important work dealing with the question was the celebrated *Vestiges of Creation*, published anonymously, but now acknowledged to have been written by the late Robert Chambers."

None are so blind as those who will not see, and it would be waste of time to argue with the invincible ignorance of one who thinks Lamarck and Buffon conceived that all species were produced from one another, more especially as I have already dealt at some length with the early evolutionists in my work *Evolution, Old and New*, first published ten years ago, and not, so far as I am aware, detected in serious error or omission. If, however, Mr. Wallace still thinks it safe to presume so far on the ignorance of his readers as to say that the only two important works on evolution before Mr. Darwin's were Lamarck's *Philosophie Zoologique* and the *Vestiges of Creation*, how fathomable is the ignorance of the average reviewer likely to have been thirty years ago, when the *Origin of Species* was first published? Mr. Darwin claimed evolution as his own theory. Of course, he would not claim it if he had no right to it. Then by all means give him the credit of it. This was the most natural view to take, and it was generally taken. It was not, moreover, surprising that people failed to appreciate all the niceties of Mr. Darwin's

The Deadlock in Darwinism

"distinctive feature" which, whether distinctive or no, was assuredly not distinct, and was never frankly contrasted with the older view, as it would have been by one who wished it to be understood and judged upon its merits. It was in consequence of this omission that people failed to note how fast and loose Mr. Darwin played with his distinctive feature, and how readily he dropped it on occasion.

It may be said that the question of what was thought by the predecessors of Mr. Darwin is, after all, personal, and of no interest to the general public, comparable to that of the main issue—whether we are to accept evolution or not. Granted that Buffon, Erasmus Darwin, and Lamarck bore the burden and heat of the day before Mr. Charles Darwin was born, they did not bring people round to their opinion, whereas Mr. Darwin and Mr. Wallace did, and the public cannot be expected to look beyond this broad and indisputable fact.

The answer to this is, that the theory which Messrs. Darwin and Wallace have persuaded the public to accept is demonstrably false, and that the opponents of evolution are certain in the end to triumph over it. Paley, in his *Natural Theology*, long since brought forward far too much evidence of design in animal organization to allow of our setting down its marvels to the accumulation of fortunate accident, undirected by will, effort, and intelligence. Those who examine the main facts of animal and vegetable organization without bias will, no doubt, ere long conclude that all animals and vegetables are derived ultimately from unicellular organisms, but they will not less readily perceive that the evolution of species without the concomitance and direction of mind and effort is as inconceivable as is the independent creation of every individual species. The two facts, evolution and design, are equally patent to plain people. There is no escaping from either. According to Messrs. Darwin and Wallace, we may have evolution, but are on no account to have it as mainly due to intelligent effort, guided by ever higher and higher range of sensations, perceptions, and ideas. We are to set it down to the shuffling of cards, or the throwing of dice without the play, and this will never stand.

According to the older men, cards did indeed count for much, but play counted for more. They denied the teleology of the time—that is to say, the teleology that saw all adaptation to surroundings as part of a plan devised long ages since by a quasi-anthropomorphic being who schemed everything out much as a man would do, but on an infinitely vaster scale. This conception they found repugnant alike to intelligence and conscience, but, though they do not seem to have perceived it, they left the door open for a design more true and more demonstrable than that which they excluded. By making their variations mainly due to effort and intelligence, they made organic development run on all fours with human progress, and with inventions which we have watched growing up from small beginnings. They made the development of man from the amoeba part and parcel of the story that may be read, though on an infinitely smaller scale, in the development of our most powerful marine engines from the common kettle, or of our finest microscopes from the dew-drop.

The development of the steam-engine and the microscope is due to intelligence and design, which did indeed utilize chance suggestions, but which improved on these, and directed each step of their accumulation, though never foreseeing more than a step or two ahead, and often not so much as this. The fact, as I have elsewhere urged, that the man who made the first kettle did not foresee the engines of the *Great Eastern*, or that he who first noted the magnifying power of the dew-drop had no conception of our present microscopes—the very limited amount, in fact, of design and intelligence that was called into play at any one point—this does not make us deny that the steam-engine and microscope owe their development to design. If each step of the road was designed, the whole journey was designed, though the particular end was not designed when the journey was begun. And so is it, according to the older view of evolution,

The Deadlock in Darwinism

with the development of those living organs, or machines, that are born with us, as part of the perambulating carpenter's chest we call our bodies. The older view gives us our design, and gives us our evolution too. If it refuses to see a quasi-anthropomorphic God modelling each species from without as a potter models clay, it gives us God as vivifying and indwelling in all His creatures—He in them, and they in Him. If it refuses to see God outside the universe, it equally refuses to see any part of the universe as outside God. If it makes the universe the body of God, it also makes God the soul of the universe. The question at issue, then, between the Darwinism of Erasmus Darwin and the neo-Darwinism of his grandson, is not a personal one, nor anything like a personal one. It not only involves the existence of evolution, but it affects the view we take of life and things in an endless variety of most interesting and important ways. It is imperative, therefore, on those who take any interest in these matters, to place side by side in the clearest contrast the views of those who refer the evolution of species mainly to accumulation of variations that have no other inception than chance, and of that older school which makes design perceive and develop still further the goods that chance provides.

But over and above this, which would be in itself sufficient, the historical mode of studying any question is the only one which will enable us to comprehend it effectually. The personal element cannot be eliminated from the consideration of works written by living persons for living persons. We want to know who is who—whom we can depend upon to have no other end than the making things clear to himself and his readers, and whom we should mistrust as having an ulterior aim on which he is more intent than on the furthering of our better understanding. We want to know who is doing his best to help us, and who is only trying to make us help him, or to bolster up the system in which his interests are vested. There is nothing that will throw more light upon these points than the way in which a man behaves towards those who have worked in the same field with him—

self, and, again, than his style. A man's style, as Buffon long since said, is the man himself. By style, I do not, of course, mean grammar or rhetoric, but that style of which Buffon again said that it is like happiness, and *vient de la douceur de l'âme*. When we find a man concealing worse than nullity of meaning under sentences that sound plausibly enough, we should distrust him much as we should a fellow-traveller whom we caught trying to steal our watch. We often cannot judge of the truth or falsehood of facts for ourselves, but we most of us know enough of human nature to be able to tell a good witness from a bad one.

However this may be, and whatever we may think of judging systems by the directness or indirectness of those who advance them, biologists, having committed themselves too rashly, would have been more than human if they had not shown some pique towards those who dared to say, first, that the theory of Messrs. Darwin and Wallace was unworkable; and secondly, that even though it were workable it would not justify either of them in claiming evolution. When biologists show pique at all they generally show a good deal of pique, but pique or no pique, they shunned Mr. Spencer's objection above referred to with a persistency more unanimous and obstinate than I ever remember to have seen displayed even by professional truth-seekers. I find no rejoinder to it from Mr. Darwin himself, between 1865 when it was first put forward, and 1882 when Mr. Darwin died. It has been similarly ostracized [1] by all the leading apologists of Darwinism, so far at least as I have been able to observe, and I have followed the matter closely for many years. Mr. Spencer has repeated and amplified it in his recent work *The Factors of Organic Evolution*, but it still remains without so much as an attempt at serious answer, for the perfunctory and illusory remarks of Mr. Wallace at the end of his *Darwinism* cannot be counted as such. The best proof

---

[1] Butler wrote "ostrichized" and "saw it twice in proof," but it was too much for the printer's reader, and was altered before the article appeared. See p. 39, *post.*—A.T.B.

of its irresistible weight is that Mr. Darwin, though maintaining silence in respect to it, retreated from his original position in the direction that would most obviate Mr. Spencer's objection.

Yet this objection has been repeatedly urged by the more prominent anti-Charles-Darwinian authorities, and there is no sign that the British public is becoming less rigorous in requiring people either to reply to objections repeatedly urged by men of even moderate weight, or to let judgement go by default. As regards Mr. Darwin's claim to the theory of evolution generally, Darwinians are beginning now to perceive that this cannot be admitted, and either say with some hardihood that Mr. Darwin never claimed it, or after a few saving clauses to the effect that this theory refers only to the particular means by which evolution has been brought about, imply forthwith thereafter none the less that evolution is Mr. Darwin's theory. Mr. Wallace has done this repeatedly in his recent *Darwinism*. Indeed, I should be by no means sure that on the first page of his preface, in the passage about "Darwin's theory," which I have already somewhat severely criticized, he was not intending evolution by "Darwin's theory," if in his preceding paragraph he had not so clearly shown that he knew evolution to be a theory of greatly older date than Mr. Darwin's.

The history of science—well exemplified by that of the development theory—is the history of eminent men who have fought against light and have been worsted. The tenacity with which Darwinians stick to their accumulation of fortuitous variations is on a par with the like tenacity shown by the illustrious Cuvier, who did his best to crush evolution altogether. It always has been thus, and always will be; nor is it desirable in the interests of Truth herself that it should be otherwise. Truth is like money—lightly come, lightly go; and if she cannot hold her own against even gross misrepresentation, she is herself not worth holding. Misrepresentation in the long run makes Truth as much as it mars her; hence our law courts do not think it desirable that pleaders should speak their *bona fide* opinions, much less that they should profess to do so. Rather let each side hoodwink judge and jury as best it can, and let truth flash out from collision of defence and accusation. When either side will not collide, it is an axiom of controversy that it desires to prevent the truth from being elicited.

Let us now note the courses forced upon biologists by the difficulties of Mr. Darwin's distinctive feature. Mr. Darwin and Mr. Wallace, as is well known, brought the feature forward simultaneously and independently of one another, but Mr. Wallace always believed in it more firmly than Mr. Darwin did. Mr. Darwin as a young man did not believe in it. He wrote before 1839, " Nature, by making habit omnipotent and its effects hereditary, has fitted the Fuegian for the climate and productions of his country," [1] a sentence than which nothing can coincide more fully with the older view that use and disuse were the main purveyors of variations, or conflict more fatally with his own subsequent distinctive feature. Moreover, as I showed in my last work on evolution,[2] in the peroration to his *Origin of Species*, he discarded his accidental variations altogether, and fell back on the older theory, so that the body of the *Origin of Species* supports one theory, and the peroration another that differs from it *toto coelo*. Finally, in his later editions, he retreated indefinitely from his original position, edging always more and more continually towards the theory of his grandfather and Lamarck. These facts convince me that he was at no time a thoroughgoing Darwinian, but was throughout an unconscious Lamarckian, though ever anxious to conceal the fact alike from himself and from his readers.

Not so with Mr. Wallace, who was both more outspoken in the first instance, and who has persevered along the path of Wallaceism just as Mr. Darwin with greater sagacity was ever on the retreat from Darwinism. Mr. Wallace's profounder faith led him in the outset to place his theory in

[1] *Voyages of the " Adventure " and " Beagle,"* iii, p. 237.
[2] *Luck, or Cunning?* pp. 179-80 [Shrewsbury Edition, pp. 134-5].

The Deadlock in Darwinism

fuller daylight than Mr. Darwin was inclined to do. Mr. Darwin just waved Lamarck aside, and said as little about him as he could, while in his earlier editions Erasmus Darwin and Buffon were not so much as named. Mr. Wallace, on the contrary, at once raised the Lamarckian spectre, and declared it exorcized. He said the Lamarckian hypothesis was "quite unnecessary." The giraffe did not "acquire its long neck by desiring to reach the foliage of the more lofty shrubs, and constantly stretching its neck for this purpose, but because any varieties which occurred among its antitypes with a longer neck than usual at once secured a fresh range of pasture over the same ground as their shorter-necked companions, and on the first scarcity of food were thus enabled to outlive them."[1]

"Which occurred" is evidently "which happened to occur" by some chance of accident unconnected with use and disuse. The word "accident" is never used, but Mr. Wallace must be credited with this instance of a desire to give his readers a chance of perceiving that according to his distinctive feature evolution is an affair of luck, rather than of cunning. Whether his readers actually did understand this as clearly as Mr. Wallace doubtless desired that they should, and whether greater development at this point would not have helped them to fuller apprehension, we need not now inquire. What was gained in distinctness might have been lost in distinctiveness, and after all he did technically put us upon our guard.

Nevertheless, he too at a pinch takes refuge in Lamarckism. In relation to the manner in which the eyes of soles, turbots, and other flat-fish travel round the head so as to become in the end unsymmetrically placed, he says:

"The eyes of these fish are curiously distorted in order that both eyes may be upon the upper side, where alone they would be of any use. . . . Now if we suppose this process, which in the young is completed in a few days or weeks, to

[1] *Journals of the Proceedings of the Linnean Society* (Zoology, vol. iii), 1859, p. 62.

have been spread over thousands of generations during the development of these fish, those usually surviving *whose eyes retained more and more of the position into which the young fish tried to twist them* [italics mine], the change becomes intelligible." [1] When it was said by Professor Ray Lankester—who knows as well as most people what Lamarck taught—that this was "flat Lamarckism," Mr. Wallace rejoined that it was the survival of the modified individuals that did it all, not the efforts of the young fish to twist their eyes, and the transmission to descendants of the effects of those efforts. But this, as I said in my book, *Evolution, Old and New*, is like saying that horses are swift runners, not by reason of the causes, whatever they were, that occasioned the direct line of their progenitors to vary towards ever greater and greater swiftness, but because their more slow-going uncles and aunts go away. Plain people will prefer to say that the main cause of any accumulation of favourable modifications consists rather in that which brings about the initial variations, and in the fact that these can be inherited at all, than in the fact that the unmodified individuals were not successful. People do not become rich because the poor in large numbers go away, but because they have been lucky, or provident, or more commonly both. If they would keep their wealth when they have made it they must exclude luck thenceforth to the utmost of their power and their children must follow their example, or they will soon lose their money. The fact that the weaker go to the wall does not bring about the greater strength of the stronger; it is the consequence of this last and not the cause—unless, indeed, it be contended that a knowledge that the weak go to the wall stimulates the strong to exertions which they would not otherwise so make, and that these exertions produce inheritable modifications. Even in this case, however, it would be the exertions, or use and disuse, that would be the main agents in the modification. But it is not often that Mr. Wallace thus backslides. His present position is that acquired (as distinguished from con-

[1] *Darwinism* (Macmillan, 1889), p. 129.

genital) modifications are not inherited at all. He does not indeed put his faith prominently forward and pin himself to it as plainly as could be wished, but under the heading " The Non-Heredity of Acquired Characters," he writes as follows on p. 440 of his recent work in reference to Professor Weismann's Theory of Heredity:

"Certain observations on the embryology of the lower animals are held to afford direct proof of this theory of heredity, but they are too technical to be made clear to ordinary readers. A logical result of the theory is the impossibility of the transmission of acquired characters, since the molecular structure of the germ-plasm is already determined within the embryo; and Weismann holds that there are no facts which really prove that acquired characters can be inherited, although their inheritance has, by most writers, been considered so probable as hardly to stand in need of direct proof.

"We have already seen in the earlier part of this chapter that many instances of change, imputed to the inheritance of acquired variations, are really cases of selection."

And the rest of the remarks tend to convey the impression that Mr. Wallace adopts Professor Weismann's view, but, curiously enough, though I have gone through Mr. Wallace's book with a special view to this particular point, I have not been able to find him definitely committing himself either to the assertion that acquired modifications never are inherited, or that they sometimes are so. It is abundantly laid down that Mr. Darwin laid too much stress on use and disuse, and a residuary impression is left that Mr. Wallace is endorsing Professor Weismann's view, but I have found it impossible to collect anything that enables me to define his position confidently in this respect.

This is natural enough, for Mr. Wallace has entitled his book *Darwinism*, and a work denying that use and disuse produced any effect could not conceivably be called Darwinism. Mr. Herbert Spencer has recently collected many passages from the *Origin of Species* and from *Animals and*

Plants under Domestication,[1] which show how largely, after all, use and disuse entered into Mr. Darwin's system, and we know that in his later years he attached still more importance to them. It was out of the question, therefore, that Mr. Wallace should categorically deny that their effects were inheritable. On the other hand, the temptation to adopt Professor Weismann's view must have been overwhelming to one who had been already inclined to minimize the effects of use and disuse. On the whole, one does not see what Mr. Wallace could do, other than what he has done—unless, of course, he changed his title, or had been no longer Mr. Wallace.

Besides, thanks to the works of Mr. Spencer, Professor Mivart, Professor Semper, and very many others, there has for some time been a growing perception that the Darwinism of Charles Darwin was doomed. Use and disuse must either do even more than is officially recognized in Mr. Darwin's later concessions, or they must do a great deal less. If they can do as much as Mr. Darwin himself said they did, why should they not do more? Why stop where Mr. Darwin did? And again, where in the name of all that is reasonable did he really stop? He drew no line, and on what principle can we say that so much is possible as effect of use and disuse, but so much more impossible? If, as Mr. Darwin contended, disuse can so far reduce an organ as to render it rudimentary, and in many cases get rid of it altogether, why cannot use create as much as disuse can destroy, provided it has anything, no matter how low in structure, to begin with? Let us know where we stand. If it is admitted that use and disuse can do a good deal, what does a good deal mean? And what is the proportion between the shares attributable to use and disuse and to natural selection respectively? If we cannot be told with absolute precision, let us at any rate have something more definite than the statement that natural selection is " the most important means of modification."

Mr. Darwin gave us no help in this respect; and worse

[1] See *Nature*, 6th March 1890.

The Deadlock in Darwinism

than this, he contradicted himself so flatly as to show that he had very little definite idea upon the subject at all. Thus in respect to the winglessness of the Madeira beetles he wrote:

"In some cases we might easily put down to disuse modifications of structure, which are wholly or mainly due to natural selection. Mr. Wollaston has discovered the remarkable fact that 200 beetles, out of the 550 species (but more are now known) inhabiting Madeira, are so far deficient in wings that they cannot fly; and that of the 29 endemic genera no less than 23 have all their species in this condition! Several facts—namely, that beetles in many parts of the world are frequently blown out to sea and perish; that the beetles in Madeira, as observed by Mr. Wollaston, lie much concealed until the wind lulls and the sun shines; that the proportion of wingless beetles is larger on the exposed Desertas than in Madeira itself; and especially the extraordinary fact, so strongly insisted on by Mr. Wollaston, that certain large groups of beetles, elsewhere excessively numerous, which absolutely require the use of their wings are here almost entirely absent;—these several considerations make me believe that the wingless condition of so many Madeira beetles is mainly due to the action of natural selection, *combined probably with disuse* [italics mine]. For during many successive generations each individual beetle which flew least, either from its wings having been ever so little less perfectly developed or from indolent habit, will have had the best chance of surviving, from not being blown out to sea; and, on the other hand, those beetles which most readily took to flight would oftenest have been blown to sea, and thus destroyed."[1]

We should like to know, first, somewhere about how much disuse was able to do after all, and moreover why, if it can do anything at all, it should not be able to do all. Mr. Darwin says: "Any change in structure and function which can be effected by small stages is within the power of natural selection." "And why not," we ask, "within the power of use

[1] *Origin of Species*, sixth edition, 1888, vol. i, p. 168.

and disuse?" Moreover, on a later page we find Mr. Darwin saying:

"*It appears probable that disuse has been the main agent in rendering organs rudimentary* [italics mine]. It would at first lead by slow steps to the more and more complete reduction of a part, until at last it has become rudimentary—as in the case of the eyes of animals inhabiting dark caverns, and of the wings of birds inhabiting oceanic islands, which have seldom been forced by beasts of prey to take flight, and have ultimately lost the power of flying. Again, an organ, useful under certain conditions, might become injurious under others, *as with the wings of beetles living on small and exposed islands*; and in this case natural selection will have aided in reducing the organ, until it was rendered harmless and rudimentary [italics mine]."[1]

So that just as an undefined amount of use and disuse was introduced on the earlier page to supplement the effects of natural selection in respect of the wings of beetles on small and exposed islands, we have here an undefined amount of natural selection introduced to supplement the effects of use and disuse in respect of the identical phenomena. In the one passage we find that natural selection has been the main agent in reducing the wings, though use and disuse have had an appreciable share in the result; in the other, it is use and disuse that have been the main agents, though an appreciable share in the result must be ascribed to natural selection.

Besides, who has seen the uncles and aunts going away with the uniformity that is necessary for Mr. Darwin's contention? We know that birds and insects do often get blown out to sea and perish, but in order to establish Mr. Darwin's position we want the evidence of those who watched the reduction of the wings during the many generations in the course of which it was being effected, and who can testify that all, or the overwhelming majority, of the beetles born with fairly well developed wings got blown out

[1] *Origin of Species*, sixth edition, 1888, vol. ii, p. 261.

The Deadlock in Darwinism

to sea, while those alone survived whose wings were congenitally degenerate. Who saw them go, or can point to analogous cases so conclusive as to compel assent from any equitable thinker?

Darwinians of the stamp of Mr. Thiselton Dyer, Professor Ray Lankester, or Mr. Romanes, insist on their pound of flesh in the matter of irrefragable demonstration. They complain of us for not bringing forward someone who has been able to detect the movement of the hour-hand of a watch during a second of time, and when we fail to do so, declare triumphantly that we have no evidence that there is any connection between the beating of a second and the movement of the hour-hand. When we say that rain comes from the condensation of moisture in the atmosphere, they demand of us a rain-drop from moisture not yet condensed. If they stickle for proof and cavil on the ninth part of a hair, as they do when we bring forward what we deem excellent instances of the transmission of an acquired characteristic, why may not we, too, demand at any rate some evidence that the unmodified beetles actually did always, or nearly always, get blown out to sea, during the reduction above referred to, and that it is to this fact, and not to the masterly inactivity of their fathers and mothers, that the Madeira beetles owe their winglessness? If we begin stickling for proof in this way, our opponents would not be long in letting us know that absolute proof is unattainable on any subject, that reasonable presumption is our highest certainty, and that crying out for too much evidence is as bad as accepting too little. Truth is like a photographic sensitized plate, which is equally ruined by over and by under exposure, and the just exposure for which can never be absolutely determined.

Surely if disuse can be credited with the vast powers involved in Mr. Darwin's statement that it has probably "been the main agent in rendering organs rudimentary," no limits are assignable to the accumulated effects of habit, provided the effects of habit, or use and disuse, are supposed, as Mr. Darwin supposed them, to be inheritable at all.

Darwinians have at length woke up to the dilemma in which they are placed by the manner in which Mr. Darwin tried to sit on the two stools of use and disuse, and natural selection of accidental variations, at the same time. The knell of Charles-Darwinism is rung in Mr. Wallace's present book, and in the general perception on the part of biologists that we must either assign to use and disuse such a predominant share in modification as to make it the feature most proper to be insisted on, or deny that the modifications, whether of mind or body, acquired during a single lifetime, are ever transmitted at all. If they can be inherited at all, they can be accumulated. If they can be accumulated at all, they can be so, for anything that appears to the contrary, to the extent of the specific and generic differences with which we are surrounded. The only thing to do is to pluck them out root and branch: they are as a cancer which, if the smallest fibre be left unexcised, will grow again, and kill any system on to which it is allowed to fasten. Mr. Wallace, therefore, may well be excused if he casts longing eyes towards Weismannism.

And what was Mr. Darwin's system? Who can make head or tail of the inextricable muddle in which he left it? The *Origin of Species* in its latest shape is the reduction of hedging to an absurdity. How did Mr. Darwin himself leave it in the last chapter of the last edition of the *Origin of Species*? He wrote:

"I have now recapitulated the facts and considerations which have thoroughly convinced me that species have been modified during a long course of descent. This has been effected chiefly through the natural selection of numerous, successive, slight, favourable variations; aided in an important manner by the inherited effects of the use and disuse of parts, and in an unimportant manner—that is, in relation to adaptive structures whether past or present—by the direct action of external conditions, and by variations which seem to us in our ignorance to arise spontaneously. It appears that I formerly underrated the frequency and value of these

The Deadlock in Darwinism

latter forms of variation, as leading to permanent modifications of structure independently of natural selection."

The "numerous, successive, slight, favourable variations" above referred to are intended to be fortuitous, accidental, spontaneous. It is the essence of Mr. Darwin's theory that this should be so. Mr. Darwin's solemn statement, therefore, of his theory, after he had done his best or his worst with it, is, when stripped of surplusage, as follows:

"The modification of species has been mainly effected by accumulation of spontaneous variations; it has been aided in an important manner by accumulation of variations due to use and disuse, and in an unimportant manner by spontaneous variations; I do not even now think that spontaneous variations have been very important, but I used once to think them less important than I do now."

It is a discouraging symptom of the age that such a system should have been so long belauded, and it is a sign of returning intelligence that even he who has been more especially the *alter ego* of Mr. Darwin should have felt constrained to close the chapter of Charles-Darwinism as a living theory, and relegate it to the important but not very creditable place in history which it must henceforth occupy. It is astonishing, however, that Mr. Wallace should have quoted the extract from the *Origin of Species* just given, as he has done on p. 412 of his *Darwinism*, without betraying any sign that he has caught its driftlessness—for drift, other than a desire to hedge, it assuredly has not got. The battle now turns on the question whether modifications of either structure or instinct due to use or disuse are ever inherited, or whether they are not. Can the effects of habit be transmitted to progeny at all? We know that more usually they are not transmitted to any perceptible extent, but we believe also that occasionally, and indeed not infrequently, they are inherited and even intensified. What are our grounds for this opinion? It will be my object to put these forward in the following number of *The Universal Review*.

Collected Essays

II[1]

At the close of my article in last month's number of *The Universal Review*, I said I would in this month's issue show why the opponents of Charles-Darwinism believe the effects of habits acquired during the lifetime of a parent to produce an effect on their subsequent offspring, in spite of the fact that we can rarely find the effect in any one generation, or even in several, sufficiently marked to arrest our attention.

I will now show that offspring can be, and not very infrequently is, affected by occurrences that have produced a deep impression on the parent organism—the effect produced on the offspring being such as leaves no doubt that it is to be connected with the impression produced on the parent. Having thus established the general proposition, I will proceed to the more particular one—that habits, involving use and disuse of special organs, with the modifications of structure thereby engendered, produce also an effect upon offspring, which, though seldom perceptible as regards structure in a single, or even in several generations, is nevertheless capable of being accumulated in successive generations till it amounts to specific and generic difference. I have found the first point as much as I can treat within the limits of this present article, and will avail myself of the hospitality of *The Universal Review* next month to deal with the second.

The proposition which I have to defend is one which no one till recently would have questioned, and even now those who look most askance at it do not venture to dispute it unreservedly; they every now and then admit it as conceivable, and even in some cases probable; nevertheless they seek to minimize it, and to make out that there is little or no connection between the great mass of the cells of which the body is composed, and those cells that are alone capable of reproducing the entire organism. The tendency is to assign to these last a life of their own, apart from, and unconnected

[1] From *The Universal Review*, May 1890.

The Deadlock in Darwinism

with that of the other cells of the body, and to cheapen all evidence that tends to prove any response on their part to the past history of the individual, and hence ultimately of the race.

Professor Weismann is the foremost exponent of those who take this line. He has naturally been welcomed by English Charles-Darwinians; for if his view can be sustained, then it can be contended that use and disuse produce no transmissible effect, and the ground is cut from under Lamarck's feet; if, on the other hand, his view is unfounded, the Lamarckian reaction, already strong, will gain still further strength. The issue, therefore, is important, and is being fiercely contested by those who have invested their all of reputation for discernment in Charles-Darwinian securities.

Professor Weismann's theory is, that at every new birth a part of the substance which proceeds from parents and which goes to form the new embryo is not used up in forming the new animal, but remains apart to generate the germ-cells — or perhaps I should say " germ-plasm "—which the new animal itself will in due course issue.

Contrasting the generally received view with his own, Professor Weismann says that according to the first of these " the organism produces germ-cells afresh again and again, and that it produces them entirely from its own substance." While by the second " the germ-cells are no longer looked upon as the product of the parent's body, at least as far as their essential part—the specific germ-plasm—is concerned; they are rather considered as something which is to be placed in contrast with the *tout ensemble* of the cells which make up the parent's body, and the germ-cells of succeeding generations stand in a similar relation to one another as a series of generations of unicellular organisms arising by a continued process of cell-division."[1]

On another page he writes:

" I believe that heredity depends upon the fact that a small portion of the effective substance of the germ, the

[1] *Essays on Heredity*, etc., Oxford, 1889, p. 171.

germ-plasm, remains unchanged during the development of the ovum into an organism, and that this part of the germ-plasm serves as a foundation from which the germ-cells of the new organism are produced. There is, therefore, continuity of the germ-plasm from one generation to another. One might represent the germ-plasm by the metaphor of a long creeping root-stock from which plants arise at intervals, these latter representing the individuals of successive generations."[1]

Mr. Wallace, who does not appear to have read Professor Weismann's essays themselves, but whose remarks are, no doubt, ultimately derived from the sequel to the passage just quoted from page 266 of Professor Weismann's book, contends that the impossibility of the transmission of acquired characters follows as a logical result from Professor Weismann's theory, inasmuch as the molecular structure of the germ-plasm that will go to form any succeeding generation is already predetermined within the still unformed embryo of its predecessor; "and Weismann," continues Mr. Wallace, "holds that there are no facts which really prove that acquired characters can be inherited, although their inheritance has, by most writers, been considered so probable as hardly to stand in need of direct proof."[2]

Professor Weismann, in passages too numerous to quote, shows that he recognizes this necessity, and acknowledges that the non-transmission of acquired characters "forms the foundation of the views" set forth in his book, p. 291.

Professor Ray Lankester does not commit himself absolutely to this view, but lends it support by saying (*Nature*, 12th December 1889): "It is hardly necessary to say that it has never yet been shown experimentally that *anything* acquired by one generation is transmitted to the next (putting aside diseases)."

Mr. Romanes, writing in *Nature*, 13th March 1890, and opposing certain details of Professor Weismann's theory, so

[1] *Essays on Heredity*, etc., Oxford, 1889, p. 266.
[2] *Darwinism*, 1889, p. 440.

far supports it as to say that "there is the gravest possible doubt lying against the supposition that any really inherited decrease is due to the inherited effects of disuse." The "gravest possible doubt" should mean that Mr. Romanes regards it as a moral certainty that disuse has no transmitted effect in reducing an organ, and it should follow that he holds use to have no transmitted effect in its development. The sequel, however, makes me uncertain how far Mr. Romanes intends this, and I would refer the reader to the article which Mr. Romanes has just published on Weismann in *The Contemporary Review* for this current month.

The burden of Mr. Thiselton Dyer's controversy with the Duke of Argyll (see *Nature*, 16th January 1890, *et seq.*) was that there was no evidence in support of the transmission of any acquired modification. The orthodoxy of science, therefore, must be held as giving at any rate a provisional support to Professor Weismann, but all of them, including even Professor Weismann himself, shrink from committing themselves to the opinion that the germ-cells of any organisms remain in all cases unaffected by the events that occur to the other cells of the same organism, and until they do this they have knocked the bottom out of their case.

From among the passages in which Professor Weismann himself shows a desire to hedge I may take the following from page 170 of his book:

"I am also far from asserting that the germ-plasm which, as I hold, is transmitted as the basis of heredity from one generation to another, is absolutely unchangeable or totally uninfluenced by forces residing in the organism within which it is transformed into germ-cells. I am also compelled to admit it as conceivable that organisms may exert a modifying influence upon their germ-cells, and even that such a process is to a certain extent inevitable. The nutrition and growth of the individual must exercise some influence upon its germ-cells . . ."

Professor Weismann does indeed go on to say that this influence must be extremely slight, but we do not care how slight the changes produced may be, provided they exist and can be transmitted. On an earlier page (p. 101) he said in regard to variations generally that we should not expect to find them conspicuous; their frequency would be enough, if they could be accumulated. The same applies here, if stirring events that occur to the somatic cells can produce any effect at all on offspring. A very small effect, provided it can be repeated and accumulated in successive generations, is all that even the most exacting Lamarckian will ask for.

Having now made the reader acquainted with the position taken by the leading Charles-Darwinian authorities, I will return to Professor Weismann himself, who declares that the transmission of acquired characters " at first sight certainly seems necessary," and that " it appears rash to attempt to dispense with its aid." He continues:

" Many phenomena only appear to be intelligible if we assume the hereditary transmission of such acquired characters as the changes which we ascribe to the use or disuse of particular organs, or to the direct influence of climate. Furthermore, how can we explain instinct as hereditary habit, unless it has gradually arisen by the accumulation, through heredity, of habits which were practised in succeeding generations?"[1]

I may say in passing that Professor Weismann appears to suppose that the view of instinct just given is part of the Charles-Darwinian system, for on page 389 of his book he says " that many observers had followed Darwin in explaining them [instincts] as inherited habits." This was not Mr. Darwin's own view of the matter. He wrote:

" If we suppose any habitual action to become inherited—and I think it can be shown that this does sometimes happen—then the resemblance between what originally was a habit and an instinct becomes so close as not to be distinguished. . . . But it would be the most serious error to suppose that the greater number of instincts have been acquired by habit in one generation, and then transmitted by inheritance to

[1] Page 83.

The Deadlock in Darwinism

succeeding generations. It can be clearly shown that the most wonderful instincts with which we are acquainted, namely, those of the hive-bee and of many ants, could not possibly have been thus acquired." (*Origin of Species*, ed. 1859, p. 209.)

Again we read: "Domestic instincts are sometimes spoken of as actions which have become inherited solely from long-continued and compulsory habit, but this, I think, is not true." (*Ibid.*, p. 214.)

Again: "I am surprised that no one has advanced this demonstrative case of neuter insects, against the well-known doctrine of inherited habit, as advanced by Lamarck." (*Ibid.*, ed. 1872, p. 233.)

I am not aware that Lamarck advanced the doctrine that instinct is inherited habit, but he may have done so in some work that I have not seen.

It is true, as I have more than once pointed out, that in the later editions of the *Origin of Species* it is no longer " the *most* serious " error to refer instincts generally to inherited habit, but it still remains " a serious error," and this slight relaxation of severity does not warrant Professor Weismann in ascribing to Mr. Darwin an opinion which he emphatically condemned. His tone, however, is so off-hand, that those who have little acquaintance with the literature of evolution would hardly guess that he is not much better informed on this subject than themselves.

Returning to the inheritance of acquired characters, Professor Weismann says that this has never been proved either by means of direct observation or by experiment. " It must be admitted," he writes, " that there are in existence numerous descriptions of cases which tend to prove that such mutilations as the loss of fingers, the scars of wounds, etc., are inherited by the offspring, but in these descriptions the previous history is invariably obscure, and hence the evidence loses all scientific value."

The experiments of M. Brown-Séquard throw so much light upon the question at issue that I will quote at some length from the summary given by Mr. Darwin in his *Variations of Animals and Plants under Domestication*.[1] Mr. Darwin writes:

"With respect to the inheritance of structures mutilated by injuries or altered by disease, it was until lately difficult to come to any definite conclusion." [Then follow several cases in which mutilations practised for many generations are not found to be transmitted.] "Notwithstanding," continues Mr. Darwin, "the above several negative cases, we now possess conclusive evidence that the effects of operations are sometimes inherited. Dr. Brown-Séquard gives the following summary of his observations on guinea-pigs, and this summary is so important that I will quote the whole:

"'1st. Appearance of epilepsy in animals born of parents having been rendered epileptic by an injury to the spinal cord.

"'2nd. Appearance of epilepsy also in animals born of parents having been rendered epileptic by the section of the sciatic nerve.

"'3rd. A change in the shape of the ear in animals born of parents in which such a change was the effect of a division of the cervical sympathetic nerve.

"'4th. Partial closure of the eyelids in animals born of parents in which that state of the eyelids had been caused either by the section of the cervical sympathetic nerve or the removal of the superior cervical ganglion.

"'5th. Exophthalmia in animals born of parents in which an injury to the restiform body had produced that protrusion of the eyeball. This interesting fact I have witnessed a good many times, and I have seen the transmission of the morbid state of the eye continue through four generations. In these animals modified by heredity, the two eyes generally protruded, although in the parents usually only one showed exophthalmia, the lesion having been made in most cases only on one of the corpora restiformia.

"'6th. Haematoma and dry gangrene of the ears in

[1] Vol. i, p. 466, etc. Ed. 1885.

animals born of parents in which these ear-alterations had been caused by an injury to the restiform body near the nib of the calamus.

"'7th. Absence of two toes out of the three of the hind leg, and sometimes of the three, in animals whose parents had eaten up their hind-leg toes which had become anaesthetic from a section of the sciatic nerve alone, or of that nerve and also of the crural. Sometimes, instead of complete absence of the toes, only a part of one or two or three was missing in the young, although in the parent not only the toes but the whole foot was absent (partly eaten off, partly destroyed by inflammation, ulceration, or gangrene).

"'8th. Appearance of various morbid states of the skin and hair of the neck and face in animals born of parents having had similar alterations in the same parts, as effects of an injury to the sciatic nerve.'

"It should be especially observed that Brown-Séquard had bred during thirty years many thousand guinea-pigs from animals which had not been operated upon, and not one of these manifested the epileptic tendency. Nor has he ever seen a guinea-pig born without toes, which was not the offspring of parents which had gnawed off their own toes owing to the sciatic nerve having been divided. Of this latter fact thirteen instances were carefully recorded, and a greater number were seen; yet Brown-Séquard speaks of such cases as one of the rarer forms of inheritance. It is a still more interesting fact, 'that the sciatic nerve in the congenitally toeless animal has inherited the power of passing through all the different morbid states which have occurred in one of its parents from the time of the division till after its reunion with the peripheric end. It is not, therefore, simply the power of performing an action which is inherited, but the power of performing a whole series of actions, in a certain order.'

"In most of the cases of inheritance recorded by Brown-Séquard only one of the two parents had been operated upon and was affected. He concludes by expressing his belief that 'what is transmitted is the morbid state of the nervous system,' due to the operation performed on the parents."

Mr. Darwin proceeds to give other instances of inherited effects of mutilations:

"With the horse there seems hardly a doubt that exostoses on the legs, caused by too much travelling on hard roads, are inherited. Blumenbach records the case of a man who had his little finger on the right hand almost cut off, and which in consequence grew crooked, and his sons had the same finger on the same hand similarly crooked. A soldier, fifteen years before his marriage, lost his left eye from purulent ophthalmia, and his two sons were microphthalmic on the same side."

The late Professor Rolleston, whose competence as an observer no one is likely to dispute, gave Mr. Darwin two cases as having fallen under his own notice, one of a man whose knee had been severely wounded, and whose child was born with the same spot marked or scarred, and the other of one who was severely cut upon the cheek, and whose child was born scarred in the same place. Mr. Darwin's conclusion was that "the effects of injuries, especially when followed by disease, or perhaps exclusively when thus followed, are occasionally inherited."

Let us now see what Professor Weismann has to say against this. He writes:

"The only cases worthy of discussion are the well-known experiments upon guinea-pigs conducted by the French physiologist, Brown-Séquard. But the explanation of his results is, in my opinion, open to discussion. In these cases we have to do with the apparent transmission of artificially produced malformations. . . . All these effects were said to be transmitted to descendants as far as the fifth or sixth generation.

"But we must inquire whether these cases are really due to heredity, and not to simple infection. In the case of epilepsy, at any rate, it is easy to imagine that the passage of some specific organism through the reproductive cells may take place, as in the case of syphilis. We are, however, entirely ignorant of the nature of the former disease. This suggested explanation may not perhaps apply to the other cases; but we must remember that animals which have been subjected to such severe operations upon the nervous system have sustained a great shock, and if they are capable of breeding, it is only probable that they will produce weak descendants, and such as are easily affected by disease. Such a result does not, however, explain why the offspring should suffer from the same disease as that which was artificially induced in the parents. But this does not appear to have been by any means invariably the case. Brown-Séquard himself says: 'The changes in the eye of the offspring were of a very variable nature, and were only occasionally exactly similar to those observed in the parents.'

"There is no doubt, however, that these experiments demand careful consideration, but before they can claim scientific recognition, they must be subjected to rigid criticism as to the precautions taken, the nature and number of the control experiments, etc.

"Up to the present time such necessary conditions have not been sufficiently observed. The recent experiments themselves are only described in short preliminary notices, which, as regards their accuracy, the possibility of mistake, the precautions taken, and the exact succession of individuals affected, afford no data on which a scientific opinion can be founded" (pp. 81, 82).

The line Professor Weismann takes, therefore, is to discredit the facts; yet on a later page we find that the experiments have since been repeated by Obersteiner, "who has described them in a very exact and unprejudiced manner," and that "the fact"—(I imagine that Professor Weismann intends "the facts")—"cannot be doubted."

On a still later page, however, we read:

"If, for instance, it could be shown that artificial mutilation spontaneously reappears in the offspring with sufficient frequency to exclude all possibilities of chance, then such proof [*i.e.*, that acquired characters can be transmitted] would be forthcoming. The transmission of mutilations has been frequently asserted, and has been even recently again brought forward, but all the supposed instances have broken down when carefully examined " (p. 390).

Here, then, we are told that proof of the occasional transmission of mutilations would be sufficient to establish the fact, but on p. 267 we find that no single fact is known which really proves that acquired characters can be transmitted, "*for the ascertained facts which seem to point to the transmission of artificially produced diseases cannot be considered as proof.*" [Italics mine.] Perhaps; but it was mutilation in many cases that Professor Weismann practically admitted to have been transmitted when he declared that Obersteiner had verified Brown-Séquard's experiments.

That Professor Weismann recognizes the vital importance to his own theory of the question whether or no mutilations can be transmitted under any circumstances, is evident from a passage on p. 425 of his work, on which he says: " It can hardly be doubted that mutilations are acquired characters; they do not arise from any tendency contained in the germ, but are merely the reaction of the body under certain external influences. They are, as I have recently expressed it, purely somatogenic characters—viz., characters which emanate from the body (*soma*) only, as opposed to the germ-cells; they are, therefore, characters that do not arise from the germ itself.

" If mutilations must necessarily be transmitted " [which no one that I know of has maintained], " or even if they might occasionally be transmitted " [which cannot, I imagine, be reasonably questioned], " a powerful support would be given to the Lamarckian principle, and the transmission of functional hypertrophy or atrophy would thus become highly probable."

I have not found any further attempt in Professor Weismann's book to deal with the evidence adduced by Mr. Darwin to show that mutilations, if followed by diseases, are sometimes inherited; and I must leave it to the reader to determine how far Professor Weismann has shown reason for rejecting Mr. Darwin's conclusion. I do not, however, dwell upon these facts now as evidence of a transmitted change of bodily form, or of instinct due to use and disuse or habit; what they prove is that the germ-cells within the parent's body do not stand apart from the other cells of the body so completely as Professor Weismann would have us believe, but that, as Professor Hering, of Prague, has aptly said, they echo with more or less frequency and force to the profounder impressions made upon other cells.

I may say that Professor Weismann does not more cavalierly wave aside the mass of evidence collected by Mr. Darwin and a host of other writers, to the effect that mutilations are sometimes inherited, than does Mr. Wallace, who says that, "as regards mutilations, it is generally admitted that they are not inherited, and there is ample evidence on this point." It is indeed generally admitted that mutilations, when not followed by disease, are very rarely, if ever, inherited; and Mr. Wallace's appeal to the "ample evidence" which he alleges to exist on this head, is much as though he should say that there is ample evidence to show that the days are longer in summer than in winter. "Nevertheless," he continues, "a few cases of apparent inheritance of mutilations have been recorded, and these, if trustworthy, are difficulties in the way of the theory." ... "The often-quoted case of a disease induced by mutilation being inherited (Brown-Séquard's epileptic guinea-pigs) has been discussed by Professor Weismann and shown to be not conclusive. The mutilation itself—a section of certain nerves—was never inherited, but the resulting epilepsy, or a general state of weakness, deformity, or sores, was sometimes inherited. It is, however, possible that the mere injury introduced and encouraged the growth of certain microbes, which, spreading through the organism, sometimes reached the germ-cells, and thus transmitted a diseased condition to the offspring."[1]

[1] *Darwinism*, p. 440.

I suppose a microbe which made guinea-pigs eat their toes off was communicated to the germ-cells of an unfortunate guinea-pig which had been already microbed by it, and made the offspring bite its toes off too. The microbe has a good deal to answer for.

On the case of the deterioration of horses in the Falkland Islands after a few generations, Professor Weismann says:

"In such a case we have only to assume that the climate which is unfavourable, and nutriment which is insufficient for horses, affect not only the animal as a whole but also its germ-cells. This would result in the diminution in size of the germ-cells, the effects upon the offspring being still further intensified by the insufficient nourishment supplied during growth. But such results would not depend upon the transmission by the germ-cells of certain peculiarities due to the unfavourable climate, which only appear in the full-grown horse."

But Professor Weismann does not like such cases, and admits that he cannot explain the facts in connection with the climatic varieties of certain butterflies, except "by supposing the passive acquisition of characters produced by the direct influence of climate."

Nevertheless, in his next paragraph but one he calls such cases "doubtful," and proposes that for the moment they should be left aside. He accordingly leaves them, but I have not yet found what other moment he considered auspicious for returning to them. He tells us that "new experiments will be necessary, and that he has himself already begun to undertake them." Perhaps he will give us the results of these experiments in some future book—for that they will prove satisfactory to him can hardly, I think, be doubted. He writes:

"Leaving on one side, for the moment, these doubtful and insufficiently investigated cases, we may still maintain that the assumption that changes induced by external conditions in the organism as a whole are communicated to the germ-cells after the manner indicated in Darwin's hypothesis of pangenesis, is wholly unnecessary for the explanation of these phenomena. Still we cannot exclude the possibility of such a transmission occasionally occurring, for even if the greater part of the effects must be attributable to natural selection, there might be a smaller part in certain cases which depends on this exceptional factor."

I repeatedly tried to understand Mr. Darwin's theory of pangenesis, and so often failed that I long since gave the matter up in despair. I did so with the less unwillingness because I saw that no one else appeared to understand the theory, and that even Mr. Darwin's warmest adherents regarded it with disfavour. If Mr. Darwin means that every cell of the body throws off minute particles that find their way to the germ-cells, and hence into the new embryo, this is indeed difficult of comprehension and belief. If he means that the rhythms or vibrations that go on ceaselessly in every cell of the body communicate themselves with greater or less accuracy or perturbation, as the case may be, to the cells that go to form offspring, and that since the characteristics of matter are determined by vibrations, in communicating vibrations they in effect communicate matter, according to the view put forward in the last chapter of my book *Luck, or Cunning?*, then we can better understand it. I have nothing, however, to do with Mr. Darwin's theory of pangenesis beyond avoiding the pretence that I understand either the theory itself or what Professor Weismann says about it; all I am concerned with is Professor Weismann's admission, made immediately afterwards, that the somatic cells may, and perhaps sometimes do, impart characteristics to the germ-cells.

"A complete and satisfactory refutation of such an opinion," he continues, " cannot be brought forward at present "; so I suppose we must wait a little longer, but in the meantime we may again remark that, if we admit even occasional communication of changes in the somatic cells to the germ-cells, we have let in the thin end of the wedge, as Mr. Darwin did when he said that use and disuse did a good deal towards modification. Buffon, in his first volume on the lower animals,[1] dwells on the impossibility of stopping the breach once made by admission of variation at all. " If the point," he writes, " were once gained, that among animals and vegetables there had been, I do not say several species, but even a single one, which had been produced in the course of direct descent from another species; if, for example, it could be once shown that the ass was but a degeneration from the horse—then there is no farther limit to be set to the power of Nature, and we should not be wrong in supposing that with sufficient time she could have evolved all other organized forms from one primordial type." So with use and disuse and transmission of acquired characteristics generally—once show that a single structure or instinct is due to habit in preceding generations, and we can impose no limit on the results achievable by accumulation in this respect, nor shall we be wrong in conceiving it as possible that all specialization, whether of structure or instinct, may be due ultimately to habit.

How far this can be shown to be probable is, of course, another matter, but I am not immediately concerned with this; all I am concerned with now is to show that the germ-cells not unfrequently become permanently affected by events that have made a profound impression upon the somatic cells, in so far that they transmit an obvious reminiscence of the impression to the embryos which they go subsequently towards forming. This is all that is necessary for my case, and I do not find that Professor Weismann, after all, disputes it.

But here, again, comes the difficulty of saying what Professor Weismann does, and what he does not, dispute. One moment he gives all that is wanted for the Lamarckian contention, the next he denies common sense the bare necessaries of life. For a more exhaustive and detailed criticism of Professor Weismann's position, I would refer the reader to an admirably clear article by Mr. Sydney H. Vines, which

[1] Tom. iv, p. 383. Ed. 1753.

The Deadlock in Darwinism

appeared in *Nature*, 24th October 1889. I can only say that while reading Professor Weismann's book, I feel as I do when I read those of Mr. Darwin, and of a good many other writers on biology whom I need not name. I become like a fly in a window-pane. I see the sunshine and freedom beyond, and buzz up and down their pages, ever hopeful to get through them to the fresh air without, but ever kept back by a mysterious something, which I feel but cannot either grasp or see. It was not thus when I read Buffon, Erasmus Darwin, and Lamarck; it is not thus when I read such articles as Mr. Vines's just referred to. Love of self-display, and the want of singleness of mind that it inevitably engenders—these, I suppose, are the sins that glaze the casements of most men's minds; and from these, no matter how hard he tries to free himself, nor how much he despises them, who is altogether exempt?

Finally, then, when we consider the immense mass of evidence referred to briefly, but sufficiently, by Mr. Charles Darwin, and referred to without other, for the most part, than off-hand dismissal by Professor Weismann in the last of the essays that have been recently translated, I do not see how anyone who brings an unbiassed mind to the question can hesitate as to the side on which the weight of testimony inclines. Professor Weismann declares that "the transmission of mutilations may be dismissed into the domain of fable."[1] If so, then, whom can we trust? What is the use of science at all if the conclusions of a man as competent as I readily admit Mr. Darwin to have been, on the evidence laid before him from countless sources, is to be set aside lightly and without giving the clearest and most cogent explanation of the why and wherefore? When we see a person "ostrichizing"[2]—if this time the printer will allow me to say so—the evidence which he has to meet, as clearly as I believe Professor Weismann to be doing, we shall in nine cases out of ten be right in supposing that he knows the evidence to be too strong for him.

[1] *Essays*, etc., p. 447.   [2] [See p. 12, *ante*.]

Collected Essays

III[1]

Now let me return to the recent division of biological opinion into two main streams—Lamarckism and Weismannism. Both Lamarckians and Weismannists, not to mention mankind in general, admit that the better adapted to its surroundings a living form may be, the more likely it is to outbreed its compeers. The world at large, again, needs not to be told that the normal course is not unfrequently deflected through the fortunes of war; nevertheless, according to Lamarckians and Erasmus-Darwinians, habitual effort, guided by ever-growing intelligence—that is to say, by continued increase of power in the matter of knowing our likes and dislikes—has been so much the main factor throughout the course of organic development, that the rest, though not lost sight of, may be allowed to go without saying. According, on the other hand, to extreme Charles-Darwinians and Weismannists, habit, effort and intelligence acquired during the experience of any one life goes for nothing. Not even a little fraction of it endures to the benefit of offspring. It dies with him in whom it is acquired, and the heirs of a man's body take no interest therein. To state this doctrine is to arouse instinctive loathing; it is my fortunate task to maintain that such a nightmare of waste and death is as baseless as it is repulsive.

The split in biological opinion occasioned by the deadlock to which Charles-Darwinism has been reduced, though comparatively recent, widens rapidly. Ten years ago Lamarck's name was mentioned only as a byword for extravagance; now, we cannot take up a number of *Nature* without seeing how hot the contention is between his followers and those of Weismann. This must be referred, as I implied earlier, to growing perception that Mr. Darwin should either have gone farther towards Lamarckism or not so far. In admitting use and disuse as freely as he did, he gave Lamarckians leverage for the overthrow of a system based

[1] From *The Universal Review*, June 1890.

The Deadlock in Darwinism

ostensibly on the accumulation of fortunate accidents. In assigning the lion's share of development to the accumulation of fortunate accidents, he tempted fortuitists to try to cut the ground from under Lamarck's feet by denying that the effects of use and disuse can be inherited at all. When the public had once got to understand what Lamarck had intended, and wherein Mr. Charles Darwin had differed from him, it became impossible for Charles-Darwinians to remain where they were, nor is it easy to see what course was open to them except to cast about for a theory by which they could get rid of use and disuse altogether. Weismannism, therefore, is the inevitable outcome of the straits to which Charles-Darwinians were reduced through the way in which their leader had halted between two opinions.

This is why Charles-Darwinians, from Professor Huxley downwards, have kept the difference between Lamarck's opinions and those of Mr. Darwin so much in the background. Unwillingness to make this understood is nowhere manifested more clearly than in Dr. Francis Darwin's life of his father. In this work Lamarck is sneered at once or twice and told to go away, but there is no attempt to state the two cases side by side; from which, as from not a little else, I conclude that Dr. Francis Darwin has descended from his father with singularly little modification.

Proceeding to the evidence for the transmissions of acquired habits, I will quote two recently adduced examples from among the many that have been credibly attested. The first was contributed to *Nature* (14th March 1889) by Professor Marcus M. Hartog, who wrote:

"A. B. is moderately myopic and very astigmatic in the left eye; extremely myopic in the right. As the left eye gave such bad images for near objects, he was compelled in childhood to mask it, and acquired the habit of leaning his head on his left arm for writing, so as to blind that eye, or of resting the left temple and eye on the hand, with the elbow on the table. At the age of fifteen the eyes were equalized by the use of suitable spectacles, and he soon lost the habit completely and permanently. He is now the father of two children, a boy and a girl, whose vision (tested repeatedly and fully) is emmetropic in both eyes, so that they have not inherited the congenital optical defect of their father. All the same, they have both of them inherited his early acquired habit, and need constant watchfulness to prevent their hiding the left eye when writing, by resting the head on the left forearm or hand. Imitation is here quite out of the question.

"Considering that every habit involves changes in the proportional development of the muscular and osseous systems, and hence probably of the nervous system also, the importance of inherited habits, natural or acquired, cannot be overlooked in the general theory of inheritance. I am fully aware that I shall be accused of flat Lamarckism, but a nickname is not an argument."

To this Professor Ray Lankester rejoined (*Nature*, 21st March 1889):

"It is not unusual for children to rest the head on the left forearm or hand when writing, and I doubt whether much value can be attached to the case described by Professor Hartog. The kind of observation which his letter suggests is, however, likely to lead to results either for or against the transmission of acquired characters. An old friend of mine lost his right arm when a schoolboy, and has ever since written with his left. He has a large family and grandchildren, but I have not heard of any of them showing a disposition to left-handedness."

From *Nature* (21st March 1889) I take the second instance communicated by Mr. J. Jenner-Weir, who wrote as follows:

"Mr. Marcus M. Hartog's letter of 6th March, inserted in last week's number (p. 462), is a very valuable contribution to the growing evidence that acquired characters may be inherited. I have long held the view that such is often the case, and I have myself observed several instances of the, at least I may say, apparent fact.

"Many years ago there was a very fine male of the *Capra*

The Deadlock in Darwinism

megaceros in the gardens of the Zoological Society. To restrain this animal from jumping over the fence of the enclosure in which he was confined, a long and heavy chain was attached to the collar round his neck. He was constantly in the habit of taking this chain up by his horns and moving it from one side to another over his back; in doing this he threw his head very much back, his horns being placed in a line with the back. The habit had become quite chronic with him, and was very tiresome to look at. I was very much astonished to observe that his offspring inherited the habit, and although it was not necessary to attach a chain to their necks, I have often seen a young male throwing his horns over his back and shifting from side to side an imaginary chain. The action was exactly the same as that of his ancestor. The case of the kid of this goat appears to me to be parallel to that of child and parent given by Mr. Hartog. I think at the time I made this observation I informed Mr. Darwin of the fact by letter, and he did not accuse me of 'flat Lamarckism.'"

To this letter there was no rejoinder. It may be said, of course, that the action of the offspring in each of these cases was due to accidental coincidence only. Anything can be said, but the question turns not on what an advocate can say, but on what a reasonably intelligent and disinterested jury will believe; granted they might be mistaken in accepting the foregoing stories, but the world of science, like that of commerce, is based on the faith or confidence which both creates and sustains them. Indeed the universe itself is but the creature of faith, for assuredly we know of no other foundation. There is nothing so generally and reasonably accepted—not even our own continued identity—but questions may be raised about it that will shortly prove unanswerable. We cannot so test every sixpence given us in change as to be sure that we never take a bad one, and had better sometimes be cheated than reduce caution to an absurdity. Moreover, we have seen from the evidence given in my preceding article that the germ-cells issuing from a parent's body can, and do, respond to profound impressions made on the somatic cells. This being so, what impressions are more profound, what needs engage more assiduous attention than those connected with self-protection, the procuring of food, and the continuation of the species? If the mere anxiety connected with an ill-healing wound inflicted on but one generation is sometimes found to have so impressed the germ-cells that they hand down its scars to offspring, how much more shall not anxieties that have directed action of all kinds from birth till death, not in one generation only but in a longer series of generations than the mind can realize to itself, modify, and indeed control, the organization of every species?

I see Professor S. H. Vines, in the article on Weismann's theory referred to in my preceding article, says Mr. Darwin "held that it was not the sudden variations due to altered external conditions which become permanent, but those slowly produced by what he termed 'the accumulative action of changed conditions of life.'" Nothing can be more soundly Lamarckian, and nothing should more conclusively show that, whatever else Mr. Darwin was, he was not a Charles-Darwinian; but what evidence other than inferential can from the nature of the case be adduced in support of this, as I believe, perfectly correct judgement? None know better than they who clamour for direct evidence that their master was right in taking the position assigned to him by Professor Vines, that they cannot reasonably look for it. With us, as with themselves, modification proceeds very gradually, and it violates our principles as much as their own to expect visible permanent progress, in any single generation, or indeed in any number of generations of wild species which we have yet had time to observe. Occasionally we can find such cases, as in that of *Branchipus stagnalis*, quoted by Mr. Wallace, or in that of the New Zealand Kea whose skin, I was assured by the late Sir Julius von Haast, has already been modified as a consequence of its change of food. Here we can show that in even a few generations structure is

The Deadlock in Darwinism

modified under changed conditions of existence, but as we believe these cases to occur comparatively rarely, so it is still more rarely that they occur when and where we can watch them. Nature is eminently conservative, and fixity of type, even under considerable change of conditions, is surely more important for the well-being of any species than an over-ready power of adaptation to, it may be, passing changes. There could be no steady progress if each generation were not mainly bound by the traditions of those that have gone before it. It is evolution and not incessant revolution that both parties are upholding; and this being so, rapid visible modification must be the exception, not the rule. I have quoted direct evidence adduced by competent observers, which is, I believe, sufficient to establish the fact that offspring can be and is sometimes modified by the acquired habits of a progenitor. I will now proceed to the still more, as it appears to me, cogent proof afforded by general considerations.

What, let me ask, are the principal phenomena of heredity? There must be physical continuity between parent, or parents, and offspring, so that the offspring is, as Erasmus Darwin well said, a kind of elongation of the life of the parent.

Erasmus Darwin put the matter so well that I may as well give his words in full; he wrote:

" Owing to the imperfection of language the offspring is termed a new animal, but is in truth a branch or elongation of the parent, since a part of the embryon animal is, or was, a part of the parent, and therefore, in strict language, cannot be said to be entirely new at the time of its production; and therefore it may retain some of the habits of the parent system.

" At the earliest period of its existence the embryon would seem to consist of a living filament with certain capabilities of irritation, sensation, volition, and association, and also with some acquired habits or propensities peculiar to the parent; the former of these are in common with other animals; the latter seem to distinguish or produce the kind of animal, whether man or quadruped, with the similarity of feature or form to the parent."[1]

Those who accept evolution insist on unbroken physical continuity between the earliest known life and ourselves, so that we both are and are not personally identical with the unicellular organism from which we have descended in the course of many millions of years, exactly in the same ways as an octogenarian both is and is not personally identical with the microscopic impregnate ovum from which he grew up. Everything both is and is not. There is no such thing as strict identity between any two things in any two consecutive seconds. In strictness they are identical and yet not identical, so that in strictness they violate a fundamental rule of strictness—namely, that a thing shall never be itself and not itself at one and the same time; we must choose between logic and dealing in a practical spirit with time and space; it is not surprising, therefore, that logic, in spite of the show of respect outwardly paid to her, is told to stand aside when people come to practice. In practice identity is generally held to exist where continuity is only broken slowly and piecemeal; nevertheless, that occasional periods of even rapid change are not held to bar identity, appears from the fact that no one denies this to hold between the microscopically small impregnate ovum and the born child that springs from it, nor yet, therefore, between the impregnate ovum and the octogenarian into which the child grows; for both ovum and octogenarian are held personally identical with the new-born baby, and things that are identical with the same are identical with one another.

The first, then, and most important element of heredity is that there should be unbroken continuity, and hence sameness of personality, between parents and offspring, in neither more nor less than the same sense as that in which any other two personalities are said to be the same. The repetition, therefore, of its developmental stages by any offspring must be regarded as something which the embryo repeating them

[1] *Zoonomia*, 1794, vol. i, p. 480.

The Deadlock in Darwinism

has already done once, in the person of one or other parent; and if once, then, as many times as there have been generations between any given embryo now repeating it, and the point in life from which we started—say, for example, the amoeba. In the case of asexually and sexually produced organisms alike, the offspring must be held to continue the personality of the parent or parents, and hence on the occasion of every fresh development, to be repeating something which in the person of its parent or parents it has done once, and if once, then any number of times, already.

It is obvious, therefore, that the germ-plasm (or whatever the fancy word for it may be) of any one generation is as physically identical with the germ-plasm of its predecessor as any two things can be. The difference between Professor Weismann and, we will say, Heringians consists in the fact that the first maintains the new germ-plasm when on the point of repeating its developmental processes to take practically no cognizance of anything that has happened to it since the last occasion on which it developed itself; while the latter maintain that offspring takes much the same kind of account of what has happened to it in the persons of its parents since the last occasion on which it developed itself, as people in ordinary life take of things that happen to them. In daily life people let fairly normal circumstances come and go without much heed as matters of course. If they have been lucky they make a note of it and try to repeat their success. If they have been unfortunate but have recovered rapidly they soon forget it; if they have suffered long and deeply they grizzle over it and are scared and scarred by it for a long time. The question is one of cognizance or non-cognizance on the part of the new germs, of the more profound impressions made on them while they were one with their parents, between the occasion of their last preceding development and the new course on which they are about to enter. Those who accept the theory put forward independently by Professor Hering of Prague (whose work on this subject is translated in my book *Unconscious Memory*) and by myself in *Life and Habit*, believe in cognizance as do Lamarckians generally. Weismannites, and with them the orthodoxy of English science, find non-cognizance more acceptable.

If the Heringian view is accepted, that heredity is only a mode of memory, and an extension of memory from one generation to another, then the repetition of its development by any embryo thus becomes only the repetition of a lesson learned by rote; and, as I have elsewhere said, our view of life is simplified by finding that it is no longer an equation of, say, a hundred unknown quantities, but of ninety-nine only, inasmuch as two of the unknown quantities prove to be substantially identical. In this case the inheritance of acquired characteristics cannot be disputed, for it is postulated in the theory that each embryo takes note of, remembers, and is guided by the profounder impressions made upon it while in the persons of its parents, between its present and last preceding development. To maintain this is to maintain use and disuse to be the main factors throughout organic development; to deny it is to deny that use and disuse can have any conceivable effect. For the detailed reasons which led me to my own conclusions I must refer the reader to my books *Life and Habit* and *Unconscious Memory*, the conclusions of which have been often adopted, but never, that I have seen, disputed. A brief résumé of the leading points in the argument is all that space will here allow me to give.

We have seen that it is a first requirement of heredity that there shall be physical continuity between parents and offspring. This holds good with memory. There must be continued identity between the person remembering and the person to whom the thing that is remembered happened. We cannot remember things that happened to someone else, and in our absence. We can only remember having heard of them. We have seen, however, that there is as much *bona fide* sameness of personality between parents and offspring up to the time at which the offspring quits the parent's body, as there is between the different states of the parent himself at any two consecutive moments; the offspring

The Deadlock in Darwinism

therefore, being one and the same person with its progenitors until it quits them, can be held to remember what happened to them within, of course, the limitations to which all memory is subject, as much as the progenitors can remember what happened earlier to themselves. Whether it does so remember can only be settled by observing whether it acts as living beings commonly do when they are acting under guidance of memory. I will endeavour to show that, though heredity and habit based on memory go about in different dresses, yet if we catch them separately—for they are never seen together—and strip them there is not a mole nor strawberry-mark nor trick nor leer of the one, but we find it in the other also.

What are the moles and strawberry-marks of habitual action, or actions remembered and thus repeated? First, the more often we repeat them the more easily and unconsciously we do them. Look at reading, writing, walking, talking, playing the piano, etc.; the longer we have practised any one of these acquired habits, the more easily, automatically and unconsciously, we perform it. Look, on the other hand, broadly, at the three points to which I called attention in *Life and Habit*:

" I. That we are most conscious of and have most control over such habits as speech, the upright position, the arts and sciences—which are acquisitions peculiar to the human race, always acquired after birth, and not common to ourselves and any ancestor who had not become entirely human.

" II. That we are less conscious of and have less control over eating and drinking [provided the food be normal], swallowing, breathing, seeing, and hearing—which were acquisitions of our prehuman ancestry, and for which we had provided ourselves with all the necessary apparatus before we saw light, but which are still, geologically speaking, recent.

" III. That we are most unconscious of and have least control over our digestion and circulation—powers possessed even by our invertebrate ancestry, and, geologically speaking, of extreme antiquity."

Collected Essays

I have put the foregoing very broadly, but enough is given to show the reader the gist of the argument. Let it be noted that disturbance and departure, to any serious extent, from normal practice tends to induce resumption of consciousness even in the case of such old habits as breathing, seeing, and hearing, digestion and the circulation of the blood. So it is with habitual actions in general. Let a player be never so proficient on any instrument, he will be put out if the normal conditions under which he plays are too widely departed from, and will then do consciously, if indeed he can do it at all, what he had hitherto been doing unconsciously. It is an axiom as regards actions acquired after birth, that we never do them automatically save as the result of long practice; the stages in the case of any acquired facility, the inception of which we have been able to watch, have invariably been from a nothingness of ignorant impotence to a little somethingness of highly self-conscious, arduous performance, and thence to the unself-consciousness of easy mastery. I saw one year a poor blind lad of about eighteen sitting on a wall by the wayside at Varese, playing the concertina with his whole body, and snorting like a child. The next year the boy no longer snorted, and he played with his fingers only; the year after that he seemed hardly to know whether he was playing or not, it came so easily to him. I know no exception to this rule. Where is the intricate and at one time difficult art in which perfect automatic ease has been reached except as the result of long practice? If, then, wherever we can trace the development of automatism we find it to have taken this course, is it not most reasonable to infer that it has taken the same even when it has risen in regions that are beyond our ken? Ought we not, whenever we see a difficult action performed automatically, to suspect antecedent practice? Granted that without the considerations in regard to identity presented above it would not have been easy to see where a baby of a day old could have had the practice which enables it to do as much as it does unconsciously, but even without these considerations it would have been more easy to suppose that the necessary opportunities had not been wanting, than that the easy performance could have been gained without practice and memory.

When I wrote *Life and Habit* (originally published in 1878) I said in slightly different words:

"Shall we say that a baby of a day old sucks (which involves the whole principle of the pump and hence a profound practical knowledge of the laws of pneumatics and hydrostatics), digests, oxygenizes its blood—millions of years before anyone had discovered oxygen—sees and hears, operations that involve an unconscious knowledge of the facts concerning optics and acoustics compared with which the conscious discoveries of Newton are insignificant—shall we say that a baby can do all these things at once, doing them so well and so regularly without being even able to give them attention, and yet without mistake, and shall we also say at the same time that it has not learnt to do them, and never did them before?

"Such an assertion would contradict the whole experience of mankind."

I have met with nothing during the thirteen years since the foregoing was published that has given me any qualms about its soundness. From the point of view of the law courts and everyday life it is, of course, nonsense; but in the kingdom of thought, as in that of heaven, there are many mansions, and what would be extravagance in the cottage or farmhouse, as it were, of daily practice, is but common decency in the palace of high philosophy, wherein dwells evolution. If we leave evolution alone, we may stick to common practice and the law courts; touch evolution and we are in another world; not higher, nor lower, but different as harmony from counterpoint. As, however, in the most absolute counterpoint there is still harmony, and in the most absolute harmony still counterpoint, so high philosophy should be still in touch with common sense, and common sense with high philosophy.

The common-sense view of the matter to people who

are not over-curious and to whom time is money, will be that a baby is not a baby until it is born, and that when born it should be born in wedlock. Nevertheless, as a sop to high philosophy, every baby is allowed to be the offspring of its father and mother.

The high-philosophy view of the matter is that every human being is still but a fresh edition of the primordial cell with the latest additions and corrections; there has been no leap nor break in continuity anywhere; the man of to-day is the primordial cell of millions of years ago as truly as he is the himself of yesterday; he can only be denied to be the one on grounds that will prove him not to be the other. Everyone is both himself and all his direct ancestors and descendants as well; therefore, if we would be logical, he is one also with all his cousins, no matter how distant, for he and they are alike identical with the primordial cell, and we have already noted it as an axiom that things which are identical with the same are identical with one another. This is practically making him one with all living things, whether animal or vegetable, that ever have existed or ever will—something of all which may have been in the mind of Sophocles when he wrote:

"Nor seest thou yet the gathering hosts of ill
That shall en-one thee both with thine own self
And with thine offspring."

And all this has come of admitting that a man may be the same person for two days running! As for sopping common sense it will be enough to say that these remarks are to be taken in a strictly scientific sense, and have no appreciable importance as regards life and conduct. True they deal with the foundations on which all life and conduct are based, but like other foundations they are hidden out of sight, and the sounder they are, the less we trouble ourselves about them.

What other main common features between heredity and memory may we note besides the fact that neither can exist

The Deadlock in Darwinism

without that kind of physical continuity which we call personal identity? First, the development of the embryo proceeds in an established order; so must all habitual actions based on memory. Disturb the normal order and the performance is arrested. The better we know "God save the Queen," the less easily can we play or sing it backwards. The return of memory again depends on the return of ideas associated with the particular thing that is remembered—we remember nothing but for the presence of these, and when enough of these are presented to us we remember everything. So, if the development of an embryo is due to memory, we should suppose the memory of the impregnate ovum to revert not to yesterday, when it was in the persons of its parents, but to the last occasion on which it was an impregnate ovum. The return of the old environment and the presence of old associations would at once involve recollection of the course that should be next taken, and the same should happen throughout the whole course of development. The actual course of development presents precisely the phenomena agreeable with this. For fuller treatment of this point I must refer the reader to the chapter on the abeyance of memory in my book *Life and Habit*, already referred to.

Secondly, we remember best our last few performances of any given kind, so our present performance will probably resemble some one or other of these; we remember our earlier performances by way of residuum only, but every now and then we revert to an earlier habit. This feature of memory is manifested in heredity by the way in which offspring commonly resembles most its nearer ancestors, but sometimes reverts to earlier ones. Brothers and sisters, each as it were giving their own version of the same story, but in different words, should generally resemble each other more closely than more distant relations. And this is what actually we find.

Thirdly, the introduction of slightly new elements into a method already established varies it beneficially; the new is soon fused with the old, and the monotony ceases to be oppressive. But if the new be too foreign, we cannot fuse the old and the new—nature seeming to hate equally too wide a deviation from ordinary practice and none at all. This fact reappears in heredity as the beneficial effects of occasional crossing on the one hand, and on the other, in the generally observed sterility of hybrids. If heredity be an affair of memory, how can an embryo, say of a mule, be expected to build up a mule on the strength of but two mule-memories? Hybridism causes a fault in the chain of memory, and it is to this cause that the usual sterility of hybrids must be referred.

Fourthly, it requires many repeated impressions to fix a method firmly, but when it has been engrained into us we cease to have much recollection of the manner in which it came to be so, or indeed of any individual repetition, but sometimes a single impression if prolonged as well as profound, produces a lasting impression and is liable to return with sudden force, and then to go on returning to us at intervals. As a general rule, however, abnormal impressions cannot long hold their own against the overwhelming preponderance of normal authority. This appears in heredity as the normal non-inheritance of mutilations on the one hand, and on the other as their occasional inheritance in the case of injuries followed by disease.

Fifthly, if heredity and memory are essentially the same, we should expect that no animal would develop new structures of importance after the age at which its species begins ordinarily to continue its race; for we cannot suppose offspring to remember anything that happens to the parent subsequently to the parent's ceasing to contain the offspring within itself. From the average age, therefore, of reproduction, offspring should cease to have any further steady, continuous memory to fall back upon; what memory there is should be full of faults, and as such unreliable. An organism ought to develop as long as it is backed by memory—that is to say, until the average age at which reproduction begins; it should then continue to go for a time on the impetus already received, and should eventually decay through failure of any memory to support it, and tell it what to do. This corresponds absolutely with what we observe in organisms generally, and explains, on the one hand, why the age of puberty marks the beginning of completed development—a riddle hitherto not only unexplained but, so far as I have seen, unasked; it explains, on the other hand, the phenomena of old age—hitherto without even attempt at explanation.

Sixthly, those organisms that are the longest in reaching maturity should on the average be the longest-lived, for they will have received the most momentous impulse from the weight of memory behind them. This harmonizes with the latest opinion as to the facts. In his article on Weismann in *The Contemporary Review* for May 1890 Mr. Romanes writes: " Professor Weismann has shown that there is throughout the metazoa a general correlation between the natural lifetime of individuals composing any given species, and the age at which they reach maturity or first become capable of procreation." This, I believe, has been the conclusion generally arrived at by biologists for some years past.

Lateness, then, in the average age of reproduction appears to be the principle underlying longevity. There does not appear at first sight to be much connection between such distinct and apparently disconnected phenomena as 1, the orderly normal progress of development; 2, atavism and the resumption of feral characteristics; 3, the more ordinary resemblance *inter se* of nearer relatives; 4, the benefit of an occasional cross, and the usual sterility of hybrids; 5, the unconsciousness with which alike bodily development and ordinary physiological functions proceed, so long as they are normal; 6, the ordinary non-inheritance, but occasional inheritance of mutilations; 7, the fact that puberty indicates the approach of maturity; 8, the phenomena of middle life and old age; 9, the principle underlying longevity. These phenomena have no conceivable bearing on one another until heredity and memory are regarded as part of the same story. Identify these two things, and I know no phenomenon of heredity that does not immediately become infinitely more intelligible. Is it conceivable that a theory which harmonizes so many facts hitherto regarded as without either connection or explanation should not deserve at any rate consideration from those who profess to take an interest in biology?

It is not as though the theory were unknown, or had been condemned by our leading men of science. Professor Ray Lankester introduced it to English readers in an appreciative notice of Professor Hering's address, which appeared in *Nature*, 13th July 1876. He wrote to *The Athenaeum*, 24th March 1884, and claimed credit for having done so, but I do not believe he has ever said more in public about it than what I have here referred to. Mr. Romanes did indeed try to crush it in *Nature*, 27th January 1881, but in 1883, in his *Mental Evolution in Animals*, he adopted its main conclusion without acknowledgement. *The Athenaeum*, to my unbounded surprise, called him to task for this (1st March 1884), and since that time he has given the Heringian theory a sufficiently wide berth. Mr. Wallace showed himself favourably enough disposed towards the view that heredity and memory are part of the same story when he reviewed my book *Life and Habit* in *Nature*, 27th March 1879, but he has never since betrayed any sign of being aware that such a theory existed. Mr. Herbert Spencer wrote to *The Athenaeum* (5th April 1884), and claimed the theory for himself, but, in spite of his doing this, he has never, that I have seen, referred to the matter again. I have dealt sufficiently with his claim in my book *Luck, or Cunning?* Lastly, Professor Hering himself has never that I know of touched his own theory since the single short address read in 1870, and translated by me in 1880. Everyone, even its originator, except myself, seems afraid to open his mouth about it. Of course the inference suggests itself that other people have more sense than I have. I readily admit it; but why have so many of our leaders shown such a strong hankering after the theory, if there is nothing in it?

The deadlock that I have pointed out as existing in Dar-

The Deadlock in Darwinism

winism will, I doubt not, lead ere long to a consideration of Professor Hering's theory. English biologists are little likely to find Weismann satisfactory for long, and if he breaks down there is nothing left for them but Lamarck, supplemented by the important and elucidatory corollary on his theory proposed by Professor Hering. When the time arrives for this to obtain a hearing it will be confirmed, doubtless, by arguments clearer and more forcible than any I have been able to adduce; I shall then be delighted to resign the championship which till then I shall continue, as for some years past, to have much pleasure in sustaining. Heretofore my satisfaction has mainly lain in the fact that more of our prominent men of science have seemed anxious to claim the theory than to refute it; in the confidence thus engendered I leave it to any fuller consideration which the outline I have above given may incline the reader to bestow upon it.

THOUGHT AND LANGUAGE

NOTE

This Lecture was given at the Working Men's College, Great Ormond Street, 15th March 1890. Afterwards Butler rewrote it and delivered it at the Somerville Club, 13th February 1894. It was included by R. A. Streatfeild in *Essays on Life, Art, and Science* (1904), and in *The Humour of Homer, and other Essays* (1913).

A.T.B.

Thought and Language

THREE WELL-KNOWN WRITERS, PROFESSOR Max Müller, Professor Mivart, and Mr. Alfred Russel Wallace, have lately maintained that though the theory of descent with modification accounts for the development of all vegetable life, and of all animals lower than man, yet that man cannot—not at least in respect of the whole of his nature—be held to have descended from any animal lower than himself, inasmuch as none lower than man possesses even the germs of language. Reason, it is contended—more especially by Professor Max Müller in his *Science of Thought*, to which I propose confining our attention this evening—is so inseparably connected with language, that the two are in point of fact identical; hence it is argued that, as the lower animals have no germs of language, they can have no germs of reason, and the inference is drawn that man cannot be conceived as having derived his own reasoning powers and command of language through descent from beings in which no germ of either can be found. The relations therefore between thought and language, interesting in themselves, acquire additional importance from the fact of their having become the battle-ground between those who say that the theory of descent breaks down with man, and those who maintain that we are descended from some ape-like ancestor long since extinct.

The contention of those who refuse to admit man unreservedly into the scheme of evolution is comparatively recent. The great propounders of evolution, Buffon, Erasmus Darwin, and Lamarck—not to mention a score of others who wrote at the close of the last and early part of this present century—had no qualms about admitting man into their system. They have been followed in this respect by the late Mr. Charles Darwin, and by the greatly more influential part of our modern biologists, who hold that whatever loss of dignity we may incur through being proved to be of humble origin, is compensated by the credit we may claim for having advanced ourselves to such a high pitch of civilization; this bids us expect still further progress, and glorifies our descendants more than it abases our ancestors. But to whichever view we may incline on sentimental grounds the fact remains that, while Charles Darwin declared language to form no impassable barrier between man and the lower animals, Professor Max Müller calls it the Rubicon which no brute dare cross, and deduces hence the conclusion that man cannot have descended from an unknown but certainly speechless ape.

It may perhaps be expected that I should begin a lecture on the relations between thought and language with some definition of both these things; but thought, as Sir William Grove said of motion, is a phenomenon " so obvious to simple apprehension that to define it would make it more obscure."[1] Definitions are useful where things are new to us, but they are superfluous about those that are already familiar, and mischievous, so far as they are possible at all, in respect of all those things that enter so profoundly and intimately into our being that in them we must either live or bear no life. To vivisect the more vital processes of thought is to suspend, if not to destroy them; for thought can think about everything more healthily and easily than about itself. It is like its instrument the brain, which knows nothing of any injuries inflicted upon itself. As regards what is new to us, a definition will sometimes dilute a difficulty, and help us to swallow that which might choke us undiluted; but to define when we have once well swallowed is to unsettle, rather than settle, our digestion. Definitions, again, are like steps cut in a steep slope of ice, or shells thrown on to a greasy pavement; they give us foothold, and enable us to advance, but when we are at our journey's end we want them no longer. Again, they are useful as mental fluxes, and as helping us to fuse new ideas with our older ones. They present us with some tags and ends of ideas that we have already mastered, on to which we can hitch our new ones; but to multiply them in respect of such a matter as thought, is like scratching the bite of a gnat; the more we scratch the

[1] *Correlation of Forces*, Longmans, 1874, p. 15.

Thought and Language

more we want to scratch; the more we define the more we shall have to go on defining the words we have used in our definitions, and shall end by setting up a serious mental raw in the place of a small uneasiness that was after all quite endurable. We know too well what thought is, to be able to know that we know it, and I am persuaded there is no one in this room but understands what is meant by thought and thinking well enough for all the purposes of this discussion. Whoever does not know this without words will not learn it for all the words and definitions that are laid before him. The more, indeed, he hears, the more confused he will become. I shall, therefore, merely premise that I use the word "thought" in the same sense as that in which it is generally used by people who say that they think this or that. At any rate, it will be enough if I take Professor Max Müller's own definition, and say that its essence consists in a bringing together of mental images and ideas with deductions therefrom, and with a corresponding power of detaching them from one another. Hobbes, the Professor tells us, maintained this long ago, when he said that all our thinking consists of addition and subtraction—that is to say, in bringing ideas together, and in detaching them from one another.

Turning from thought to language, we observe that the word is derived from the French *langue*, or "tongue." Strictly, therefore, it means "tonguage." This, however, takes account of but a very small part of the ideas that underlie the word. It does, indeed, seize a familiar and important detail of everyday speech, though it may be doubted whether the tongue has more to do with speaking than lips, teeth, and throat have, but it makes no attempt at grasping and expressing the essential characteristic of speech. Anything done with the tongue, even though it involve no speaking at all, is "tonguage"; eating oranges is as much tonguage as speech is. The word, therefore, though it tells us in part how speech is effected, reveals nothing of that ulterior meaning which is nevertheless inseparable from any right use of the words either "speech" or "language." It presents us with what is indeed a very frequent adjunct of conversation, but the use of written characters, or the finger-speech of deaf mutes, is enough to show that the word "language" omits all reference to the most essential characteristics of the idea, which in practice it nevertheless very sufficiently presents to us. I hope presently to make it clear to you how and why it should do so. The word is incomplete in the first place, because it omits all reference to the ideas which words, speech, or language are intended to convey, and there can be no true word without its actually or potentially conveying an idea. Secondly, it makes no allusion to the person or persons to whom the ideas are to be conveyed. Language is not language unless it not only expresses fairly definite and coherent ideas, but unless it also conveys these ideas to some other living intelligent being, either man or brute, that can understand them. We may speak to a dog or horse, but not to a stone. If we make pretence of doing so we are in reality only talking to ourselves. The person or animal spoken to is half the battle—a half, moreover, which is essential to there being any battle at all. It takes two people to say a thing—a sayee as well as a sayer. The one is as essential to any true saying as the other. A. may have spoken, but if B. has not heard there has been nothing said, and he must speak again. True, the belief on A.'s part that he had a *bona fide* sayee in B., saves his speech *qua* him, but it has been barren and left no fertile issue. It has failed to fulfil the conditions of true speech, which involve not only that A. should speak, but also that B. should hear. True, again, we often speak of loose, incoherent, indefinite language; but by doing so we imply, and rightly, that we are calling that language which is not true language at all. People, again, sometimes talk to themselves without intending that any other person should hear them, but this is not well done, and does harm to those who practise it. It is abnormal, whereas our concern is with normal and essential characteristics; we may, therefore, neglect both delirious babblings, and the cases in which a person is regarding him

Thought and Language

or herself, as it were, from outside, and treating himself as though he were someone else.

Inquiring, then, what are the essentials, the presence of which constitutes language, while their absence negatives it altogether, we find that Professor Max Müller restricts them to the use of grammatical articulate words that we can write or speak, and denies that anything can be called language unless it can be written or spoken in articulate words and sentences. He also denies that we can think at all unless we do so in words; that is to say, in sentences with verbs and nouns. Indeed, he goes so far as to say upon his title-page that there can be no reason—which I imagine comes to much the same thing as thought—without language, and no language without reason.

Against the assertion that there can be no true language without reason I have nothing to say. But when the Professor says that there can be no reason, or thought, without language, his opponents contend, as it seems to me, with greater force, that thought, though infinitely aided, extended and rendered definite through the invention of words, nevertheless existed so fully as to deserve no other name thousands, if not millions, of years before words had entered into it at all. Words, they say, are a comparatively recent invention, for the fuller expression of something that was already in existence.

Children, they urge, are often evidently thinking and reasoning, though they can neither think nor speak in words. If you ask me to define reason, I answer as before that this can no more be done than thought, truth, or motion can be defined. Who has answered the question, " What is truth? " Man cannot see God and live. We cannot go so far back upon ourselves as to undermine our own foundations; if we try to do so we topple over, and lose that very reason about which we vainly try to reason. If we let the foundations be, we know well enough that they are there, and we can build upon them in all security. We cannot, then, define reason nor crib, cabin, and confine it within a thus-far-shalt-thou-go-

and-no-farther. Who can define heat or cold, or night or day? Yet, so long as we hold fast by current consent, our chances of error for want of better definition are so small that no sensible person will consider them. In like manner, if we hold by current consent or common sense, which is the same thing, about reason, we shall not find the want of an academic definition hinder us from a reasonable conclusion. What nurse or mother will doubt that her infant child can reason within the limits of its own experience, long before it can formulate its reason in articulately worded thought? If the development of any given animal is, as our opponents themselves admit, an epitome of the history of its whole anterior development, surely the fact that speech is an accomplishment acquired after birth so artificially that children who have gone wild in the woods lose it if they have ever learned it, points to the conclusion that man's ancestors only learned to express themselves in articulate language at a comparatively recent period. Granted that they learn to think and reason continually the more and more fully for having done so, will common sense permit us to suppose that they could neither think nor reason at all till they could convey their ideas in words?

I will return later to the reason of the lower animals, but will now deal with the question what it is that constitutes language in the most comprehensive sense that can be properly attached to it. I have said already that language to be language at all must not only convey fairly definite coherent ideas, but must also convey them to another living being. Whenever two living beings have conveyed and received ideas, there has been language, whether looks or gestures or words spoken or written have been the vehicle by means of which the ideas have travelled. Some ideas crawl, some run, some fly; and in this case words are the wings they fly with, but they are only the wings of thought or of ideas, they are not the thought or ideas themselves, nor yet, as Professor Max Müller would have it, inseparably connected with them. Last summer I was at an inn in Sicily,

Thought and Language

where there was a deaf and dumb waiter; he had been born so, and could neither write nor read. What had he to do with words or words with him? Are we to say, then, that this most active, amiable, and intelligent fellow could neither think nor reason? One day I had had my dinner and had left the hotel. A friend came in, and the waiter saw him look for me in the place I generally occupied. He instantly came up to my friend and moved his two forefingers in a way that suggested two people going about together, this meant " your friend "; he then moved his forefingers horizontally across his eyes, this meant, " who wears divided spectacles "; he made two fierce marks over the sockets of his eyes, this meant, " with the heavy eyebrows "; he pulled his chin, and then touched his white shirt, to say that my beard was white. Having thus identified me as a friend of the person he was speaking to, and as having a white beard, heavy eyebrows, and wearing divided spectacles, he made a munching movement with his jaws to say that I had had my dinner; and finally, by making two fingers imitate walking on the table, he explained that I had gone away. My friend, however, wanted to know how long I had been gone, so he pulled out his watch and looked inquiringly. The man at once slapped himself on the back, and held up the five fingers of one hand, to say it was five minutes ago. All this was done as rapidly as though it had been said in words; and my friend, who knew the man well, understood without a moment's hesitation. Are we to say that this man had no thought, nor reason, nor language, merely because he had not a single word of any kind in his head, which I am assured he had not; for, I should add, he could not speak with his fingers? Is it possible to deny that a dialogue—an intelligent conversation—had passed between the two men? And if conversation, then surely it is technical and pedantic to deny that all the essential elements of language were present. The signs and tokens used by this poor fellow were as rude an instrument of expression, in comparison with ordinary language, as going on one's hands and knees is in comparison with walking, or as walking compared with going by train; but it is as great an abuse of words to limit the word " language " to mere words written or spoken, as it would be to limit the idea of a locomotive to a railway engine. This may indeed pass in ordinary conversation, where so much must be suppressed if talk is to be got through at all, but it is intolerable when we are inquiring about the relations between thought and words. To do so is to let words become as it were the masters of thought, on the ground that the fact of their being only its servants and appendages is so obvious that it is generally allowed to go without saying.

If all that Professor Max Müller means to say is, that no animal but man commands an articulate language, with verbs and nouns, or is ever likely to command one (and I question whether in reality he means much more than this), no one will differ from him. No dog or elephant has one word for bread, another for meat, and another for water. Yet, when we watch a cat or dog dreaming, as they often evidently do, can we doubt that the dream is accompanied by a mental image of the thing that is dreamed of, much like what we experience in dreams ourselves, and much doubtless like the mental images which must have passed through the mind of my deaf and dumb waiter? If they have mental images in sleep, can we doubt that waking, also, they picture things before their mind's eyes, and see them much as we do—too vaguely indeed to admit of our thinking that we actually see the objects themselves, but definitely enough for us to be able to recognize the idea or object of which we are thinking, and to connect it with any other idea, object, or sign that we may think appropriate?

Here we have touched on the second essential element of language. We laid it down, that its essence lay in the communication of an idea from one intelligent being to another; but no ideas can be communicated at all except by the aid of conventions to which both parties have agreed to attach an identical meaning. The agreement may be very informal,

Thought and Language

and may pass so unconsciously from one generation to another that its existence can only be recognized by the aid of much introspection, but it will be always there. A sayer, a sayee, and a convention, no matter what, agreed upon between them as inseparably attached to the idea which it is intended to convey—these comprise all the essentials of language. Where these are present there is language; where any of them are wanting there is no language. It is not necessary for the sayee to be able to speak and become a sayer. If he comprehends the sayer—that is to say, if he attaches the same meaning to a certain symbol as the sayer does—if he is a party to the bargain whereby it is agreed upon by both that any given symbol shall be attached invariably to a certain idea, so that in virtue of the principle of associated ideas the symbol shall never be present without immediately carrying the idea along with it, then all the essentials of language are complied with, and there has been true speech though never a word was spoken.

The lower animals, therefore, many of them, possess a part of our own language, though they cannot speak it, and hence do not possess it so fully as we do. They cannot say "bread," "meat," or "water," but there are many that readily learn what ideas they ought to attach to these symbols when they are presented to them. It is idle to say that a cat does not know what the cat's-meat man means when he says "meat." The cat knows just as well, neither better nor worse than the cat's-meat man does, and a great deal better than I myself understand much that is said by some very clever people at Oxford or Cambridge. There is more true employment of language, more *bona fide* currency of speech, between a sayer and a sayee who understand each other, though neither of them can speak a word, than between a sayer who can speak with the tongues of men and of angels without being clear about his own meaning, and a sayee who can himself utter the same words, but who is only in imperfect agreement with the sayer as to the ideas which the words or symbols that he utters are intended to convey. The nature of the symbols counts for nothing; the gist of the matter is in the perfect harmony between sayer and sayee as to the significance that is to be associated with them.

Professor Max Müller admits that we share with the lower animals what he calls an emotional language, and continues that we may call their interjections and imitations language if we like, as we speak of the language of the eyes or the eloquence of mute nature, but he warns us against mistaking metaphor for fact. It is indeed mere metaphor to talk of the eloquence of mute nature, or the language of winds and waves. There is no intercommunion of mind with mind by means of a covenanted symbol; but it is only an apparent, not a real, metaphor to say that two pairs of eyes have spoken when they have signalled to one another something which they both understand. A schoolboy at home for the holidays wants another plate of pudding, and does not like to apply officially for more. He catches the servant's eye and looks at the pudding; the servant understands, takes his plate without a word, and gets him some. Is it metaphor to say that the boy asked the servant to do this, or is it not rather pedantry to insist on the letter of a bond and deny its spirit, by denying that language passed, on the ground that the symbols covenanted upon and assented to by both were uttered and received by eyes and not by mouth and ears? When the lady drank to the gentleman only with her eyes, and he pledged with his, was there no conversation because there was neither noun nor verb? Eyes are verbs, and glasses of wine are good nouns enough as between those who understand one another. Whether the ideas underlying them are expressed and conveyed by eyeage or by tonguage is a detail that matters nothing.

But everything we say is metaphorical if we choose to be captious. Scratch the simplest expressions, and you will find the metaphor. Written words are handage, inkage, and paperage; it is only by metaphor, or substitution and transposition of ideas, that we can call them language. They are indeed potential language, and the symbols employed presuppose nouns, verbs, and the other parts of speech; but for the most part it is in what we read between the lines that the profounder meaning of any letter is conveyed. There are words unwritten and untranslatable into any nouns that are nevertheless felt as above, about, and underneath the gross material symbols that lie scrawled upon the paper; and the deeper the feeling with which anything is written the more pregnant will it be of meaning which can be conveyed securely enough, but which loses rather than gains if it is squeezed into a sentence, and limited by the parts of speech. The language is not in the words but in the heart-to-heartness of the thing, which is helped by words, but is nearer and farther than they. A correspondent wrote to me once, many years ago, " If I could think to you without words you would understand me better." But surely in this he was thinking to me, and without words, and I did understand him better. . . . So it is not by the words that I am too presumptuously venturing to speak to-night that your opinions will be formed or modified. They will be formed or modified, if either, by something that you will feel, but which I have not spoken, to the full as much as by anything that I have actually uttered. You may say that this borders on mysticism. Perhaps it does, but there really is some mysticism in nature.

To return, however, to *terra firma*. I believe I am right in saying that the essence of language lies in the intentional conveyance of ideas from one living being to another through the instrumentality of arbitrary tokens or symbols agreed upon and understood by both as being associated with the particular ideas in question. The nature of the symbol chosen is a matter of indifference; it may be anything that appeals to human senses, and is not too hot or too heavy; the essence of the matter lies in a mutual covenant that whatever it is shall stand invariably for the same thing, or nearly so.

We shall see this more easily if we observe the differences between written and spoken language. The written word " stone," and the spoken word, are each of them symbols arrived at in the first instance arbitrarily. They are neither of them more like the other than they are to the idea of a stone which rises before our minds, when we either see or hear the word, or than this idea again is like the actual stone itself, but nevertheless the spoken symbol and the written one each alike convey with certainty the combination of ideas to which we have agreed to attach them.

The written symbol is formed with the hand, appeals to the eye, leaves a material trace as long as paper and ink last, can travel as far as paper and ink can travel, and can be imprinted on eye after eye practically *ad infinitum* both as regards time and space.

The spoken symbol is formed by means of various organs in or about the mouth, appeals to the ear, not the eye, perishes instantly without material trace, and if it lives at all does so only in the minds of those who heard it. The range of its action is no wider than that within which a voice can be heard; and every time a fresh impression is wanted the type must be set up anew.

The written symbol extends infinitely, as regards time and space, the range within which one mind can communicate with another; it gives the writer's mind a life limited by the duration of ink, paper, and readers, as against that of his flesh and blood body. On the other hand, it takes longer to learn the rules so as to be able to apply them with ease and security, and even then they cannot be applied so quickly and easily as those attaching to spoken symbols. Moreover, the spoken symbols admit of a hundred quick and subtle adjuncts by way of action, tone, and expression, so that no one will use written symbols unless either for the special advantages of permanence and travelling power, or because he is incapacitated from using spoken ones. This, however, is hardly to the point; the point is that these two conventional combinations of symbols, that are as unlike one another as the Hallelujah Chorus is to St. Paul's Cathedral, are the one as much language as the other; and we therefore inquire what this very patent fact reveals to us about the more essential characteristics of language itself. What is the common bond that unites these two classes of symbols that seem at first sight to have nothing in common, and makes the one raise the idea of language in our minds as readily as the other? The bond lies in the fact that both are a set of conventional tokens or symbols, agreed upon between the parties to whom they appeal as being attached invariably to the same ideas, and because they are being made as a means of communion between one mind and another—for a memorandum made for a person's own later use is nothing but a communication from an earlier mind to a later and modified one; it is therefore in reality a communication from one mind to another as much as though it had been addressed to another person.

We see, therefore, that the nature of the outward and visible sign to which the inward and spiritual idea of language is attached does not matter. It may be the firing of a gun; it may be an old semaphore telegraph; it may be the movements of a needle; a look, a gesture, the breaking of a twig by an Indian to tell someone that he has passed that way: a twig broken designedly with this end in view is a letter addressed to whomsoever it may concern, as much as though it had been written out in full on bark or paper. It does not matter one straw what it is, provided it is agreed upon in concert, and stuck to. Just as the lowest forms of life nevertheless present us with all the essential characteristics of livingness, and are as much alive in their own humble way as the most highly developed organisms, so the rudest intentional and effectual communication between two minds through the instrumentality of a concerted symbol is as much language as the most finished oratory of Mr. Gladstone. I demur therefore to the assertion that the lower animals have no language, inasmuch as they cannot themselves articulate a grammatical sentence. I do not indeed pretend that when the cat calls upon the tiles it uses what it consciously and introspectively recognizes as language; it says what it has to say without introspection, and in the ordinary course of business, as one of the common forms of courtship. It no more knows that it has been using language than M. Jourdain knew he had been speaking prose, but M. Jourdain's knowing or not knowing was neither here nor there.

Anything which can be made to hitch on invariably to a definite idea that can carry some distance—say an inch at the least, and which can be repeated at pleasure, can be pressed into the service of language. Mrs. Bentley, wife of the famous Dr. Bentley of Trinity College, Cambridge, used to send her snuff-box to the college buttery when she wanted beer, instead of a written order. If the snuff-box came the beer was sent, but if there was no snuff-box there was no beer. Wherein did the snuff-box differ more from a written order, than a written order differs from a spoken one? The snuff-box was for the time being language. It sounds strange to say that one might take a pinch of snuff out of a sentence, but if the servant had helped him or herself to a pinch while carrying it to the buttery this is what would have been done; for if a snuff-box can say "Send me a quart of beer," so efficiently that the beer is sent, it is impossible to say that it is not a *bona fide* sentence. As for the recipient of the message, the butler did not probably translate the snuff-box into articulate nouns and verbs; as soon as he saw it he just went down into the cellar and drew the beer, and if he thought at all, it was probably about something else. Yet he must have been thinking without words, or he would have drawn too much beer or too little, or have spilt it in the bringing it up, and we may be sure that he did none of these things.

You will, of course, observe that if Mrs. Bentley had sent the snuff-box to the buttery of St. John's College instead of Trinity, it would not have been language, for there would have been no covenant between sayer and sayee as to what the symbol should represent, there would have been no previously established association of ideas in the mind of the butler of St. John's between beer and snuff-box; the con-

Thought and Language

nection was artificial, arbitrary, and by no means one of those in respect of which an impromptu bargain might be proposed by the very symbol itself, and assented to without previous formality by the person to whom it was presented. More briefly, the butler of St. John's would not have been able to understand and read it aright. It would have been a dead letter to him—a snuff-box and not a letter; whereas to the butler of Trinity it was a letter and not a snuff-box. You will also note that it was only at the moment when he was looking at it and accepting it as a message that it flashed forth from snuff-box-hood into the light and life of living utterance. As soon as it had kindled the butler into sending a single quart of beer, its force was spent until Mrs. Bentley threw her soul into it again and charged it anew by wanting more beer, and sending it down accordingly.

Again, take the ring which the Earl of Essex sent to Queen Elizabeth, but which the queen did not receive. This was intended as a sentence, but failed to become effectual language because the sensible material symbol never reached those sentient organs which it was intended to affect. A book, again, however full of excellent words it may be, is not language when it is merely standing on a bookshelf. It speaks to no one, unless when being actually read, or quoted from by an act of memory. It is potential language as a lucifer-match is potential fire, but it is no more language till it is in contact with a recipient mind, than a match is fire till it is struck, and is being consumed.

A piece of music, again, without any words at all, or a song with words that have nothing in the world to do with the ideas which it is nevertheless made to convey, is very often effectual language. Much lying, and all irony depends on tampering with covenanted symbols, and making those that are usually associated with one set of ideas convey by a sleight of mind others of a different nature. That is why irony is intolerably fatiguing unless very sparingly used. Take the song which Blondel sang under the window of King Richard's prison. There was not one syllable in it to say that Blondel was there, and was going to help the king to get out of prison. It was about some silly love affair, but it was a letter all the same, and the king made language of what would otherwise have been no language, by guessing the meaning, that is to say, by perceiving that he was expected to enter then and there into a new covenant as to the meaning of the symbols that were presented to him, understanding what this covenant was to be, and acquiescing in it.

On the other hand, no ingenuity can torture " language " into being a fit word to use in connection with either sounds or any other symbols that have not been intended to convey a meaning, or again in connection with either sounds or symbols in respect of which there has been no covenant between sayer and sayee. When we hear people speaking a foreign language—we will say Welsh—we feel that though they are no doubt using what is very good language as between themselves, there is no language whatever as far as we are concerned. We call it lingo, not language. The Chinese letters on a tea-chest might as well not be there, for all that they say to us, though the Chinese find them very much to the purpose. They are a covenant to which we have been no parties—to which our intelligence has affixed no signature.

We have already seen that it is in virtue of such an understood covenant that symbols so unlike one another as the written word " stone " and the spoken word alike at once raise the idea of a stone in our minds. See how the same holds good as regards the different languages that pass current in different nations. The letters p, i, e, r, r, e convey the idea of a stone to a Frenchman as readily as s, t, o, n, e do to ourselves. And why? because that is the covenant that has been struck between those who speak and those who are spoken to. Our " stone " conveys no idea to a Frenchman, nor his " pierre " to us, unless we have done what is commonly called acquiring one another's language. To acquire a foreign language is only to learn and adhere to the covenants in respect of symbols which the nation in question has adopted and adheres to. Till we have done this we neither of us know the rules, so to speak, of the game that the other is playing, and cannot, therefore, play together; but the convention being once known and consented to, it does not matter whether we raise the idea of a stone by the words "lapis," or by "lithos," "pietra," "pierre," "stein," "stane," or "stone"; we may choose what symbols written or spoken we choose, and one set, unless they are of unwieldy length, will do as well as another, if we can get other people to choose the same and stick to them; it is the accepting and sticking to them that matters, not the symbols. The whole power of spoken language is vested in the invariableness with which certain symbols are associated with certain ideas. If we are strict in always connecting the same symbols with the same ideas, we speak well, keep our meaning clear to ourselves, and convey it readily and accurately to anyone who is also fairly strict. If, on the other hand, we use the same combination of symbols for one thing one day and for another the next, we abuse our symbols instead of using them, and those who indulge in slovenly habits in this respect ere long lose the power alike of thinking and of expressing themselves correctly. The symbols, however, in the first instance, may be anything in the wide world that we have a fancy for. They have no more to do with the ideas they serve to convey than money has with the things that it serves to buy.

The principle of association, as everyone knows, involves that whenever two things have been associated sufficiently together, the suggestion of one of them to the mind shall immediately raise a suggestion of the other. It is in virtue of this principle that language, as we so call it, exists at all, for the essence of language consists, as I have said perhaps already too often, in the fixity with which certain ideas are invariably connected with certain symbols. But this being so, it is hard to see how we can deny that the lower animals possess the germs of a highly rude and unspecialized, but still true language, unless we also deny that they have any ideas at all; and this I gather is what Professor Max Müller in a quiet way rather wishes to do. Thus he says, "It is easy enough to show that animals communicate, but this is a fact which has never been doubted. Dogs who growl and bark leave no doubt in the minds of other dogs or cats, or even of man, of what they mean, but growling and barking are not language, nor do they even contain the elements of language."[1]

I observe the Professor says that animals communicate without saying what it is that they communicate. I believe this to have been because if he said that the lower animals communicate their ideas, this would be to admit that they have ideas; if so, and if, as they present every appearance of doing, they can remember, reflect upon, modify these ideas according to modified surroundings, and interchange them with one another, how is it possible to deny them the germs of thought, language, and reason—not to say a good deal more than the germs? It seems to me that not knowing what else to say that animals communicated if it was not ideas, and not knowing what mess he might not get into if he admitted that they had ideas at all, he thought it safer to omit his accusative case altogether.

That growling and barking cannot be called a very highly specialized language goes without saying; they are, however, so much diversified in character, according to circumstances, that they place a considerable number of symbols at an animal's command, and he invariably attaches the same symbol to the same idea. A cat never purrs when she is angry, nor spits when she is pleased. When she rubs her head against anyone affectionately it is her symbol for saying that she is very fond of him, and she expects, and usually finds that it will be understood. If she sees her mistress raise her hand as though to pretend to strike her, she knows that it is the symbol her mistress invariably attaches to the idea of sending her away, and as such she accepts it. Granted that the symbols in use among the lower animals are fewer

[1] *Three Lectures on the Science of Language*, Longmans, 1889, p. 4.

and less highly differentiated than in the case of any known human language, and therefore that animal language is incomparably less subtle and less capable of expressing delicate shades of meaning than our own, these differences are nevertheless only those that exist between highly developed and inchoate language; they do not involve those that distinguish language from no language. They are the differences between the undifferentiated protoplasm of the amoeba and our own complex organization; they are not the differences between life and no life. In animal language as much as in human there is a mind intentionally making use of a symbol accepted by another mind as invariably attached to a certain idea, in order to produce that idea in the mind which it is desired to affect—more briefly, there is a sayer, a sayee, and a covenanted symbol designedly applied. Our own speech is vertebrated and articulated by means of nouns, verbs, and the rules of grammar. A dog's speech is invertebrate, but I do not see how it is possible to deny that it possesses all the essential elements of language.

I have said nothing about Professor R. L. Garner's researches into the language of apes, because they have not yet been so far verified and accepted as to make it safe to rely upon them; but when he lays it down that all voluntary sounds are the products of thought, and that, if they convey a meaning to another, they perform the functions of human speech, he says what I believe will commend itself to any unsophisticated mind. I could have wished, however, that he had not limited himself to sounds, and should have preferred his saying what I doubt not he would readily accept—I mean, that all symbols or tokens of whatever kind, if voluntarily adopted as such, are the products of thought, and perform the functions of human speech; but I cannot too often remind you that nothing can be considered as fulfilling the conditions of language, except a voluntary application of a recognized token in order to convey a more or less definite meaning, with the intention doubtless of thus purchasing as it were some other desired meaning and consequent sensation. It is astonishing how closely in this respect money and words resemble one another. Money indeed may be considered as the most universal and expressive of all languages. For gold and silver coins are no more money when not in the actual process of being voluntarily used in purchase, than words not so in use are language. Pounds, shillings, and pence are recognized covenanted tokens, the outward and visible signs of an inward and spiritual purchasing power, but till in actual use they are only potential money, as the symbols of language, whatever they may be, are only potential language till they are passing between two minds. It is the power and will to apply the symbols that alone gives life to money, and as long as these are in abeyance the money is in abeyance also; the coins may be safe in one's pocket, but they are as dead as a log till they begin to burn in it, and so are our words till they begin to burn within us.

The real question, however, as to the substantial underlying identity between the language of the lower animals and our own, turns upon that other question whether or no, in spite of an immeasurable difference of degree, the thought and reason of man and of the lower animals is essentially the same. No one will expect a dog to master and express the varied ideas that are incessantly arising in connection with human affairs. He is a pauper as against a millionaire. To ask him to do so would be like giving a street-boy sixpence and telling him to go and buy himself a founder's share in the New River Company. He would not even know what was meant, and even if he did it would take several millions of sixpences to buy one. It is astonishing what a clever workman will do with very modest tools, or again how far a thrifty housewife will make a very small sum of money go, or again in like manner how many ideas an intelligent brute can receive and convey with its very limited vocabulary; but no one will pretend that a dog's intelligence can ever reach the level of a man's. What we do maintain is that, within its own limited range, it is of the same essential character as our own, and that though a dog's ideas in respect of human affairs are both vague and narrow, yet in respect of canine affairs they are precise enough and extensive enough to deserve no other name than thought or reason. We hold moreover that they communicate their ideas in essentially the same manner as we do—that is to say, by the instrumentality of a code of symbols attached to certain states of mind and material objects, in the first instance arbitrarily, but so persistently, that the presentation of the symbol immediately carries with it the idea which it is intended to convey. Animals can thus receive and impart ideas on all that most concerns them. As my great namesake said some two hundred years ago, they know " what's what, and that's as high as metaphysic wit can fly." And they not only know what's what themselves, but can impart to one another any new what's-whatness that they may have acquired, for they are notoriously able to instruct and correct one another.

Against this Professor Max Müller contends that we can know nothing of what goes on in the mind of any lower animal, inasmuch as we are not lower animals ourselves. " We can imagine anything we like about what passes in the mind of an animal," he writes, " we can know absolutely nothing."[1] It is something to have it in evidence that he conceives animals as having a mind at all, but it is not easy to see how they can be supposed to have a mind, without being able to acquire ideas, and having acquired, to read, mark, learn, and inwardly digest them. Surely the mistake of requiring too much evidence is hardly less great than that of being contented with too little. We, too, are animals, and can no more refuse to infer reason from certain visible actions in their case than we can in our own. If Professor Max Müller's plea were allowed, we should have to deny our right to infer confidently what passes in the mind of anyone not ourselves, inasmuch as we are not that person. We never, indeed, can obtain irrefragable certainty about this or any other matter, but we can be sure enough in many cases to

[1] *Science of Thought*, Longmans, 1887, p. 9.

warrant our staking all that is most precious to us on the soundness of our opinion. Moreover, if the Professor denies our right to infer that animals reason, on the ground that we are not animals enough ourselves to be able to form an opinion, with what right does he infer so confidently himself that they do not reason? And how, if they present every one of those appearances which we are accustomed to connect with the communication of an idea from one mind to another, can we deny that they have a language of their own, though it is one which in most cases we can neither speak nor understand? How can we say that a sentinel rook, when it sees a man with a gun and warns the other rooks by a concerted note which they all show that they understand by immediately taking flight, should not be credited both with reason and the germs of language?

After all, a professor, whether of philology, psychology, biology, or any other ology, is hardly the kind of person to whom we should appeal on such an elementary question as that of animal intelligence and language. We might as well ask a botanist to tell us whether grass grows, or a meteorologist to tell us if it has left off raining. If it is necessary to appeal to anyone, I should prefer the opinion of an intelligent gamekeeper to that of any professor, however learned. The keepers, again, at the Zoological Gardens, have exceptional opportunities for studying the minds of animals—modified, indeed, by captivity, but still minds of animals. Grooms, again, and dog-fanciers, are to the full as able to form an intelligent opinion on the reason and language of animals as any University Professor, and so are cat's-meat men. I have repeatedly asked gamekeepers and keepers at the Zoological Gardens whether animals could reason and converse with one another, and have always found myself regarded somewhat contemptuously for having even asked the question. I once said to a friend, in the hearing of a keeper at the Zoological Gardens, that the penguin was very stupid. The man was furious, and jumped upon me at once. "He's not stupid at all," said he; "he's very intelligent."

Thought and Language

Who has not seen a cat, when it wishes to go out, raise its fore paws on to the handle of the door, or as near as it can get, and look round, evidently asking someone to turn it for her? Is it reasonable to deny that a reasoning process is going on in the cat's mind, whereby she connects her wish with the steps necessary for its fulfilment, and also with certain invariable symbols which she knows her master or mistress will interpret? Once, in company with a friend, I watched a cat playing with a house-fly in the window of a ground-floor room. We were in the street, while the cat was inside. When we came up to the window she gave us one searching look, and, having satisfied herself that we had nothing for her, went on with her game. She knew all about the glass in the window, and was sure we could do nothing to molest her, so she treated us with absolute contempt, never even looking at us again.

The game was this. She was to catch the fly and roll it round and round under her paw along the window-sill, but so gently as not to injure it nor prevent it from being able to fly again when she had done rolling it. It was very early spring, and flies were scarce, in fact there was not another in the whole window. She knew that if she crippled this one, it would not be able to amuse her further, and that she would not readily get another instead, and she liked the feel of it under her paw. It was soft and living, and the quivering of its wings tickled the ball of her foot in a manner that she found particularly grateful; so she rolled it gently along the whole length of the window-sill. It then became the fly's turn. He was to get up and fly about in the window, so as to recover himself a little; then she was to catch him again, and roll him softly all along the window-sill, as she had done before.

It was plain that the cat knew the rules of her game perfectly well, and enjoyed it keenly. It was equally plain that the fly could not make head or tail of what it was all about. If it had been able to do so it would have gone to play in the upper part of the window, where the cat could not reach it.

Collected Essays

Perhaps it was always hoping to get through the glass, and escape that way; anyhow, it kept pretty much to the same pane, no matter how often it was rolled. At last, however, the fly, for some reason or another, did not reappear on the pane, and the cat began looking everywhere to find it. Her annoyance when she failed to do so was extreme. It was not only that she had lost her fly, but that she could not conceive how she should have ever come to do so. Presently she noted a small knot in the woodwork of the sill, and it flashed upon her that she had accidentally killed the fly, and that this was its dead body. She tried to move it gently with her paw, but it was no use, and for the time she satisfied herself that the knot and the fly had nothing to do with one another. Every now and then, however, she returned to it as though it were the only thing she could think of, and she would try it again. She seemed to say she was certain there had been no knot there before—she must have seen it if there had been; and yet, the fly could hardly have got jammed so firmly into the wood. She was puzzled and irritated beyond measure, and kept looking in the same place again and again, just as we do when we have mislaid something. She was rapidly losing temper and dignity when suddenly we saw the fly reappear from under the cat's stomach and make for the window-pane, at the very moment when the cat herself was exclaiming for the fiftieth time that she wondered where that stupid fly ever could have got to. No man who has been hunting twenty minutes for his spectacles could be more delighted when he suddenly finds them on his own forehead. "So that's where you were," we seemed to hear her say, as she proceeded to catch it, and again began rolling it very softly without hurting it, under her paw.

My friend and I both noticed that the cat, in spite of her perplexity, never so much as hinted that we were the culprits. The question whether anything outside the window could do her good or harm had long since been settled by her in the negative, and she was not going to reopen it; she simply cut us dead, and though her annoyance was so great that she

Thought and Language

was manifestly ready to lay the blame on anybody or anything with or without reason, and though she must have perfectly well known that we were watching the whole affair with amusement, she never either asked us if we had happened to see such a thing as a fly go down our way lately, or accused us of having taken it from her—both of which ideas she would, I am confident, have been very well able to convey to us if she had been so minded.

Now what are thought and reason if the processes that were going through this cat's mind were not both one and the other? If would be childish to suppose that the cat thought in words of its own, or in anything like words. Its thinking was probably conducted through the instrumentality of a series of mental images. We so habitually think in words ourselves that we find it difficult to realize thought without words at all; our difficulty, however, in imagining the particular manner in which the cat thinks has nothing to do with the matter. We must answer the question whether she thinks or no, not according to our own ease or difficulty in understanding the particular manner of her thinking, but according as her action does or does not appear to be of the same character as other action that we commonly call thoughtful. To say that the cat is not intelligent, merely on the ground that we cannot ourselves fathom her intelligence —this, as I have elsewhere said, is to make intelligence mean the power of being understood, rather than the power of understanding. This nevertheless is what, for all our boasted intelligence, we generally do. The more we can understand an animal's ways, the more intelligent we call it, and the less we can understand these, the more stupid do we declare it to be. As for plants—whose punctuality and attention to all the details and routine of their somewhat restricted lines of business is as obvious as it is beyond all praise—we understand the working of their minds so little that by common consent we declare them to have no intelligence at all.

Before concluding I should wish to deal a little more fully with Professor Max Müller's contention that there can be no reason without language, and no language without reason. Surely when two practised pugilists are fighting, parrying each other's blows, and watching keenly for an unguarded point, they are thinking and reasoning very subtly the whole time, without doing so in words. The machination of their thoughts, as well as its expression, is actual—I mean, effectuated and expressed by action and deed, not words. They are unaware or any logical sequence of thought that they could follow in words as passing through their minds at all. They may perhaps think consciously in words now and again, but such thought will be intermittent, and the main part of the fighting will be done without any internal concomitance of articulated phrases. Yet we cannot doubt that their action, however much we may disapprove of it, is guided by intelligence and reason; nor should we doubt that a reasoning process of the same character goes on in the minds of two dogs or fighting-cocks when they are striving to master their opponents.

Do we think in words, again, when we wind up our watches, put on our clothes, or eat our breakfasts? If we do, it is generally about something else. We do these things almost as much without the help of words as we wink or yawn, or perform any of those other actions that we call reflex, as it would almost seem because they are done without reflection. They are not, however, the less reasonable because wordless.

Even when we think we are thinking in words, we do so only in half measure. A running accompaniment of words no doubt frequently attends our thoughts; but, unless we are writing or speaking, this accompaniment is of the vaguest and most fitful kind, as we often find out when we try to write down or say what we are thinking about, though we have a fairly definite notion of it, or fancy that we have one, all the time. The thought is not steadily and coherently governed by and moulded in words, nor does it steadily govern them. Words and thought interact upon and help one another, as any other mechanical appliances interact on

Thought and Language

and help the invention that first hit upon them; but reason or thought, for the most part, flies along over the heads of words, working its own mysterious way in paths that are beyond our ken, though whether some of our departmental personalities are as unconscious of what is passing, as that central government is which we alone dub with the name of " we " or " us," is a point on which I will not now touch.

I cannot think, then, that Professor Max Müller's contention that thought and language are identical—and he has repeatedly affirmed this—will ever be generally accepted. Thought is no more identical with language than feeling is identical with the nervous system. True, we can no more feel without a nervous system than we can discern certain minute organisms without a microscope. Destroy the nervous system, and we destroy feeling. Destroy the microscope, and we can no longer see the animalcules; but our sight of the animalcules is not the microscope, though it is effectuated by means of the microscope, and our feeling is not the nervous system, though the nervous system is the instrument that enables us to feel.

The nervous system is a device which living beings have gradually perfected—I believe I may say quite truly—through the will and power which they have derived from a fountain-head, the existence of which we can infer, but which we can never apprehend. By the help of this device, and in proportion as they have perfected it, living beings feel ever with great definiteness, and hence formulate their feelings in thought with more and more precision. The higher evolution of thought has reacted on the nervous system, and the consequent higher evolution of the nervous system has again reacted upon thought. These things are as power and desire, or supply and demand, each one of which is continually outstripping, and being in turn outstripped by the other; but, in spite of their close connection and interaction, power is not desire, nor demand supply. Language is a device evolved sometimes by leaps and bounds, and sometimes exceedingly slowly, whereby we help ourselves alike to greater ease, precision, and complexity of thought, and also to more convenient interchange of thought among ourselves. Thought found rude expression, which gradually among other forms assumed that of words. These reacted upon thought, and thought again on them, but thought is no more identical with words than words are with the separate letters of which they are composed.

To sum up, then, and to conclude. I would ask you to see the connection between words and ideas as in the first instance arbitrary. No doubt in some cases an imitation of the cry of some bird or wild beast would suggest the name that should be attached to it; occasionally the sound of an operation such as grinding may have influenced the choice of the letters g, r, as the root of many words that denote a grinding, grating, grasping, crushing action; but I understand that the number of words due to direct imitation is comparatively few in number, and that they have been mainly coined as the result of connections so far-fetched and fanciful as to amount practically to no connection at all. Once chosen, however, they were adhered to for a considerable time among the dwellers in any given place, so as to become acknowledged as the vulgar tongue, and raise readily in the mind of the inhabitants of that place the ideas with which they had been artificially associated.

As regards our being able to think and reason without words, the Duke of Argyll has put the matter as soundly as I have yet seen it stated. "It seems to me," he wrote, " quite certain that we can and do constantly think of things without thinking of any sound or word as designating them. Language seems to me to be necessary for the progress of thought, but not at all for the mere act of thinking. It is a product of thought, an expression of it, a vehicle for the communication of it, and an embodiment which is essential to its growth and continuity; but it seems to me altogether erroneous to regard it as an inseparable part of cogitation."

The following passages, again, are quoted from Sir William Hamilton in Professor Max Müller's own book, with so much approval as to lead one to suppose that the differences between himself and his opponents are in reality less than he believes them to be.

"Language," says Sir W. Hamilton, "is the attribution of signs to our cognitions of things. But as a cognition must have already been there before it could receive a sign, consequently that knowledge which is denoted by the formation and application of a word must have preceded the symbol that denotes it. A sign, however, is necessary to give stability to our intellectual progress—to establish each step in our advance as a new starting-point for our advance to another beyond. A country may be overrun by an armed host, but it is only conquered by the establishment of fortresses. Words are the fortresses of thought. They enable us to realize our dominion over what we have already overrun in thought; to make every intellectual conquest the base of operations for others still beyond."

"This," says Professor Max Müller, "is a most happy illustration," and he proceeds to quote the following, also from Sir William Hamilton, which he declares to be even happier still.

"You have all heard," says Sir William Hamilton, "of the process of tunnelling through a sandbank. In this operation it is impossible to succeed unless every foot, nay, almost every inch of our progress be secured by an arch of masonry before we attempted the excavation of another. Now language is to the mind precisely what the arch is to the tunnel. The power of thinking and the power of excavation are not dependent on the words in the one case or on the mason-work in the other; but without these subsidiaries neither could be carried on beyond its rudimentary commencement. Though, therefore, we allow that every movement forward in language must be determined by an antecedent movement forward in thought, still, unless thought be accompanied at each point of its evolutions by a corresponding evolution of language, its further development is arrested."

Collected Essays

Man has evolved an articulate language, whereas the lower animals seem to be without one. Man, therefore, has far outstripped them in reasoning faculty as well as in power of expression. This, however, does not bar the communications which the lower animals make to one another from possessing all the essential characteristics of language, and, as a matter of fact, wherever we can follow them we find such communications effectuated by the aid of arbitrary symbols covenanted upon by the living beings that wish to communicate, and persistently associated with certain corresponding feelings, states of mind, or material objects. Human language is nothing more than this in principle, however much further the principle has been carried in our own case than in that of the lower animals.

This being admitted, we should infer that the thought or reason on which the language of men and animals is alike founded differs as between men and brutes in degree but not in kind. More than this cannot be claimed on behalf of the lower animals, even by their most enthusiastic admirer.

HOW TO MAKE THE BEST OF LIFE

NOTE

BUTLER gave this Address at the Somerville Club, 27th February 1895. It was included by R. A. Streatfeild in his two collections of Butler's essays—*Essays on Life, Art, and Science* (1904), and *The Humour of Homer, and other Essays* (1913).

A.T.B.

How to Make the Best of Life

I HAVE BEEN ASKED TO SPEAK ON THE QUEStion how to make the best of life, but may as well confess at once that I know nothing about it. I cannot think that I have made the best of my own life, nor is it likely that I shall make much better of what may or may not remain to me. I do not even know how to make the best of the twenty minutes that your committee has placed at my disposal, and as for life as a whole, who ever yet made the best of such a colossal opportunity by conscious effort and deliberation? In little things no doubt deliberate and conscious effort will help us, but we are speaking of large issues, and such kingdoms of heaven as the making the best of these come not by observation.

The question, therefore, on which I have undertaken to address you is, as you must all know, fatuous, if it be faced seriously. Life is like playing a violin solo in public and learning the instrument as one goes on. One cannot make the best of such impossibilities, and the question is doubly fatuous until we are told which of our two lives—the conscious or the unconscious—is held by the asker to be the truer life. Which does the question contemplate—the life we know, or the life which others may know, but which we know not?

Death gives a life to some men and women compared with which their so-called existence here is as nothing. Which is the truer life of Shakespeare, Handel, that divine woman who wrote the Odyssey, and of Jane Austen—the life which palpitated with sensible warm motion within their own bodies, or that in virtue of which they are still palpitating in ours? In whose consciousness does their truest life consist—their own, or ours? Can Shakespeare be said to have begun his true life till a hundred years or so after he was dead and buried? His physical life was but as an embryonic stage, a coming up out of darkness, a twilight and dawn before the sunrise of that life of the world to come which he was to enjoy hereafter. We all live for a while after we are gone hence, but we are for the most part stillborn, or at any rate die in infancy, as regards that life which every age and country has recognized as higher and truer than the one of which we are now sentient. As the life of the race is larger, longer, and in all respects more to be considered than that of the individual, so is the life we live in others larger and more important than the one we live in ourselves. This appears nowhere perhaps more plainly than in the case of great teachers, who often in the lives of their pupils produce an effect that reaches far beyond anything produced while their single lives were yet unsupplemented by those other lives into which they infused their own.

Death to such people is the ending of a short life, but it does not touch the life they are already living in those whom they have taught; and happily, as none can know when he shall die, so none can make sure that he too shall not live long beyond the grave; for the life after death is like money before it—no one can be sure that it may not fall to him or her even at the eleventh hour. Money and immortality come in such odd unaccountable ways that no one is cut off from hope. We may not have made either of them for ourselves, but yet another may give them to us in virtue of his or her love, which shall illumine us for ever, and establish us in some heavenly mansion whereof we neither dreamed nor shall ever dream. Look at the Doge Loredano Loredani, the old man's smile upon whose face has been reproduced so faithfully in so many lands that it can never henceforth be forgotten—would he have had one hundredth part of the life he now lives had he not been linked awhile with one of those heaven-sent men who know *che cosa è amor* ? Look at Rembrandt's old woman in our National Gallery; had she died before she was eighty-three years old she would not have been living now. Then, when she was eighty-three, immortality perched upon her as a bird on a withered bough.

I seem to hear someone say that this is a mockery, a piece of special pleading, a giving of stones to those that ask for bread. Life is not life unless we can feel it, and a life limited to a knowledge of such fraction of our work as may happen

How to Make the Best of Life

to survive us is no true life in other people; salve it as we may, death is not life any more than black is white.

The objection is not so true as it sounds. I do not deny that we had rather not die, nor do I pretend that much even in the case of the most favoured few can survive them beyond the grave. It is only because this is so that our own life is possible; others have made room for us, and we should make room for others in our turn without undue repining. What I maintain is that a not inconsiderable number of people do actually attain to a life beyond the grave which we can all feel forcibly enough, whether they can do so or not—that this life tends with increasing civilization to become more and more potent, and that it is better worth considering, in spite of its being unfelt by ourselves, than any which we have felt or can ever feel in our own persons.

Take an extreme case. A group of people are photographed by Edison's new process—say Titiens, Trebelli, and Jenny Lind, with any two of the finest men singers the age has known—let them be photographed incessantly for half an hour while they perform a scene in *Lohengrin*; let all be done stereoscopically. Let them be phonographed at the same time so that their minutest shades of intonation are preserved, let the slides be coloured by a competent artist, and then let the scene be called suddenly into sight and sound, say a hundred years hence. Are those people dead or alive? Dead to themselves they are, but while they live so powerfully and so livingly in us, which is the greater paradox—to say that they are alive or that they are dead? To myself it seems that their life in others would be more truly life than their death to themselves is death. Granted that they do not present all the phenomena of life—who ever does so even when he is held to be alive? We are held to be alive because we present a sufficient number of living phenomena to let the others go without saying; those who see us take the part for the whole here as in everything else, and surely, in the case supposed above, the phenomena of life predominate so powerfully over those of death, that the people themselves must be held to be more alive than dead. Our living personality is, as the word implies, only our mask, and those who still own such a mask as I have supposed have a living personality. Granted again that the case just put is an extreme one; still many a man and many a woman has so stamped him or herself on his work that, though we would gladly have the aid of such accessories as we doubtless presently shall have to the livingness of our great dead, we can see them very sufficiently through the masterpieces they have left us.

As for their own unconsciousness I do not deny it. The life of the embryo was unconscious before birth, and so is the life—I am speaking only of the life revealed to us by natural religion—after death. But as the embryonic and infant life of which we were unconscious was the most potent factor in our after life of consciousness, so the effect which we may unconsciously produce in others after death, and it may be even before it on those who have never seen us, is in all sober seriousness our truer and more abiding life, and the one which those who would make the best of their sojourn here will take most into their consideration.

Unconsciousness is no bar to livingness. Our conscious actions are a drop in the sea as compared with our unconscious ones. Could we know all the life that is in us by way of circulation, nutrition, breathing, waste, and repair, we should learn what an infinitesimally small part consciousness plays in our present existence; yet our unconscious life is as truly life as our conscious life, and though it is unconscious to itself it emerges into an indirect and vicarious consciousness in our other and conscious self, which exists but in virtue of our unconscious self. So we have also a vicarious consciousness in others. The unconscious life of those that have gone before us has in great part moulded us into such men and women as we are, and our own unconscious lives will in like manner have a vicarious consciousness in others, though we be dead enough to it in ourselves.

If it is again urged that it matters not to us how much we

How to Make the Best of Life

may be alive in others, if we are to know nothing about it, I reply that the common instinct of all who are worth considering gives the lie to such cynicism. I see here present some who have achieved, and others who no doubt will achieve, success in literature. Will one of them hesitate to admit that it is a lively pleasure to her to feel that on the other side of the world someone may be smiling happily over her work, and that she is thus living in that person though she knows nothing about it? Here it seems to me that true faith comes in. Faith does not consist, as the Sunday School pupil said, " in the power of believing that which we know to be untrue." It consists in holding fast that which the healthiest and most kindly instincts of the best and most sensible men and women are intuitively possessed of, without caring to require much evidence further than the fact that such people are so convinced; and for my own part I find the best men and women I know unanimous in feeling that life in others, even though we know nothing about it, is nevertheless a thing to be desired and gratefully accepted if we can get it either before death or after. I observe also that a large number of men and women do actually attain to such life, and in some cases continue so to live, if not for ever, yet to what is practically much the same thing. Our life then in this world is, to natural religion as much as to revealed, a period of probation. The use we make of it is to settle how far we are to enter into another, and whether that other is to be a heaven of just affection or a hell of righteous condemnation.

Who, then, are the most likely so to run that they may obtain this veritable prize of our high calling? Setting aside such lucky numbers, drawn as it were in the lottery of immortality, which I have referred to casually above, and setting aside also the chances and changes from which even immortality is not exempt, who on the whole are most likely to live anew in the affectionate thoughts of those who never so much as saw them in the flesh, and know not even their names? There is a *nisus*, a straining in the dull dumb economy of things, in virtue of which some, whether they will it and know it or no, are more likely to live after death than others, and who are these? Those who aimed at it as by some great thing that they would do to make them famous? Those who have lived most in themselves and for themselves, or those who have been most ensouled consciously, but perhaps better unconsciously, directly but more often indirectly, by the most living souls past and present that have flitted near them? Can we think of a man or woman who grips us firmly, at the thought of whom we kindle when we are alone in our honest daw's plumes, with none to admire or shrug his shoulders, can we think of one such, the secret of whose power does not lie in the charm of his or her personality—that is to say, in the wideness of his or her sympathy with, and therefore life in and communion with other people? In the wreckage that comes ashore from the sea of time there is much tinsel stuff that we must preserve and study if we would know our own times and people; granted that many a dead charlatan lives long and enters largely and necessarily into our own lives; we use them and throw them away when we have done with them. I do not speak of these, I do not speak of the Virgils and Alexander Popes, and who can say how many more whose names I dare not mention for fear of offending. They are as stuffed birds or beasts in a museum; serviceable no doubt from a scientific standpoint, but with no vivid or vivifying hold upon us. They seem to be alive, but are not. I am speaking of those who do actually live in us, and move us to higher achievements though they be long dead, whose life thrusts out our own and overrides it. I speak of those who draw us ever more towards them from youth to age, and to think of whom is to feel at once that we are in the hands of those we love, and whom we would most wish to resemble. What is the secret of the hold that these people have upon us? Is it not that while, conventionally speaking, alive, they most merged their lives in, and were in fullest communion with those among whom they lived? They found their lives in losing

How to Make the Best of Life

them. We never love the memory of anyone unless we feel that he or she was himself or herself a lover.

I have seen it urged, again, in querulous accents, that the so-called immortality even of the most immortal is not for ever. I see a passage to this effect in a book that is making a stir as I write. I will quote it. The writer says:

"So, it seems to me, is the immortality we so glibly predicate of departed artists. If they survive at all, it is but a shadowy life they live, moving on through the gradations of slow decay to distant but inevitable death. They can no longer, as heretofore, speak directly to the hearts of their fellow-men, evoking their tears or laughter, and all the pleasures, be they sad or merry, of which imagination holds the secret. Driven from the market-place they become first the companions of the student, then the victims of the specialist. He who would still hold familiar intercourse with them must train himself to penetrate the veil which in ever-thickening folds conceals them from the ordinary gaze; he must catch the tone of a vanished society, he must move in a circle of alien associations, he must think in a language not his own." [1]

This is crying for the moon, or rather pretending to cry for it, for the writer is obviously insincere. I see *The Saturday Review* says the passage I have just quoted " reaches almost to poetry," and indeed I find many blank verses in it, some of them very aggressive. No prose is free from an occasional blank verse, and a good writer will not go hunting over his work to rout them out, but nine or ten in little more than as many lines is indeed reaching too near to poetry for good prose. This, however, is a trifle, and might pass if the tone of the writer was not so obviously that of cheap pessimism. I know not which is cheapest, pessimism or optimism. One forces lights, the other darks; both are equally untrue to good art, and equally sure of their effect with the groundlings. The one extenuates, the other sets down in malice. The first

[1] *The Foundations of Belief*, by the Right Hon. A. J. Balfour. Longmans, 1895, p. 48.

is the more amiable lie, but both are lies, and are known to be so by those who utter them. Talk about catching the tone of a vanished society to understand Rembrandt or Giovanni Bellini! It is nonsense—the folds do not thicken in front of these men; we understand them as well as those among whom they went about in the flesh, and perhaps better. Homer and Shakespeare speak to us probably far more effectually than they did to the men of their own time, and most likely we have them at their best. I cannot think that Shakespeare talked better than we hear him now in *Hamlet* or *Henry the Fourth*; like enough he would have been found a very disappointing person in a drawing-room. People stamp themselves on their work; if they have not done so they are naught, if they have we have them; and for the most part they stamp themselves deeper on their work than on their talk. No doubt Shakespeare and Handel will be one day clean forgotten, as though they had never been born. The world will in the end die; mortality therefore itself is not immortal, and when death dies the life of these men will die with it—but not sooner. It is enough that they should live within us and move us for many ages as they have and will. Such immortality, therefore, as some men and women are born to achieve, or have thrust upon them, is a practical if not a technical immortality, and he who would have more let him have nothing.

I see I have drifted into speaking rather of how to make the best of death than of life, but who can speak of life without his thoughts turning instantly to that which is beyond it? He or she who has made the best of the life after death has made the best of the life before it; who cares one straw for any such chances and changes as will commonly befall him here if he is upheld by the full and certain hope of everlasting life in the affections of those that shall come after? If the life after death is happy in the hearts of others, it matters little how unhappy was the life before it.

And now I leave my subject, not without misgiving that I shall have disappointed you. But for the great attention which

How to Make the Best of Life

is being paid to the work from which I have quoted above, I should not have thought it well to insist on points with which you are, I doubt not, as fully impressed as I am: but that book weakens the sanctions of natural religion, and minimizes the comfort which it affords us, while it does more to undermine than to support the foundations of what is commonly called belief. Therefore I was glad to embrace this opportunity of protesting. Otherwise I should not have been so serious on a matter that transcends all seriousness. Lord Beaconsfield cut it shorter with more effect. When asked to give a rule of life for the son of a friend he said, " Do not let him try and find out who wrote the *Letters of Junius*." Pressed for further counsel, he added, " Nor yet who was the Man in the Iron Mask "—and he would say no more. Don't bore people. And yet I am by no means sure that a good many people do not think themselves ill-used unless he who addresses them has thoroughly well bored them—especially if they have paid any money for hearing him. My great namesake said, " Surely the pleasure is as great of being cheated as to cheat," and great as the pleasure both of cheating and boring undoubtedly is, I believe he was right. So I remember a poem which came out some thirty years ago in *Punch*, about a young lady who went forth in quest to " Some burden make or burden bear, but which she did not greatly care, O Miserie." So, again, all the holy men and women who in the Middle Ages professed to have discovered how to make the best of life took care that being bored, if not cheated, should have a large place in their programme. Still there are limits, and I close not without fear that I may have exceeded them.

QUIS DESIDERIO . . . ?

NOTE

BUTLER contributed this paper to the third number of *The Universal Review* (July 1888). It was included in the two collections of Butler's essays brought out by R. A. Streatfeild in 1904 and 1913 – *viz.*, *Essays on Life, Art, and Science*, and *The Humour of Homer, and other Essays*. For further information as to Dr. John Frost, the author of *Lives of Eminent Christians*, the reader is referred to an article entitled " The Real Use of a Book " in *The Bodleian Quarterly Record*, vol. ii, nos 16 and 17.

A.T.B.

Quis Desiderio . . . ? [1]

LIKE MR. WILKIE COLLINS, I, TOO, HAVE BEEN asked to lay some of my literary experiences before the readers of *The Universal Review*. It occurred to me that the Review must be indeed universal before it could open its pages to one so obscure as myself; but, nothing daunted by the distinguished company among which I was for the first time asked to move, I resolved to do as I was told, and went to the British Museum to see what books I had written. Having refreshed my memory by a glance at the catalogue, I was about to try and diminish the large and ever-increasing circle of my non-readers when I became aware of a calamity that brought me to a standstill, and indeed bids fair, so far as I can see at present, to put an end to my literary existence altogether.

I should explain that I cannot write unless I have a sloping desk, and the reading-room of the British Museum, where alone I can compose freely, is unprovided with sloping desks. Like every other organism, if I cannot get exactly what I want I make shift with the next thing to it; true, there are no desks in the reading-room, but, as I once heard a visitor from the country say, " it contains a large number of very interesting works." I know it was not right, and hope the Museum authorities will not be severe upon me if any of them reads this confession; but I wanted a desk, and set myself to consider which of the many very interesting works which a grateful nation places at the disposal of its would-be authors was best suited for my purpose.

For mere reading I suppose one book is pretty much as good as another; but the choice of a desk-book is a more serious matter. It must be neither too thick nor too thin; it must be large enough to make a substantial support; it must be strongly bound so as not to yield or give; it must not be too troublesome to carry backwards and forwards; and it must live on shelf C, D, or E, so that there need be no stooping or reaching too high. These are the conditions which a really good book must fulfil; simple, however, as they are,

[1] From *The Universal Review*, July 1888.

it is surprising how few volumes comply with them satisfactorily; moreover, being perhaps too sensitively conscientious, I allowed another consideration to influence me, and was sincerely anxious not to take a book which would be in constant use for reference by readers, more especially as, if I did this, I might find myself disturbed by the officials.

For weeks I made experiments upon sundry poetical and philosophical works, whose names I have forgotten, but could not succeed in finding my ideal desk, until at length, more by luck than cunning, I happened to light upon Frost's *Lives of Eminent Christians*, which I had no sooner tried than I discovered it to be the very perfection and *ne plus ultra* of everything that a book should be. It lived in Case No. 2008, and I accordingly took at once to sitting in Row B, where for the last dozen years or so I have sat ever since.

The first thing I have done whenever I went to the Museum has been to take down Frost's *Lives of Eminent Christians* and carry it to my seat. It is not the custom of modern writers to refer to the works to which they are most deeply indebted, and I have never, that I remember, mentioned it by name before; but it is to this book alone that I have looked for support during many years of literary labour, and it is round this to me invaluable volume that all my own have, page by page, grown up. There is none in the Museum to which I have been under anything like such constant obligation, none which I can so ill spare, and none which I would choose so readily if I were allowed to select one single volume and keep it for my own.

On finding myself asked for a contribution to *The Universal Review*, I went, as I have explained, to the Museum, and presently repaired to bookcase No. 2008 to get my favourite volume. Alas! it was in the room no longer. It was not in use, for its place was filled up already; besides, no one ever used it but myself. Whether the ghost of the late Mr. Frost has been so eminently unchristian as to interfere, or whether the authorities have removed the book in ignorance of the steady demand which there has been for it on the part of at

Quis Desiderio . . . ?

least one reader, are points I cannot determine. All I know is that the book is gone, and I feel as Wordsworth is generally supposed to have felt when he became aware that Lucy was in her grave, and exclaimed so emphatically that this would make a considerable difference to him, or words to that effect.

Now I think of it, Frost's *Lives of Eminent Christians* was very like Lucy. The one resided at Dovedale in Derbyshire, the other in Great Russell Street, Bloomsbury. I admit that I do not see the resemblance here at this moment, but if I try to develop my perception I shall doubtless ere long find a marvellously striking one. In other respects, however, than mere local habitat the likeness is obvious. Lucy was not particularly attractive either inside or out—no more was Frost's *Lives of Eminent Christians*; there were few to praise her, and of those few still fewer could bring themselves to like her; indeed, Wordsworth himself seems to have been the only person who thought much about her one way or the other. In like manner, I believe I was the only reader who thought much one way or the other about Frost's *Lives of Eminent Christians*, but this in itself was one of the attractions of the book; and as for the grief we respectively felt and feel, I believe my own to be as deep as Wordsworth's, if not more so.

I said above, " as Wordsworth is generally supposed to have felt "; for anyone imbued with the spirit of modern science will read Wordsworth's poem with different eyes from those of a mere literary critic. He will note that Wordsworth is most careful not to explain the nature of the difference which the death of Lucy will occasion to him. He tells us that there will be a difference; but there the matter ends. The superficial reader takes it that he was very sorry she was dead; it is, of course, possible that he may have actually been so, but he has not said this. On the contrary, he has hinted plainly that she was ugly, and generally disliked; she was only like a violet when she was half-hidden from the view, and only fair as a star when there were so few stars out that it was practically impossible to make an invidious comparison. If there were as many as even two stars the likeness was felt to be at an end. If Wordsworth had imprudently promised to marry this young person during a time when he had been unusually long in keeping to good resolutions, and had afterwards seen someone whom he liked better, then Lucy's death would undoubtedly have made a considerable difference to him, and this is all that he has ever said that it would do. What right have we to put glosses upon the masterly reticence of a poet, and credit him with feelings possibly the very reverse of those he actually entertained?

Sometimes, indeed, I have been inclined to think that a mystery is being hinted at more dark than any critic has suspected. I do not happen to possess a copy of the poem, but the writer, if I am not mistaken, says that "few could know when Lucy ceased to be." "Ceased to be" is a suspiciously euphemistic expression, and the words "few could know" are not applicable to the ordinary peaceful death of a domestic servant such as Lucy appears to have been. No matter how obscure the deceased, any number of people commonly can know the day and hour of his or her demise, whereas in this case we are expressly told it would be impossible for them to do so. Wordsworth was nothing if not accurate, and would not have said that few could know, but that few actually did know, unless he was aware of circumstances that precluded all but those implicated in the crime of her death from knowing the precise moment of its occurrence. If Lucy was the kind of person not obscurely portrayed in the poem; if Wordsworth had murdered her, either by cutting her throat or smothering her, in concert, perhaps, with his friends Southey and Coleridge; and if he had thus found himself released from an engagement which had become irksome to him, or possibly from the threat of an action for breach of promise, then there is not a syllable in the poem with which he crowns his crime that is not alive with meaning. On any other supposition to the general reader it is unintelligible.

Quis Desiderio . . . ?

We cannot be too guarded in the interpretations we put upon the words of great poets. Take the young lady who never loved the dear gazelle—and I don't believe she did; we are apt to think that Moore intended us to see in this creation of his fancy a sweet, amiable, but most unfortunate young woman, whereas all he has told us about her points to an exactly opposite conclusion. In reality, he wished us to see a young lady who had been a habitual complainer from her earliest childhood; whose plants had always died as soon as she bought them, while those belonging to her neighbours had flourished. The inference is obvious, nor can we reasonably doubt that Moore intended us to draw it; if her plants were the very first to fade away, she was evidently the very first to neglect or otherwise maltreat them. She did not give them enough water, or left the door of her fern-case open when she was cooking her dinner at the gas stove, or kept them too near the paraffin oil, or other like folly; and as for her temper, see what the gazelles did; as long as they did not know her "well," they could just manage to exist, but when they got to understand her real character, one after another felt that death was the only course open to it, and accordingly died rather than live with such a mistress. True, the young lady herself said the gazelles loved her; but disagreeable people are apt to think themselves amiable, and in view of the course invariably taken by the gazelles themselves anyone accustomed to weigh evidence will hold that she was probably mistaken.

I must, however, return to Frost's *Lives of Eminent Christians*. I will leave none of the ambiguity about my words in which Moore and Wordsworth seem to have delighted. I am very sorry the book is gone, and know not where to turn for its successor. Till I have found a substitute I can write no more, and I do not know how to find even a tolerable one. I should try a volume of Migne's *Complete Course of Patrology*, but I do not like books in more than one volume, for the volumes vary in thickness, and one never can remember which one took; the four volumes, however, of

Bede in Giles's *Anglican Fathers* are not open to this objection, and I have reserved them for favourable consideration. Mather's *Magnalia* might do, but the binding does not please me; Cureton's *Corpus Ignatianum* might also do if it were not too thin. I do not like taking Norton's *Genuineness of the Gospels*, as it is just possible someone may be wanting to know whether the Gospels are genuine or not, and be unable to find out because I have got Mr. Norton's book. Baxter's *Church History of England*, Lingard's *Anglo-Saxon Church*, and Cardwell's *Documentary Annals*, though none of them as good as Frost, are works of considerable merit; but on the whole I think Arvine's *Cyclopedia of Moral and Religious Anecdote* is perhaps the one book in the room which comes within measurable distance of Frost. I should probably try this book first, but it has a fatal objection in its too seductive title. " I am not curious," as Miss Lottie Venne says in one of her parts, " but I like to know," and I might be tempted to pervert the book from its natural uses and open it, so as to find out what kind of a thing a moral and religious anecdote is. I know, of course, that there are a great many anecdotes in the Bible, but no one thinks of calling them either moral or religious, though some of them certainly seem as if they might fairly find a place in Mr. Arvine's work. There are some things, however, which it is better not to know, and take it all round I do not think I should be wise in putting myself in the way of temptation, and adopting Arvine as the successor to my beloved and lamented Frost.

Some successor I must find, or I must give up writing altogether, and this I should be sorry to do. I have only as yet written about a third, or from that—counting works written but not published—to a half of the books which I have set myself to write. It would not so much matter if old age was not staring me in the face. Dr. Parr said it was " a beastly shame for an old man not to have laid down a good cellar of port in his youth "; I, like the greater number, I suppose, of those who write books at all, write in order that I may have something to read in my old age when I can write no longer. I know what I shall like better than anyone can tell me, and write accordingly; if my career is nipped in the bud, as seems only too likely, I really do not know where else I can turn for present agreeable occupation, nor yet how to make suitable provision for my later years. Other writers can, of course, make excellent provision for their own old ages, but they cannot do so for mine, any more than I should succeed if I were to try to cater for theirs. It is one of those cases in which no man can make agreement for his brother.

I have no heart for continuing this article, and if I had, I have nothing of interest to say. No one's literary career can have been smoother or more unchequered than mine. I have published all my books at my own expense, and paid for them in due course. What can be conceivably more unromantic? For some years I had a little literary grievance against the authorities of the British Museum because they would insist on saying in their catalogue that I had published three sermons on Infidelity in the year 1820. I thought I had not, and got them out to see. They were rather funny, but they were not mine. Now, however, this grievance has been removed. I had another little quarrel with them because they would describe me as " of St. John's College, Cambridge," an establishment for which I have the most profound veneration, but with which I have not had the honour to be connected for some quarter of a century. At last they said they would change this description if I would only tell them what I was, for, though they had done their best to find out, they had themselves failed. I replied with modest pride that I was a Bachelor of Arts. I keep all my other letters inside my name, not outside. They mused and said it was unfortunate that I was not a Master of Arts. Could I not get myself made a Master? I said I understood that a Mastership was an article the University could not do under about five pounds, and that I was not disposed to go sixpence higher than three ten. They again said it was a pity, for it would be very inconvenient to them if I did not keep to something between a bishop and a poet. I might be anything I liked in reason, provided I showed proper respect for the alphabet; but they had got me between "Samuel Butler, bishop," and "Samuel Butler, poet." It would be very troublesome to shift me, and "bachelor" came before "bishop." This was reasonable, so I replied that, under those circumstances, if they pleased, I thought I would like to be a "philosophical writer." They embraced the solution, and, no matter what I write now, I must remain a "philosophical writer" as long as I live, for the alphabet will hardly be altered in my time, and I must be something between "bis" and "poe." If I could get a volume of my excellent namesake's *Hudibras* out of the list of my works, I should be robbed of my last shred of literary grievance, so I say nothing about this, but keep it secret, lest some worse thing should happen to me. Besides, I have a great respect for my namesake, and always say that if *Erewhon* had been a racehorse it would have been got by *Hudibras* out of *Analogy*. Someone said this to me many years ago, and I felt so much flattered that I have been repeating the remark as my own ever since.

But how small are these grievances as compared with those endured without a murmur by hundreds of writers far more deserving than myself. When I see the scores and hundreds of workers in the reading-room who have done so much more than I have, but whose work is absolutely fruitless to themselves, and when I think of the prompt recognition obtained by my own work, I ask myself what I have done to be thus rewarded. On the other hand, the feeling that I have succeeded far beyond my deserts hitherto, makes it all the harder for me to acquiesce without complaint in the extinction of a career which I honestly believe to be a promising one; and once more I repeat that, unless the Museum authorities give me back my Frost, or put a locked clasp on Arvine, my career must be extinguished. Give me back Frost, and, if life and health are spared, I will write another dozen of volumes yet before I hang up my fiddle—if so serious a confusion of metaphors may be pardoned. I know from long experience how kind and considerate both the

Quis Desiderio . . . ?

late and present superintendents of the reading-room were and are, but I doubt how far either of them would be disposed to help me on this occasion; continue, however, to rob me of my Frost, and, whatever else I may do, I will write no more books.

Note by Dr. Garnett, British Museum. The frost has broken up. Mr. Butler is restored to literature. Mr. Mudie may make himself easy. England will still boast a humorist; and the late Mr. Darwin (to whose posthumous machinations the removal of the book was owing) will continue to be confounded.—R. GARNETT.

THE AUNT, THE NIECES, AND THE DOG

NOTE

This piece appeared in *The Universal Review* for May 1889. It was included by R. A. Streatfeild in the two collections of Butler's essays which he brought out in 1904 and 1913 respectively, with the following note:

"As I have several times been asked if the letters here reprinted were not fabricated by Butler himself, I take this opportunity of stating that they are authentic in every particular, and that the originals are now in my possession."

The reader will find the true history of these letters in H. F. Jones's *Memoir*, ii, 82-84. In *The Universal Review* an attempt was made to reproduce typographically the queer appearance of the originals, but the attempt was a failure and was abandoned when the letters were reprinted.

A.T.B.

The Aunt, the Nieces, and the Dog[1]

WHEN A THING IS OLD, BROKEN, AND useless we throw it on the dust-heap, but when it is sufficiently old, sufficiently broken, and sufficiently useless we give money for it, put it into a museum, and read papers over it which people come long distances to hear. By and by, when the whirligig of time has brought on another revenge, the museum itself becomes a dust-heap, and remains so till after long ages it is rediscovered, and valued as belonging to a neo-rubbish age—containing, perhaps, traces of a still older paleo-rubbish civilization. So when people are old, indigent, and in all respects incapable, we hold them in greater and greater contempt as their poverty and impotence increase, till they reach the pitch when they are actually at the point to die, whereon they become sublime. Then we place every resource our hospitals can command at their disposal, and show no stint in our consideration for them.

It is the same with all our interests. We care most about extremes of importance and of unimportance; but extremes of importance are tainted with fear, and a very imperfect fear casteth out love. Extremes of unimportance cannot hurt us, therefore we are well disposed towards them; the means may come to do so, therefore we do not love them. Hence we pick a fly out of a milk-jug and watch with pleasure over its recovery, for we are confident that under no conceivable circumstances will it want to borrow money from us; but we feel less sure about a mouse, so we show it no quarter. The compilers of our almanacs well know this tendency of our natures, so they tell us, not when Noah went into the ark, nor when the temple of Jerusalem was dedicated, but that Lindley Murray, grammarian, died 16th January 1826. This is not because they could not find so many as three hundred and sixty-five events of considerable interest since the creation of the world, but because they well know we would rather hear of something less interesting. We care most about what concerns us either very closely,

[1] From *The Universal Review*, May 1889.

or so little that practically we have nothing whatever to do with it.

I once asked a young Italian, who professed to have a considerable knowledge of English literature, which of all our poems pleased him best. He replied without a moment's hesitation:

> "Hey diddle diddle, the cat and the fiddle,
>   The cow jumped over the moon;
>   The little dog laughed to see such sport,
>   And the dish ran away with the spoon."

He said this was better than anything in Italian. They had Dante and Tasso, and ever so many more great poets, but they had nothing comparable to "Hey diddle diddle," nor had he been able to conceive how anyone could have written it. Did I know the author's name, and had we given him a statue? On this I told him of the young lady of Harrow who would go to church in a barrow, and plied him with whatever rhyming nonsense I could call to mind, but it was no use; all of these things had an element of reality that robbed them of half their charm, whereas "Hey diddle diddle" had nothing in it that could conceivably concern him.

So again it is with the things that gall us most. What is it that rises up against us at odd times and smites us in the face again and again for years after it has happened? That we spent all the best years of our life in learning what we have found to be a swindle, and to have been known to be a swindle by those who took money for misleading us? That those on whom we most leaned most betrayed us? That we have only come to feel our strength when there is little strength left of any kind to feel? These things will hardly much disturb a man of ordinary good temper. But that he should have said this or that little unkind and wanton saying; that he should have gone away from this or that hotel and given a shilling too little to the waiter; that his clothes were shabby at such or such a garden-party—these things gall us

The Aunt, the Nieces, and the Dog

as a corn will sometimes do, though the loss of a limb may not be seriously felt.

I have been reminded lately of these considerations with more than common force by reading the very voluminous correspondence left by my grandfather, Dr. Butler, of Shrewsbury, whose memoirs I am engaged in writing. I have found a large number of interesting letters on subjects of serious import, but must confess that it is to the hardly less numerous lighter letters that I have been most attracted, nor do I feel sure that my eminent namesake did not share my predilection. Among other letters in my possession I have one bundle that has been kept apart, and has evidently no connection with Dr. Butler's own life. I cannot use these letters, therefore, for my book, but over and above the charm of their inspired spelling, I find them of such an extremely trivial nature that I incline to hope the reader may derive as much amusement from them as I have done myself, and venture to give them the publicity here which I must refuse them in my book. The dates and signatures have, with the exception of Mrs. Newton's, been carefully erased, but I have collected that they were written by the two servants of a single lady who resided at no great distance from London, to two nieces of the said lady who lived in London itself. The aunt never writes, but always gets one of the servants to do so for her. She appears either as " your aunt " or as " She "; her name is not given, but she is evidently looked upon with a good deal of awe by all who had to do with her.

The letters almost all of them relate to visits either of the aunt to London, or of the nieces to the aunt's home, which, from occasional allusions to hopping, I gather to have been in Kent, Sussex, or Surrey. I have arranged them to the best of my power, and take the following to be the earliest. It has no signature, but is not in the handwriting of the servant who styles herself Elizabeth, or Mrs. Newton. It runs:

" MADAM, Your Aunt Wishes me to inform you she will be glad if you will let hir know if you think of coming To hir House thiss month or Next as she cannot have you in September on a kount of the Hoping If you ar coming she thinkes she had batter Go to London on the Day you com to hir House she says you shall have everry Thing raddy for you at hir House and Mrs. Newton to meet you and stay with you till She returnes a gann.

" if you arnot Coming thiss Summer She will be in London before thiss Month is out and will Sleep on the Sofy As She willnot be in London more thann two nits. and She Says she willnot truble you on anny a kount as She Will returne the Same Day before She will plage you anny more. but She thanks you for asking hir to London. but She says She cannot leve the house at prassant She sayhir Survants ar to do for you as she cannot lodge yours nor she willnot have thim in at the house anny more to brake and destroy hir thinks and beslive hir and make up Lies by hir and Skandel as your too did She says she mens to pay fore 2 Nits and one day, She says the Pepelwill let hir have it if you ask thim to let hir: you Will be so good as to let hir know sun: wish She is to do, as She says She dos not care anny thing a bout it. which way tiss she is batter than She was and desirs hir Love to bouth bouth.

" Your aunt wises to know how the silk Clocks ar madup [how the silk cloaks are made up] with a Cape or a wood as she is a goin to have one madeup to rideout in in hir littel shas [chaise].

" Charles is a butty and so good.

" Mr & Mrs Newton ar quite wall & desires to be remembered to you."

I can throw no light on the meaning of the verb to "beslive." Each letter in the MS. is so admirably formed that there can be no question about the word being as I have given it. Nor have I been able to discover what is referred to by the words " Charles is a butty and so good." We shall presently meet with a Charles who " flies in the

The Aunt, the Nieces, and the Dog

Fier," but that Charles appears to have been in London, whereas this one is evidently in Kent, or wherever the aunt lived.

The next letter is from Mrs. Newton:

"DER MISS ——, I Receve your Letter your Aunt is vary Ill and Lowspireted I Donte think your Aunt wood Git up all Day if My Sister Wasnot to Persage her We all Think hir lif is two monopolous. you Wish to know Who Was Liveing With your Aunt. that is My Sister and Willian — and Cariline — as Cock and Old Poll Pepper is Come to Stay With her a Littel Wile and I hoped [hopped] for Your Aunt, and Harry has Worked for your Aunt all the Summer. Your Aunt and Harry Whent to the Wells Races and Spent a very Pleasant Day your Aunt has Lost Old Fanney Sow She Died about a Week a Go Harry he Wanted your Aunt to have her killed and send her to London and Shee Wold Fech her £11 the Farmers have Lost a Great Deal of Cattel such as Hogs and Cows What theay call the Plage I Whent to your Aunt as you Wish Mee to Do But She Told Mee She Did not wont aney Boddy She Told Mee She Should Like to Come up to see you But She Cant Come know for she is Boddyley ill and Harry Donte Work there know But he Go up there Once in Two or Three Day Harry Offered is self to Go up to Live With your Aunt But She Made him know Ancer. I hav Been up to your Aunt at Work for 5 Weeks Hopping and Ragluting Your Aunt Donte Eat nor Drink But vary Littel indeed.

"I am Happy to Say We are Both Quite Well and I am Glad to hear you are Both Quite Well

"MRS NEWTON."

This seems to have made the nieces propose to pay a visit to their aunt, perhaps to try and relieve the monopoly of her existence and cheer her up a little. In their letter, doubtless, the dog motive is introduced that is so finely developed presently by Mrs. Newton. I should like to have been able to give the theme as enounced by the nieces themselves, but their letters are not before me. Mrs. Newton writes:

"MY DEAR GIRLS, Your Aunt receiv your Letter your Aunt will Be vary glad to see you as it quite a greeable if it tis to you and Shee is Quite Willing to Eair the beds and the Rooms if you Like to Trust to hir and the Servantes; if not I may Go up there as you Wish. My Sister Sleeps in the Best Room as she allways Did and the Coock in the garret and you Can have the Rooms the same as you allways Did as your Aunt Donte set in the Parlour She Continlery Sets in the Ciching. your Aunt says she Cannot Part from the dog know hows and She Says he will not hurt you for he is Like a Child and I can safeley say My Self he wonte hurt you as She Cannot Sleep in the Room With out him as he allWay Sleep in the Same Room as She Dose. your Aunt is agreeable to Git in What Coles and Wood you Wish for I am know happy to say your Aunt is in as Good health as ever She Was and She is happy to hear you are Both Well your Aunt Wishes for Ancer By Return of Post."

The nieces replied that their aunt must choose between the dog and them, and Mrs. Newton sends a second letter which brings her development to a climax. It runs:

"DEAR MISS —, I have Receve your Letter and i Whent up to your Aunt as you Wish me and i Try to Perveal With her about the Dog But she Wold not Put the Dog away nor it alow him to Be Tied up But She Still Wishes you to Come as Shee says the Dog Shall not interrup you for She Donte alow the Dog nor it the Cats to Go in the Parlour never sence She has had it Donup ferfere of Spoiling the Paint your Aunt think it vary Strange you Should Be so vary Much afraid of a Dog and She says you Cant Go out in London But What you are up a gance one and She says She Wonte Trust the Dog in know one hands But her Owne for She is afraid theay

The Aunt, the Nieces, and the Dog

Will not fill is Belley as he Lives upon Rost Beeff and Rost and Boil Moutten Wich he Eats More then the Servantes in the House there is not aney One Wold Beable to Give Sattefacktion upon that account Harry offerd to Take the Dog But She Wood not Trust him in our hands so I Cold not Do aney thing With her your Aunt youse to Tell Me When we was at your House in London She Did not know how to make you amens and i Told her know it was the Time to Do it But i Considder She sets the Dog Before you your Aunt keep know Beer know Sprits know Wines in the House of aney Sort Oneley a Little Barl of Wine I made her in the Summer the Workmen and servantes are a Blige to Drink wauter Morning Noon and Night your Aunt the Same She Donte Low her Self aney Tee nor Coffee But is Loocking Wonderful Well

"I Still Remane your Humble Servant Mrs Newton

"I am vary sorry to think the Dog Perventes your Comeing

"I am Glad to hear you are Both Well and we are the same."

The nieces remained firm, and from the following letter it is plain the aunt gave way. The dog motive is repeated *pianissimo*, and is not returned to—not at least by Mrs. Newton.

"DEAR MISS —, I Receve your Letter on Thursday i Whent to your Aunt and i see her and She is a Greable to every thing i asked her and seme so vary Much Please to see you Both Next Tuseday and she has sent for the Faggots to Day and she Will Send for the Coles to Morrow and i will Go up there to Morrow Morning and Make the Fiers and Tend to the Beds and sleep in it Till you Come Down your Aunt sends her Love to you Both and she is Quite well your Aunt Wishes you wold Write againe Before you Come as she ma Expeckye and the Dog is not to Gointo the Parlor a Tall

"your Aunt kind Love to you Both & hopes you Wonte Fail in Coming according to Prommis

"MRS NEWTON."

From a later letter it appears that the nieces did not pay their visit after all, and what is worse a letter had miscarried, and the aunt sat up expecting them from seven till twelve at night, and Harry had paid for "Faggots and Coles quarter of Hund. Faggots Half tun of Coles 1*l*. 1*s*. 3*d*." Shortly afterwards, however, " She " again talks of coming up to London herself and writes through her servant:

" My Dear girls i Receve your kind letter & I am happy to hear you ar both Well and I Was in hopes of seeing of you Both Down at My House this spring to stay a Wile I am Quite well my self in Helth But vary Low Spireted I am vary sorry to hear the Misforting of Poor charles & how he cum to flie in the Fier I cannot think. I should like to know if he is dead or a Live, and I shall come to London in August & stay three or four daies if it is agreable to you. Mrs. Newton has lost her mother in Law 4 day March & I hope you send me word Wather charles is Dead or a Live as soon as possible, and will you send me word what little Betty is for I cannot make her out."

The next letter is a new handwriting, and tells the nieces of their aunt's death in the following terms:

" DEAR MISS —, It is my most painful duty to inform you that your dear aunt expired this morning comparatively easy as Hannah informs me and in so doing restored her soul to the custody of him whom she considered to be alone worthy of its care.

" The doctor had visited her about five minutes previously and had applied a blister.

" You and your sister will I am sure excuse further details at present and believe me with kindest remembrances to remain

" Yours truly, etc."

After a few days a lawyer's letter informs the nieces that their aunt had left them the bulk of her not very considerable

The Aunt, the Nieces, and the Dog

property, but had charged them with an annuity of £1 a week to be paid to Harry and Mrs. Newton so long as the dog lived.

The only other letters by Mrs. Newton are written on paper of a different and more modern size; they leave an impression of having been written a good many years later. I take them as they come. The first is very short:

" DEAR MISS —, i write to say i cannot possiblely come on Wednesday as we have killed a pig. your's truely,
" ELIZABETH NEWTON."

The second runs:

" DEAR MISS —, i hope you are both quite well in health & your Leg much better i am happy to say i am getting quite well again i hope Amandy has reached you safe by this time i sent a small parcle by Amandy, there was half a dozen Pats of butter & the Cakes was very homely and not so light as i could wish i hope by this time Sarah Ann has promised she will stay untill next monday as i think a few daies longer will not make much diferance and as her young man has been very considerate to wait so long as he has i think he would for a few days Longer dear Miss — I wash for William and i have not got his clothes yet as it has been delayed by the carrier & i cannot possiblely get it done before Sunday and i do not Like traviling on a Sunday but to oblige you i would come but to come sooner i cannot possiblely but i hope Sarah Ann will be prevailed on once more as She has so many times i feel sure if she tells her young man he will have patient for he is a very kind young man
" i remain your sincerely
" ELIZABETH NEWTON."

The last letter in my collection seems written almost within measurable distance of the Christmas-card era. The sheet is headed by a beautifully embossed device of some holly in red and green, wishing the recipient of the letter a merry Xmas and a happy new year, while the border is crimped and edged with blue. I know not what it is, but there is something in the writer's highly finished style that reminds me of Mendelssohn. It would almost do for the words of one of his celebrated " Lieder ohne Worte ":

"DEAR MISS MARIA, I hasten to acknowledge the receipt of your kind note with the inclosure for which I return my best thanks. I need scarcely say how glad I was to know that the volumes secured your approval, and that the announcement of the improvement in the condition of your Sister's legs afforded me infinite pleasure. The gratifying news encouraged me in the hope that now the nature of the disorder is comprehended her legs will—notwithstanding the process may be gradual—ultimately get quite well. The pretty Robin Redbreast which lay ensconced in your epistle, conveyed to me, in terms more eloquent than words, how much you desired me those Compliments which the little missive he bore in his bill expressed; the emblem is sweetly pretty, and now that we are again allowed to felicitate each other on another recurrence of the season of the Christian's rejoicing, permit me to tender to yourself, and by you to your Sister, mine and my Wife's heartfelt congratulations and warmest wishes with respect to the coming year. It is a common belief that if we take a retrospective view of each departing year, as it behoves us annually to do, we shall find the blessings which we have received to immeasurably outnumber our causes of sorrow. Speaking for myself I can fully subscribe to that sentiment, and doubtless neither Miss — nor yourself are exceptions. Miss —'s illness and consequent confinement to the house has been a severe trial, but in that trouble an opportunity was afforded you to prove a Sister's devotion and she has been enabled to realize a larger (if possible) display of sisterly affection.

"A happy Christmas to you both, and may the new year prove a Cornucopia from which still greater blessings than even those we have hitherto received, shall issue, to benefit

The Aunt, the Nieces, and the Dog

us all by contributing to our temporal happiness and, what is of higher importance, conducing to our felicity hereafter.

"I was sorry to hear that you were so annoyed with mice and rats, and if I should have an opportunity to obtain a nice cat I will do so and send my boy to your house with it.

"I remain,

"Yours truly."

How little what is commonly called education can do after all towards the formation of a good style, and what a delightful volume might not be entitled "Half Hours with the Worst Authors." Why, the finest word I know of in the English language was coined, not by my poor old grandfather, whose education had left little to desire, nor by any of the admirable scholars whom he in his turn educated, but by an old matron who presided over one of the halls, or houses of his school. This good lady, whose name by the way was Bromfield, had a fine high temper of her own, or thought it politic to affect one. One night when the boys were particularly noisy she burst like a hurricane into the hall, collared a youngster, and told him he was the "rampingest-scampingest-rackety-tackety-tow-row-roaringest boy in the whole school." Would Mrs. Newton have been able to set the aunt and the dog before us so vividly if she had been more highly educated? Would Mrs. Bromfield have been able to forge and hurl her thunderbolt of a word if she had been taught how to do so, or indeed been at much pains to create it at all? It came. It was her χάρισμα. She did not probably know that she had done what the greatest scholar would have had to rack his brains over for many an hour before he could even approach. Tradition says that having brought down her boy she looked round the hall in triumph, and then after a moment's lull said, "Young gentlemen, prayers are excused," and left them.

I have sometimes thought that, after all, the main use of a classical education consists in the check it gives to originality, and the way in which it prevents an inconvenient number of people from using their own eyes. That we will not be at the trouble of looking at things for ourselves if we can get anyone to tell us what we ought to see goes without saying, and it is the business of schools and universities to assist us in this respect. The theory of evolution teaches that any power not worked at pretty high pressure will deteriorate: originality and freedom from affectation are all very well in their way, but we can easily have too much of them, and it is better that none should be either original or free from cant but those who insist on being so, no matter what hindrances obstruct, nor what incentives are offered them to see things through the regulation medium. To insist on seeing things for oneself is to be an ἰδιώτης, or in plain English, an idiot; nor do I see any safer check against general vigour and clearness of thought, with consequent terseness of expression, than that provided by the curricula of our universities and schools of public instruction. If a young man, in spite of every effort to fit him with blinkers, will insist on getting rid of them, he must do so at his own risk. He will not be long in finding out his mistake. Our public schools and universities play the beneficent part in our social scheme that cattle do in forests: they browse the seedlings down and prevent the growth of all but the luckiest and sturdiest. Of course, if there are too many either cattle or schools, they browse so effectually that they find no more food, and starve till equilibrium is restored; but it seems to be a provision of nature that there should always be these alternate periods, during which either the cattle or the trees are getting the best of it; and, indeed, without such provision we should have neither the one nor the other. At this moment the cattle, doubtless, are in the ascendant, and if university extension proceeds much farther, we shall assuredly have no more Mrs. Newtons and Mrs. Bromfields; but whatever is is best, and, on the whole, I should propose to let things find pretty much their own level.

However this may be, who can question that the treasures hidden in many a country house contain sleeping beauties

The Aunt, the Nieces, and the Dog

even fairer than those that I have endeavoured to waken from long sleep in the foregoing article? How many Mrs. Quicklys are there not living in London at this present moment? For that Mrs. Quickly was an invention of Shakespeare's I will not believe. The old woman from whom he drew said every word that he put into Mrs. Quickly's mouth, and a great deal more which he did not and perhaps could not make use of. This question, however, would again lead me far from my subject, which I should mar were I to dwell upon it longer, and therefore leave with the hope that it may give my readers absolutely no food whatever for reflection.

NOTE

This piece was published in *The Universal Review* for December 1890. It was reprinted in the two collections of Butler's essays which R. A. Streatfeild brought out in 1904 and 1913 respectively. In reprinting it Streatfeild omitted Goethe and Mr. Pitt (see p. 137, *post*), and added, from Butler's Note-Books, the two passages printed between asterisks on pp. 137 and 138. It is clear from a note pasted into his copy of Butler's *Universal Review* articles that Streatfeild intended to amplify the history of the ingenious parrots, but he did not do so. The passage printed within double asterisks (p. 143, *post*) is, therefore, now included for the first time. See H. F. Jones's *Memoir*, i, 421.

A.T.B.

Ramblings in Cheapside [1]

WALKING THE OTHER DAY IN CHEAPSIDE I saw some turtles in Mr. Sweeting's window, and was tempted to stay and look at them. As I did so I was struck not more by the defences with which they were hedged about, than by the fatuousness of trying to hedge that in at all which, if hedged thoroughly, must die of its own defencefulness. The holes for the head and feet through which the turtle leaks out, as it were, on to the exterior world, and through which it again absorbs the exterior world into itself—" catching on " through them to things that are thus both turtle and not turtle at one and the same time—these holes stultify the armour, and show it to have been designed by a creature with more of faithfulness to a fixed idea, and hence onesidedness, than of that quick sense of relative importances and their changes, which is the main factor of good living.

The turtle obviously had no sense of proportion; it differed so widely from myself that I could not comprehend it; and as this word occurred to me, it occurred also that until my body comprehended its body in a physical material sense, neither would my mind be able to comprehend its mind with any thoroughness. For unity of mind can only be consummated by unity of body; everything, therefore, must be in some respects both knave and fool to all that which has not eaten it, or by which it has not been eaten. As long as the turtle was in the window and I in the street outside, there was no chance of our comprehending one another.

Nevertheless, I knew that I could get it to agree with me if I could so effectually buttonhole and fasten on to it as to eat it. Most men have an easy method with turtle soup, and I had no misgiving but that if I could bring my first premise to bear I should prove the better reasoner. My difficulty lay in this initial process, for I had not with me the argument that would alone compel Mr. Sweeting to think that I ought to be allowed to convert the turtles—I mean I had no money

[1] From *The Universal Review*, December 1890.

in my pocket. No missionary enterprise can be carried on without any money at all, but even so small a sum as half a crown would, I suppose, have enabled me to bring the turtle partly round, and with many half-crowns I could in time no doubt convert the lot, for the turtle needs must go where the money drives. If, as is alleged, the world stands on a turtle, the turtle stands on money. No money no turtle. As for money, that stands on opinion, credit, trust, faith—things that, though highly material in connection with money, are still of immaterial essence.

The steps are perfectly plain. The men who caught the turtles brought a fairly strong and definite opinion to bear upon them, that passed into action, and later on into money. They thought the turtles would come that way, and verified their opinion; on this, will and action were generated, with the result that the men turned the turtles on their backs and carried them off. Mr. Sweeting touched these men with money, which is the outward and visible sign of verified opinion. The customer touches Mr. Sweeting with money, Mr. Sweeting touches the waiter and the cook with money. They touch the turtle with skill and verified opinion. Finally, the customer applies the clinching argument that brushes all sophisms aside, and bids the turtle stand protoplasm to protoplasm with himself, to know even as it is known.

But it must be all touch, touch, touch; skill, opinion, power, and money, passing in and out with one another in any order we like, but still link to link and touch to touch. If there is failure anywhere in respect of opinion, skill, power, or money, either as regards quantity or quality, the chain can be no stronger than its weakest link, and the turtle and the clinching argument will fly asunder. Of course, if there is an initial failure in connection, through defect in any member of the chain, or of connection between the links, it will no more be attempted to bring the turtle and the clinching argument together, than it will to chain up a dog with two pieces of broken chain that are disconnected. The contact

Ramblings in Cheapside

throughout must be conceived as absolute; and yet perfect contact is inconceivable by us, for on becoming perfect it ceases to be contact, and becomes essential, once for all inseverable, identity. The most absolute contact short of this is still contact by courtesy only. So here, as everywhere else, Eurydice glides off as we are about to grasp her. We can see nothing face to face; our utmost seeing is but a fumbling of blind finger-ends in an overcrowded pocket.

Presently my own blind finger-ends fished up the conclusion, that as I had neither time nor money to spend on perfecting the chain that would put me in full spiritual contact with Mr. Sweeting's turtles, I had better leave them to complete their education at someone else's expense rather than mine, so I walked on towards the Bank. As I did so it struck me how continually we are met by this melting of one existence into another. The limits of the body seem well defined enough as definitions go, but definitions seldom go far. What, for example, can seem more distinct from a man than his banker or his solicitor? Yet these are commonly so much parts of him that he can no more cut them off and grow new ones, than he can grow new legs or arms; neither must he wound his solicitor; a wound in the solicitor is a very serious thing. As for his bank—failure of his bank's action may be as fatal to a man as failure of his heart. I have said nothing about the medical or spiritual adviser, but most men grow into the society that surrounds them by the help of these four main tap-roots, and not only into the world of humanity, but into the universe at large. We can, indeed, grow butchers, bakers, and greengrocers, almost *ad libitum*, but these are low developments, and correspond to skin, hair, or finger-nails. Those of us again who are not highly enough organized to have grown a solicitor or banker can generally repair the loss of whatever social organization they may possess as freely as lizards are said to grow new tails; but this with the higher social, as well as organic, developments is only possible to a very limited extent.

The doctrine of metempsychosis, or transmigration of

souls—a doctrine to which the foregoing considerations are for the most part easy corollaries—crops up no matter in what direction we allow our thoughts to wander. And we meet instances of transmigration of body as well as of soul. I do not mean that both body and soul have transmigrated together, far from it; but that, as we can often recognize a transmigrated mind in an alien body, so we not less often see a body that is clearly only a transmigration, linked on to someone else's new and alien soul. We meet people every day whose bodies are evidently those of men and women long dead, but whose appearance we know through their portraits. We see them going about in omnibuses, railway carriages, and in all public places. The cards have been shuffled, and they have drawn fresh lots in life and nationalities, but anyone fairly well up in mediaeval and last-century portraiture knows them at a glance.

Going down once towards Italy I saw a young man in the train whom I recognized, only he seemed to have got younger. He was with a friend, and his face was in continual play, but for some little time I puzzled in vain to recollect where it was that I had seen him before. All of a sudden I remembered he was King Francis I of France. I had hitherto thought the face of this king impossible, but when I saw it in play I understood it. His great contemporary Henry VIII keeps a restaurant in Oxford Street. Falstaff drove one of the St. Gothard diligences for many years, and only retired when the railway was opened. Titian once made me a pair of boots at Vicenza, and not very good ones. At Modena I had my hair cut by a young man whom I perceived to be Raffaelle. The model who sat to him for his celebrated Madonnas is first lady in a confectionery establishment at Montreal. She has a little motherly pimple on the left side of her nose that is misleading at first, but on examination she is readily recognized; probably Raffaelle's model had the pimple too, but Raffaelle left it out—as he would.

Handel, of course, is Madame Patey. Give Madame Patey Handel's wig and clothes, and there would be no telling her

Ramblings in Cheapside

from Handel. It is not only that the features and the shape of the head are the same, but there is a certain imperiousness of expression and attitude about Handel which he hardly attempts to conceal in Madame Patey. It is a curious coincidence that he should continue to be such an incomparable renderer of his own music. Pope Julius II was the late Mr. Darwin. I met Goethe once coming down Ludgate Hill, and glared at him, but he would not look at me. Mr. Pitt is a clerk in a solicitor's office, and neither drinks nor gambles. *Rameses II is a blind woman now, and stands in Holborn, holding a tin mug. I never could understand why I always found myself humming " They oppressed them with burthens " when I passed her, till one day I was looking in Mr. Spooner's window in the Strand, and saw a photograph of Rameses II. Mary Queen of Scots wears surgical boots and is subject to fits, near the Horse Shoe in Tottenham Court Road.*

Michael Angelo is a commissionaire; I saw him on board the *Glen Rosa*, which used to run every day from London to Clacton-on-Sea and back. It gave me quite a turn when I saw him coming down the stairs from the upper deck, with his bronzed face, flattened nose, and with the familiar bar upon his forehead. I never liked Michael Angelo, and never shall, but I am afraid of him, and was near trying to hide when I saw him coming towards me. He had not got his commissionaire's uniform on, and I did not know he was one till I met him a month or so later in the Strand. When we got to Blackwall the music struck up and people began to dance. I never saw a man dance so much in my life. He did not miss a dance all the way to Clacton, nor all the way back again, and when not dancing he was flirting and cracking jokes. I could hardly believe my eyes when I reflected that this man had painted the famous " Last Judgement," and had made all those statues.

Dante is, or was a year or two ago, a waiter at Brissago on the Lago Maggiore, only he is better-tempered-looking, and has a more intellectual expression. He gave me his ideas

137

upon beauty: " Tutto ch' è vero è bello," he exclaimed, with all his old self-confidence. I am not afraid of Dante. I know people by their friends, and he went about with Virgil, so I said with some severity, " No, Dante, il naso della Signora Robinson è vero, ma non è bello "; and he admitted I was right. Beatrice's name is Towler; she is waitress at a small inn in German Switzerland. I used to sit at my window and hear people call " Towler, Towler, Towler," fifty times in a forenoon. She was the exact antithesis to Abra; Abra, if I remember, used to come before they called her name, but no matter how often they called Towler, everyone came before she did. I suppose they spelt her name Taula, but to me it sounded Towler; I never, however, met anyone else with this name. She was a sweet, artless little hussy, who made me play the piano to her, and she said it was lovely. Of course I only played my own compositions; so I believed her, and it all went off very nicely. I thought it might save trouble if I did not tell her who she really was, so I said nothing about it.

*I met Socrates once. He was my muleteer on an excursion which I will not name, for fear it should identify the man. The moment I saw my guide I knew he was somebody, but for the life of me I could not remember who. All of a sudden it flashed across me that he was Socrates. He talked enough for six, but it was all in *dialetto*, so I could not understand him, nor, when I had discovered who he was, did I much try to do so. He was a good creature, a trifle given to stealing fruit and vegetables, but an amiable man enough. He had had a long day with his mule and me, and he only asked me five francs. I gave him ten, for I pitied his poor old patched boots, and there was a meekness about him that touched me. " And now, Socrates," said I at parting, " we go on our several ways, you to steal tomatoes, I to filch ideas from other people; for the rest—which of these two roads will be the better going, our father which is in heaven knows, but we know not." *

I have never seen Mendelssohn, but there is a fresco of

Ramblings in Cheapside

him on the terrace, or open-air dining-room, of an inn at Chiavenna. He is not called Mendelssohn, but I knew him by his legs. He is in the costume of a dandy of some five-and-forty years ago, is smoking a cigar, and appears to be making an offer of marriage to his cook. Beethoven both my friend Mr. H. Festing Jones and I have had the good fortune to meet; he is an engineer now, and does not know one note from another; he has quite lost his deafness, is married, and is, of course, a little squat man with the same refractory hair that he always had. It was very interesting to watch him, and Jones remarked that before the end of dinner he had become positively posthumous. One morning I was told the Beethovens were going away, and before long I met their two heavy boxes being carried down the stairs. The boxes were so squab and like their owners, that I half thought for a moment that they were inside, and should hardly have been surprised to see them spring up like a couple of Jacks-in-the-box. "Sono indentro?" said I, with a frown of wonder, pointing to the boxes. The porters knew what I meant, and laughed. But there is no end to the list of people whom I have been able to recognize, and before I had got through it myself, I found I had walked some distance, and had involuntarily paused in front of a second-hand bookstall.

I do not like books. I believe I have the smallest library of any literary man in London, and I have no wish to increase it. I keep my books at the British Museum and at Mudie's, and it makes me very angry if anyone gives me one for my private library. I once heard two ladies disputing in a railway carriage as to whether one of them had or had not been wasting money. "I spent it in books," said the accused, "and it's not wasting money to buy books." "Indeed, my dear, I think it is," was the rejoinder, and in practice I agree with it. Webster's Dictionary, Whitaker's Almanack, and Bradshaw's Railway Guide should be sufficient for any ordinary library; it will be time enough to go beyond these when the mass of useful and entertaining matter which they provide has been mastered. Nevertheless, I admit that sometimes, if not particularly busy, I stop at a second-hand bookstall and turn over a book or two from mere force of habit.

I know not what made me pick up a copy of Aeschylus—of course in an English version—or rather I know not what made Aeschylus take up with me, for he took me rather than I him; but no sooner had he got me than he began puzzling me, as he has done any time this forty years, to know wherein his transcendent merit can be supposed to lie. To me he is, like the greater number of classics in all ages and countries, a literary Struldbrug, rather than a true ambrosia-fed immortal. There are true immortals, but they are few and far between; most classics are as great impostors dead as they were when living, and while posing as gods are, five-sevenths of them, only Struldbrugs. It comforts me to remember that Aristophanes liked Aeschylus no better than I do. True, he praises him by comparison with Sophocles and Euripides, but he only does so that he may run down these last more effectively. Aristophanes is a safe man to follow, nor do I see why it should not be as correct to laugh with him as to pull a long face with the Greek Professors; but this is neither here nor there, for no one really cares about Aeschylus; the more interesting question is how he contrived to make so many people for so many years pretend to care about him.

Perhaps he married somebody's daughter. If a man would get hold of the public ear, he must pay, marry, or fight. I have never understood that Aeschylus was a man of means, and the fighters do not write poetry, so I suppose he must have married a theatrical manager's daughter, and got his plays brought out that way. The ear of any age or country is like its land, air, and water; it seems limitless but is really limited, and is already in the keeping of those who naturally enough will have no squatting on such valuable property. It is written and talked up to as closely as the means of subsistence are bred up to by a teeming population. There is not a square inch of it but is in private hands, and he who

Ramblings in Cheapside

would freehold any part of it must do so by purchase, marriage, or fighting, in the usual way—and fighting gives the longest, safest tenure. The public itself has hardly more voice in the question who shall have its ear, than the land has in choosing its owners. It is farmed as those who own it think most profitable to themselves, and small blame to them; nevertheless, it has a residuum of mulishness which the land has not, and does sometimes dispossess its tenants. It is in this residuum that those who fight place their hope and trust.

Or perhaps Aeschylus squared the leading critics of his time. When one comes to think of it, he must have done so, for how is it conceivable that such plays should have had such runs if he had not? I met a lady one year in Switzerland who had some parrots that always travelled with her and were the idols of her life. These parrots would not let anyone read aloud in their presence, unless they heard their own names introduced from time to time. If these were freely interpolated into the text they would remain as still as stones, for they thought the reading was about themselves. If it was not about them it could not be allowed. The leaders of literature are like these parrots; they do not look at what a man writes, nor if they did would they understand it much better than the parrots do; but they like the sound of their own names, and if these are freely interpolated in a tone they take as friendly, they may even give ear to an outsider. Otherwise they will scream him off if they can.

I should not advise anyone with ordinary independence of mind to attempt the public ear unless he is confident that he can out-lung and out-last his own generation; for if he has any force, people will and ought to be on their guard against him, inasmuch as there is no knowing where he may not take them. Besides, they have staked their money on the wrong men so often without suspecting it, that when there comes one whom they do suspect it would be madness not to bet against him. True, he may die before he has outscreamed his opponents, but that has nothing to do with it. If his scream was well pitched it will sound clearer when he is dead. We do not know what death is. If we know so little about life which we have experienced, how shall we know about death which we have not—and in the nature of things never can? Everyone, as I said years ago in *Alps and Sanctuaries*, is an immortal to himself, for he cannot know that he is dead until he is dead, and when dead how can he know anything about anything? All we know is, that even the humblest dead may live long after all trace of the body has disappeared; we see them doing it in the bodies and memories of those that come after them; and not a few live so much longer and more effectually than is desirable, that it has been necessary to get rid of them by Act of Parliament. It is love that alone gives life, and the truest life is that which we live not in ourselves but vicariously in others, and with which we have no concern. Our concern is so to order ourselves that we may be of the number of them that enter into life—although we know it not.

Aeschylus did so order himself; but his life is not of that inspiring kind that can be won through fighting the good fight only—or being believed to have fought it. His voice is the echo of a drone, drone-begotten and drone-sustained. It is not a tone that a man must utter or die—nay, even though he die; and likely enough half the allusions and hard passages in Aeschylus of which we can make neither head nor tail are in reality only puffs of some of the literary leaders of his time.

The lady above referred to told me more about her parrots. She was like a Nasmyth hammer going slow—very gentle, but irresistible. She always read the newspaper to them. What was the use of having a newspaper if one did not read it to one's parrots?

"And have you divined," I asked, "to which side they incline in politics?"

"They do not like Mr. Gladstone," was the somewhat freezing answer; "this is the only point on which we disagree, for I adore him. Don't ask more about this, it is a

Ramblings in Cheapside

great grief to me. I tell them everything," she continued, " and hide no secret from them."

" But can any parrot be trusted to keep a secret?"

" Mine can."

" And on Sundays do you give them the same course of reading as on a week-day, or do you make a difference?"

" On Sundays I always read them a genealogical chapter from the Old or New Testament, for I can thus introduce their names without profanity. I always keep tea by me in case they should ask for it in the night, and I have an Etna to warm it for them; they take milk and sugar. The old white-headed clergyman came to see them last night; it was very painful, for Jocko reminded him so strongly of his late . . ."

I thought she was going to say " wife," but it proved to have been only of a parrot that he had once known and loved.

** " They expect a cup of tea every afternoon at half-past four. Last year, when we were staying on the Lake of Como, we went for an excursion one day and unfortunately missed the boat, so that we did not return until nearly six o'clock; then the waiter told us that punctually at half-past four he had heard our bell ring and on going up to our room had found the door locked, for we always lock the parrots into our room and take the key with us when we go out. He went downstairs thinking he must have made a mistake, but in a few minutes our bell rang again, and again he went upstairs and found the door locked! This appeared to him so mysterious that he got a ladder and climbed up to the window. As soon as the parrots saw him they exclaimed, ' Bring tea, if you please.' Oh! they know very well when it is tea-time." **

One evening she was in difficulties about the quarantine, which was enforced that year on the Italian frontier. The local doctor had gone down that morning to see the Italian doctor and arrange some details. " Then, perhaps, my dear," she said to her husband, " he is the quarantine." " No, my love," replied her husband; "the quarantine is not a person, it is a place where they put people"; but she would not be comforted, and suspected the quarantine as an enemy that might at any moment pounce out upon her and her parrots. So a lady told me once that she had been in like trouble about the anthem. She read in her Prayer Book that in choirs and places where they sing "here followeth the anthem," yet the person with this most mysteriously sounding name never did follow. They had a choir, and no one could say the church was not a place where they sang, for they did sing—both chants and hymns. Why, then, this persistent slackness on the part of the anthem, who at this juncture should follow her papa, the rector, into the reading-desk? No doubt he would come some day, and then what would he be like? Fair or dark? Tall or short? Would he be bald and wear spectacles like papa, or would he be young and good-looking? Anyhow, there was something wrong, for it was announced that he would follow, and he never did follow; therefore there was no knowing what he might not do next.

I heard of the parrots a year or two later as giving lessons in Italian to an English maid. I do not know what their terms were. Alas! since then both they and their mistress have joined the majority. When the poor lady felt her end was near she desired (and the responsibility for this must rest with her, not me) that the birds might be destroyed, as fearing that they might come to be neglected, and knowing that they could never be loved again as she had loved them. On being told that all was over, she said, "Thank you," and immediately expired.

Reflecting in such random fashion, and strolling with no greater method, I worked my way back through Cheapside and found myself once more in front of Sweeting's window. Again the turtles attracted me. They were alive, and so far at any rate they agreed with me. Nay, they had eyes, mouths, legs, if not arms, and feet, so there was much in which we were both of a mind, but surely they must be mistaken in

Ramblings in Cheapside

arming themselves so very heavily. Any creature on getting what the turtle aimed at would overreach itself and be landed not in safety but annihilation. It should have no communion with the outside world at all, for death could creep in wherever the creature could creep out; and it must creep out somewhere if it was to hook on to outside things. What death can be more absolute than such absolute isolation? Perfect death, indeed, if it were attainable (which it is not), is as near perfect security as we can reach, but it is not the kind of security aimed at by any animal that is at the pains of defending itself. For such want to have things both ways, desiring the livingness of life without its perils, and the safety of death without its deadness, and some of us do actually get this for a considerable time, but we do not get it by plating ourselves with armour as the turtle does. We tried this in the Middle Ages, and no longer mock ourselves with the weight of armour that our forefathers carried in battle. Indeed the more deadly the weapons of attack become the more we go into the fight slug-wise.

Slugs have ridden their contempt for defensive armour as much to death as the turtles their pursuit of it. They have hardly more than skin enough to hold themselves together; they court death every time they cross the road. Yet death comes not to them more than to the turtle, whose defences are so great that there is little left inside to be defended. Moreover, the slugs fare best in the long run, for turtles are dying out, while slugs are not, and there must be millions of slugs all the world over for every single turtle. Of the two vanities, therefore, that of the slug seems most substantial.

In either case the creature thinks itself safe, but is sure to be found out sooner or later; nor is it easy to explain this mockery save by reflecting that everything must have its meat in due season, and that meat can only be found for such a multitude of mouths by giving everything as meat in due season to something else. This is like the Kilkenny cats, or robbing Peter to pay Paul; but it is the way of the world, and as every animal must contribute in kind to the picnic of the universe, one does not see what better arrangement could be made than the providing each race with a hereditary fallacy, which shall in the end get it into a scrape, but which shall generally stand the wear and tear of life for some time. "*Do ut des*" is the writing on all flesh to him that eats it; and no creature is dearer to itself than it is to some other that would devour it.

Nor is there any statement or proposition more invulnerable than living forms are. Propositions prey upon and are grounded upon one another just like living forms. They support one another as plants and animals do; they are based ultimately on credit, or faith, rather than the cash of irrefragable conviction. The whole universe is carried on on the credit system, and if the mutual confidence on which it is based were to collapse, it must itself collapse immediately. Just or unjust, it lives by faith; it is based on vague and impalpable opinion that by some inscrutable process passes into will and action, and is made manifest in matter and in flesh: it is meteoric—suspended in mid-air; it is the baseless fabric of a vision so vast, so vivid, and so gorgeous that no base can seem more broad than such stupendous baselessness, and yet any man can bring it about his ears by being over-curious; when faith fails, a system based on faith fails also.

Whether the universe is really a paying concern, or whether it is an inflated bubble that must burst sooner or later, this is another matter. If people were to demand cash payment in irrefragable certainty for everything that they have taken hitherto as paper money on the credit of the bank of public opinion, is there money enough behind it all to stand so great a drain even on so great a reserve? Probably there is not, but happily there can be no such panic, for even though the cultured classes may do so, the uncultured are too dull to have brains enough to commit such stupendous folly. It takes a long course of academic training to educate a man up to the standard which he must reach before he can entertain such questions seriously, and by a merciful dispensation of Providence university training is almost as costly as it is unprofitable. The majority will thus be always unable to afford it, and will base their opinions on mother wit and current opinion rather than on demonstration.

So I turned my steps homewards; I saw a good many more things on my way home, but I was told that I was not to see more this time than I could get into twelve pages of *The Universal Review*; I must therefore reserve any remark which I think might perhaps entertain the reader for another occasion.

PORTRAITS OF GENTILE AND GIOVANNI BELLINI

NOTE

THE two pieces which follow appeared, respectively, in *The Athenaeum*, 20th February 1886, and *The Academy*, 14th May 1887. They are now for the first time reprinted.

It appears from notes found among Butler's papers that he intended to write an article on the Bellini heads, perhaps for *The Universal Review*. These notes are undated, but probably belong to the year 1888. They include the draft of a letter to the Directeur des Musées Nationaux, sent 5th October 1887, from which it is clear that the Louvre authorities then once more attributed their picture to Gentile Bellini, but denied that it represented the painter and his brother Giovanni. In 1914 this was still the case; but in 1924 the picture was called " Portraits d'hommes," and attributed to Cariani.

A.T.B.

THE "BELLINI HEADS"
From the painting in the Louvre

Portraits of Gentile and Giovanni Bellini[1]

I

SOME TIME AGO, HAVING OCCASION TO REFER to Messrs. Crowe and Cavalcaselle's chapter on Gentile Bellini, I saw with regret that doubt was thrown upon the picture in the Salon Carré of the Louvre which till lately was ascribed to Gentile Bellini, and was supposed to represent Giovanni and himself. " Here," say Messrs. Crowe and Cavalcaselle, " we miss the firm hand of Bellini, and stand face to face with the melting and coloured tinting of Cariani " (*History of Painting in Northern Italy*, ed. 1871, p. 134). In a note, again, on the same page, the authors say: " We are far here from the firm and decided touch and outline of Gentile Bellini. Cariani of Bergamo would be found here in his earliest phase, one but little known, but familiar to those who are acquainted with all his works."

I am unwilling to differ from Messrs. Crowe and Cavalcaselle, but believe I can show conclusively that they have been too hasty in disturbing the old opinion about the picture in question. They appear to have overlooked the fact that these same two heads are to be found in Gentile Bellini's undoubted picture of " St. Mark's Sermon," now in the Brera. The figure to the extreme left of this picture has the auburn-haired head which we find given to the older of the two portraits in the Louvre, while immediately next him — the head alone being shown — appears the black-haired man of the Louvre picture. The resemblance is so striking that I do not think any doubt can exist about the same people being intended in the two pictures. I have observed it for fully twenty years, but, not knowing that the Louvre picture had been doubted, did not think it necessary to call attention to it. When I saw what Messrs. Crowe and Cavalcaselle had said, I was at first inclined to think I must be mistaken, but, on seeing the Brera picture again last summer, found it impossible to entertain any doubt upon the matter.

The " Sermon of St. Mark " was Gentile Bellini's last

[1] From *The Athenaeum*, 20th February 1886.

work; he left it unfinished, and by his will desired his brother Giovanni to finish it, at the same time bequeathing him their father Jacopo's sketch-book on condition that he did so. It is in a high degree likely that he should have wished his own and his brother's portraits to appear in this his crowning work, which is obviously full of the portraits of men of his time, and the place in which we find these two people is just the one which a painter would be likely to choose for himself and his nearest friend. In both the Louvre and Brera pictures pre-eminence is given to Gentile, who in each case is the reputed painter, and was also the elder brother. I submit, therefore, that if I am right in supposing the same people to be intended in the two pictures, there can be little doubt that the old belief concerning the Louvre picture—namely, that it represented Gentile and Giovanni Bellini—was well founded.

Whoever these two men were, they must have been well-known characters, and well known, moreover, as closely associated, for they appear again in Carpaccio's "Dispute of St. Stephen," also in the Brera; they are the two penultimate bystanders (but this time Gentile's figure is not given, the preference, as was natural, being given to Giovanni) to the right of the picture, immediately to the right of a head something like Mr. Gladstone's. These two heads are not so like the Louvre picture as those in the "St. Mark" by Gentile Bellini are, but this is only what might be expected, for Carpaccio must have been painting from memory a residuum of impressions only. In 1514, when Carpaccio painted the "Dispute of St. Stephen" (which is signed and dated), Gentile Bellini had been dead seven years, and Giovanni was far older than Carpaccio represents him; so also Gentile must have been giving a residuum of impressions, for though the heads are considerably older in the Brera than in the Louvre picture, yet they are not at all those of the octogenarians that both himself and his brother in reality were in 1507. In the Louvre picture we probably have the most painstakingly exact portraits that Gentile could turn out of himself

Portraits of Gentile and Giovanni Bellini

and his brother when they were about thirty-five and thirty years of age respectively; in this case the picture was painted about the year 1460. In the " St. Mark " the painter hands himself down to posterity not as the dying man in the decrepitude of extreme old age, which he then actually was, but as those would remember him who knew him in later middle life. But however this may be, I find it impossible to doubt that the same two men are intended, and intentionally associated in each of the three pictures we have been considering, and am hence assured that the one in which the sitters are represented as still young—I mean the Louvre picture—was painted many years before 1507. One of these pictures is unquestionably by Gentile Bellini, and another was till recently so fully believed to be by him that, after having been for some years assigned to his brother Giovanni, it was on consideration ascribed to Gentile in deference to the weight of evidence in its favour; who, then, are the two men so likely to have been as the *doyens* of Venetian painting—one of whom, indeed, though lately dead, was still not to be dissociated from the brother whom he loved so well—not, at least, while that brother was living?

Let us now turn to the external evidence in favour of the Louvre picture having been painted by Gentile Bellini. In the 1865 edition of the Louvre catalogue we find Félibien quoted as having written in 1666 as follows: " L'on voit dans le cabinet du roy les portraits de ces deux frères (Jean et Gentil) dans un même tableau que Gentil a fait "; and it is not disputed that the picture here referred to is the one now in the Louvre. I have not the 1666 edition of Félibien's work before me, but will quote more fully from the 1685 edition, which alone I have been able to obtain. Félibien there says: " ' Je sçay bien,' dît Pymandre [a fictitious character introduced by Félibien], ' que beaucoup de sçavans hommes ont parlé de Jean avec éloge, entre autres le Cardinal Bembo et l'Arioste, mais je ne croy pas avoir jamais rien vêu de la main de ces Peintres et je pense que leurs tableaux sont très rares en ce päis.' ' L'on voit,' repartis-je, ' dans le

Cabinet du Roy les portraits de ces deux freres dans un mesme tableau que Gentil a fait lors qu'ils estoient encore fort jeunes'" (*Entretiens sur les Vies*, etc., Paris, 1685, vol. i, p. 163).

Félibien does not, indeed, pretend to know much about the Bellini, nor does he talk about " stern sobriety," " stern and solid power," "a touch rich, copious, firm, and decisive," nor use any of those somewhat easily acquired turns of phrase with which we now impress our readers at once with the fineness of our perceptions and our felicity of expression; but, on the other hand, he does not ascribe his picture to a man who was not born till twenty years or so after it was painted, and if he does not claim acquaintance with all, even the early, works of a second-rate Bergamasc painter, he at least gives us the opinion of an age which was within measurable distance of the Bellini themselves, of an age in which there were still old men living who as children must have seen Titian. Surely the assertion which he so unhesitatingly makes should not be set aside without stronger reasons than any assigned by Messrs. Crowe and Cavalcaselle. It is on the authority of Messrs. Crowe and Cavalcaselle as experts, and on this, so far as I can gather, only, that the Louvre picture has been taken from Gentile Bellini. I venture respectfully to demur to that authority on this occasion. I cannot, indeed, claim to be an authority myself, but I know the greater part of what remains to us of Gentile Bellini's pictures, and know no painter whom the Louvre picture suggests to me so strongly. I find myself supported here by the Frenchman who, of all others, is best entitled to be listened to on the matter, but whose name I must not give inasmuch as I forgot to ask his permission. He said to me a short time since, speaking of the technique of the picture only, " Je trouve le tableau très bien attribué à Gentil Bellin." I grant it is richer in colour and lower in tone than is usual with this painter, but I do not find this ground enough for rechristening a picture, every other feature of which satisfies me that it is not a sixteenth-century work from

Portraits of Gentile and Giovanni Bellini

either Bergamo or Venice, but certainly a fifteenth-century one, and no less certainly from Venice. Those who wish to find an early work of Cariani, to whom Messrs. Crowe and Cavalcaselle ascribe the picture, will find the only one to which an early date can be plausibly assigned in the Brera at Milan. It represents the Virgin enthroned with a landscape background. For an account of it see Locatelli's *Illustri Bergamaschi*, ii, 34. There is also other work by Cariani in the Brera, but none that can, so far as I have been able to ascertain, be authenticated as early.

I last summer searched the pictures by Gentile Bellini in the Accademia at Venice, and, indeed, all the pictures there, and among the hundreds of heads examined found only two which at all reminded me of the Louvre and Brera portraits, nor do I feel sufficiently sure about these to call attention to them. The only place where I have been strongly reminded of the Bellini portraits is in the Scuola di S. Antonio at Padua. In the first fresco by Titian as the room is entered, immediately on the right hand, we have two prominent figures—a yellow-red haired man and a black-haired one side by side—who might very well be the Bellini. Titian painted this fresco in 1511, four years after the death of Gentile, and makes Giovanni a man of not more than forty; he must, therefore (if the Bellini were in his mind at all), have been giving a general impression of what he supposed them to have been like as comparatively young men. Nevertheless, as I looked at the fresco, I found myself reminded of the Louvre portraits with some force.

II [1]

IN *The Athenaeum* of 20th February 1886 I showed cause for thinking that the picture in the Salon Carré of the Louvre, till lately ascribed to Gentile Bellini, and said to represent his brother Giovanni and himself, was a genuine work, and should continue to be ascribed as till within the last few years.

[1] From *The Academy*, 14th May 1887.

I called attention to the fact that the two people portrayed in that work were also seen in the two extreme left-hand figures of Gentile Bellini's undoubted picture of "St. Mark's Sermon," his last and crowning work, now in the Brera; that they were found side by side in Carpaccio's "Dispute of St. Stephen," also in the Brera; and that a strong reminiscence of them was observable in a fresco by Titian, painted in 1511, in the Scuola di S. Antonio at Padua.

I have as yet met with nothing to shake my confidence in the soundness of the conclusion I arrived at; but it has been lately pointed out to me by my friend Mr. T. Ballard that two heads in Marco Marziale's picture of "The Circumcision" in the National Gallery, which bears date 1500, are also strongly suggestive of the two people represented in the Salon Carré picture. These heads are to be found on the right of the central group as one faces the picture, one of them being partly hidden by the hood of the officiating priest. They are those of a yellow-red-haired, fair-complexioned, square-faced man (so far as the face can be seen), with a rather straight nose; and an oval-faced, black-haired, dark-complexioned man, with a nose the bridge of which is decidedly convex. The heads are very badly painted, as are all the others in the picture, and it cannot be pretended that they are comparable to those in the Louvre; nevertheless the onerous conditions on the combined fulfilment of which we may suspect that portraiture of the brothers Bellini is intended are here all complied with—namely, the picture is Venetian, it is painted between the years say 1460 and 1520, and it gives us two men side by side with all the characteristics which we have reason to believe were those of Gentile and Giovanni Bellini.

I should add that Mr. Ballard arrived at the conclusion above stated several years ago, entirely without concert with myself.

26th April 1887.

THE SANCTUARY OF MONTRIGONE

NOTE

This is the second part of an article which appeared in *The Universal Review* for November 1888, entitled "A Sculptor and a Shrine." The first part is not reprinted for reasons set forth by Streatfeild, vol. i, *ante*. The reader is further referred to the Shrewsbury Edition of *Ex Voto*, where Butler's corrected views on Tabachetti's life and career will be found. When the article appeared in *The Universal Review* Butler prefixed to it the following characteristic note:

"A friend to whom I submitted my MS. told me that the first of the two following articles was dry and would fail to please the public, who knew little and cared less about Tabachetti. I said I was afraid this was so. 'Then,' said he, 'why not put the second article, which your readers may like, first, so as to tempt them on to the second?' I said I was not going to put D'Enrico and Giacomo Ferro before Tabachetti, and that after all, in my first part, I was giving people a new life-sized statue of Leonardo da Vinci by Gaudenzio Ferrari. He said nothing, but gave me a look which seemed to say that Leonardo da Vinci was hardly a safe draw. I am again afraid he must be right, and will own that my first part is perhaps a little dry, but I could no more poke fun at Tabachetti than at Handel, Shakespeare, Holbein, Rembrandt, Giovanni Bellini, or De Hooghe, and compromised by saying that I would write a few lines of apologetic preface to warn the reader that he will probably find 'The Shrine' less 'dry' reading than 'The Sculptor.'"

"The Sanctuary of Montrigone" was reprinted in the two collections of Butler's essays brought out by Streatfeild in 1904 and 1913 respectively, but without illustrations. These are now restored.

A.T.B.

The Sanctuary of Montrigone [1]

THE ONLY PLACE IN THE VALSESIA, EXCEPT Varallo, where I at present suspect the presence of Tabachetti [2] is at Montrigone, a little-known sanctuary dedicated to St. Anne, about three-quarters of a mile south of Borgo-Sesia station. The situation is, of course, lovely, but the sanctuary does not offer any features of architectural interest. The sacristan told me it was founded in 1631; and in 1644 Giovanni D'Enrico, while engaged in superintending and completing the work undertaken here by himself and Giacomo Ferro, fell ill and died. I do not know whether or no there was an earlier sanctuary on the same site, but was told it was built on the demolition of a stronghold belonging to the Counts of Biandrate.

The incidents which it illustrates are treated with even more than the homeliness usual in works of this description when not dealing with such solemn events as the death and passion of Christ. Except when these subjects were being represented, something of the latitude, and even humour, allowed in the old mystery plays was permitted, doubtless from a desire to render the work more attractive to the peasants, who were the most numerous and most important pilgrims. It is not until faith begins to be weak that it fears an occasionally lighter treatment of semi-sacred subjects, and it is impossible to convey an accurate idea of the spirit prevailing at this hamlet of sanctuary without attuning oneself somewhat to the more pagan character of the place. Of irreverence, in the sense of a desire to laugh at things that are of high and serious import, there is not a trace, but at the same time there is a certain unbending of the bow at Montrigone which is not perceivable at Varallo.

[1] From *The Universal Review*, November 1888.
[2] Since this essay was written it has been ascertained by Cavaliere Francesco Negri, of Casale Monferrato, that Tabachetti died in 1615. If, therefore, the Sanctuary of Montrigone was not founded until 1631, it is plain that Tabachetti cannot have worked there. All the latest discoveries about Tabachetti's career will be found in Cavaliere Negri's pamphlet *Il Santuario di Crea* (Alessandria, 1902). See also note on p. 224.—R.A.S.

The first chapel to the left on entering the church is that of the Birth of the Virgin. St. Anne is sitting up in bed. She is not at all ill—in fact, considering that the Virgin has only been born about five minutes, she is wonderful; still the doctors think it may be perhaps better that she should keep her room for half an hour longer, so the bed has been festooned with red and white paper roses, and the counterpane is covered with bouquets in baskets and in vases of glass and china. These cannot have been there during the actual birth of the Virgin, so I suppose they had been in readiness, and were brought in from an adjoining room as soon as the baby had been born. A lady on her left is bringing in some more flowers, which St. Anne is receiving with a smile and most gracious gesture of the hands. The first thing she asked for, when the birth was over, was for her three silver hearts. These were immediately brought to her, and she has got them all on, tied round her neck with a piece of blue silk ribbon.

Dear mamma has come. We felt sure she would, and that any little misunderstandings between her and Joachim would ere long be forgotten and forgiven. They are both so good and sensible, if they would only understand one another. At any rate, here she is, in high state at the right hand of the bed. She is dressed in black, for she has lost her husband some few years previously, but I do not believe a smarter, spryer old lady for her years could be found in Palestine, nor yet that either Giovanni D'Enrico or Giacomo Ferro could have conceived or executed such a character. The sacristan wanted to have it that she was not a woman at all, but was a portrait of St. Joachim, the Virgin's father. "Sembra una donna," he pleaded more than once, " ma non è donna." Surely, however, in works of art even more than in other things, there is no " is " but seeming, and if a figure seems female it must be taken as such. Besides, I asked one of the leading doctors at Varallo whether the figure was man or woman. He said it was evident I was not married, for that if I had been I should have seen at once that she was not

ST. ANNE

(Chapel of the Birth of the Virgin)

The Sanctuary of Montrigone

only a woman but a mother-in-law of the first magnitude, or, as he called it, "una suocera tremenda," and this without knowing that I wanted her to be a mother-in-law myself. Unfortunately she had no real drapery, so I could not settle the question as my friend Mr. H. F. Jones and I had been able to do at Varallo with the figure of Eve that had been turned into a Roman soldier assisting at the capture of Christ. I am not, however, disposed to waste more time upon anything so obvious, and will content myself with saying that we have here the Virgin's grandmother. I had never had the pleasure, so far as I remembered, of meeting this lady before, and was glad to have an opportunity of making her acquaintance.

Tradition says that it was she who chose the Virgin's name, and if so, what a debt of gratitude do we not owe her for her judicious selection! It makes one shudder to think what might have happened if she had named the child Keren-Happuch, as poor Job's daughter was called. How could we have said, "Ave Keren-Happuch!" What would the musicians have done? I forget whether Maher-Shalal-Hash-Baz was a man or a woman, but there were plenty of names quite as unmanageable at the Virgin's grandmother's option, and we cannot sufficiently thank her for having chosen one that is so euphonious in every language which we need take into account. For this reason alone we should not grudge her her portrait, but we should try to draw the line here. I do not think we ought to give the Virgin's great-grandmother a statue. Where is it to end? It is like Mr. Crookes's ultimissimate atoms; we used to draw the line at ultimate atoms, and now it seems we are to go a step farther back and have ultimissimate atoms. How long, I wonder, will it be before we feel that it will be a material help to us to have ultimissimissimate atoms? Quavers stopped at demi-semi-demi, but there is no reason to suppose that either atoms or ancestresses of the Virgin will be so complacent.

I have said that on St. Anne's left hand there is a lady who is bringing in some flowers. St. Anne was always passionately fond of flowers. There is a pretty story told about her in one of the Fathers, I forget which, to the effect that when a child she was asked which she liked best—cakes or flowers? She could not yet speak plainly and lisped out, " Oh fowses, pretty fowses "; she added, however, with a sigh and as a kind of wistful corollary, " but cakes are very nice." She is not to have any cakes just now, but as soon as she has done thanking the lady for her beautiful nosegay, she is to have a couple of nice new-laid eggs, that are being brought her by another lady. Valsesian women immediately after their confinement always have eggs beaten up with wine and sugar, and one can tell a Valsesian Birth of the Virgin from a Venetian or a Florentine by the presence of the eggs. I learned this from an eminent Valsesian professor of medicine, who told me that, though not according to received rules, the eggs never seemed to do any harm. Here they are evidently to be beaten up, for there is neither spoon nor egg-cup, and we cannot suppose that they were hard-boiled. On the other hand, in the Middle Ages Italians never used egg-cups and spoons for boiled eggs. The mediaeval boiled egg was always eaten by dipping bread into the yolk.

Behind the lady who is bringing in the eggs is the under-under-nurse who is at the fire warming a towel. In the foreground we have the regulation midwife holding the regulation baby (who, by the way, was an astonishingly fine child for only five minutes old). Then comes the under-nurse—a good buxom creature who, as usual, is feeling the water in the bath to see that it is of the right temperature. Next to her is the head-nurse, who is arranging the cradle. Behind the head-nurse is the under-under-nurse's drudge, who is just going out upon some errands. Lastly—for by this time we have got all round the chapel—we arrive at the Virgin's grandmother's body-guard, a stately, responsible-looking lady, standing in waiting upon her mistress. I put it to the reader—is it conceivable that St. Joachim should have been allowed in such a room at such a time, or that he should have had the courage to avail himself of the permission, even

THE VIRGIN'S GRANDMOTHER
(Chapel of the Birth of the Virgin)

The Sanctuary of Montrigone

though it had been extended to him? At any rate, is it conceivable that he should have been allowed to sit on St. Anne's right hand, laying down the law with a " Marry, come up " here, and a " Marry, go down " there, and a couple of such unabashed collars as are shown in my illustration?

Moreover (for I may as well demolish this mischievous confusion between St. Joachim and his mother-in-law once and for all), the merest tyro in hagiology knows that St. Joachim was not at home when the Virgin was born. He had been hustled out of the temple for having no children, and had fled desolate and dismayed into the wilderness. It shows how silly people are, for all the time he was going, if they had only waited a little, to be the father of the most remarkable person of purely human origin who had ever been born, and such a parent as this should surely not be hurried. The story is told in the frescoes of the chapel of Loreto, only a quarter of an hour's walk from Varallo, and no one can have known it better than D'Enrico. The frescoes are explained by written passages that tell us how, when Joachim was in the desert, an angel came to him in the guise of a fair, civil young gentleman, and told him the Virgin was to be born. Then, later on, the same young gentleman appeared to him again, and bade him " in God's name be comforted, and turn again to his content," for the Virgin had been actually born. On which St. Joachim, who seems to have been of opinion that marriage after all *was* rather a failure, said that, as things were going on so nicely without him, he would stay in the desert just a little longer, and offered up a lamb as a pretext to gain time. Perhaps he guessed about his mother-in-law, or he may have asked the angel. Of course, even in spite of such evidence as this, I may be mistaken about the Virgin's grandmother's sex, and the sacristan may be right; but I can only say that if the lady sitting by St. Anne's bedside at Montrigone is the Virgin's father—well, in that case I must reconsider a good deal that I have been accustomed to believe was beyond question.

Collected Essays

Taken singly, I suppose that none of the figures in the chapel, except the Virgin's grandmother, should be rated very highly. The under-nurse is the next best figure, and might very well be Tabachetti's, for neither Giovanni D'Enrico nor Giacomo Ferro was successful with his female characters. There is not a single really comfortable woman in any chapel by either of them on the Sacro Monte at Varallo. Tabachetti, on the other hand, delighted in women; if they were young he made them comely and engaging, if they were old he gave them dignity and individual character, and the under-nurse is much more in accordance with Tabachetti's habitual mental attitude than with D'Enrico's or Giacomo Ferro's. Still there are only four figures out of the eleven that are mere otiose supers, and taking the work as a whole it leaves a pleasant impression as being throughout naïve and homely, and sometimes, which is of less importance, technically excellent.

Allowance must, of course, be made for tawdry accessories and repeated coats of shiny oleaginous paint—very disagreeable where it has peeled off and almost more so where it has not. What work could stand against such treatment as the Valsesian terra-cotta figures have had to put up with? Take the Venus of Milo; let her be done in terra-cotta, and have run, not much, but still something, in the baking; paint her pink, two oils, all over, and then varnish her—it will help to preserve the paint; glue a lot of horsehair on to her pate, half of which shall have come off, leaving the glue still showing; scrape her, not too thoroughly, get the village drawing-master to paint her again, and the drawing-master in the next provincial town to put a forest background behind her with the brightest emerald-green leaves that he can do for the money; let this painting and scraping and repainting be repeated several times over; festoon her with pink and white flowers made of tissue paper; surround her with the cheapest German imitations of the cheapest decorations that Birmingham can produce; let the night air and winter fogs get at her for three hundred years, and how easy,

The Sanctuary of Montrigone

I wonder, will it be to see the goddess who will be still in great part there? True, in the case of the Birth of the Virgin chapel at Montrigone, there is no real hair and no fresco background, but time has had abundant opportunities without these. I will conclude my notice of this chapel by saying that on the left, above the door through which the under-under-nurse's drudge is about to pass, there is a good painted terra-cotta bust, said—but I believe on no authority— to be a portrait of Giovanni D'Enrico. Others say that the Virgin's grandmother is Giovanni D'Enrico, but this is even more absurd than supposing her to be St. Joachim.

The next chapel to the Birth of the Virgin is that of the "Sposalizio." There is no figure here which suggests Tabachetti, but still there are some very good ones. The best have no taint of *barocco*; the man who did them, whoever he may have been, had evidently a good deal of life and go, was taking reasonable pains, and did not know too much. Where this is the case no work can fail to please. Some of the figures have real hair and some terra-cotta. There is no fresco background worth mentioning. A man sitting on the steps of the altar with a book on his lap, and holding up his hand to another, who is leaning over him and talking to him, is among the best figures; some of the disappointed suitors who are breaking their wands are also very good.

The angel in the Annunciation chapel, which comes next in order, is a fine, burly, ship's-figurehead, commercial-hotel sort of being enough, but the Virgin is very ordinary. There is no real hair and no fresco background, only three dingy old blistered pictures of no interest whatever.

In the Visit of Mary to Elizabeth there are three pleasing subordinate lady attendants, two to the left and one to the right of the principal figures; but these figures themselves are not satisfactory. There is no fresco background. Some of the figures have real hair and some terra-cotta.

In the Circumcision and Purification chapel—for both these events seem contemplated in the one that follows— there are doves, but there is neither dog nor knife. Still

Simeon, who has the infant Saviour in his arms, is looking at him in a way which can only mean that, knife or no knife, the matter is not going to end here. At Varallo they have now got a dreadful knife for the Circumcision chapel. They had none last winter. What they have now got would do very well to kill a bullock with, but could not be used professionally with safety for any animal smaller than a rhinoceros. I imagine that someone was sent to Novara to buy a knife, and that, thinking it was for the Massacre of the Innocents chapel, he got the biggest he could see. Then when he brought it back people said " Chow " several times, and put it upon the table and went away.

Returning to Montrigone, the Simeon is an excellent figure, and the Virgin is fairly good, but the prophetess Anna, who stands just behind her, is by far the most interesting in the group, and is alone enough to make me feel sure that Tabachetti gave more or less help here, as he had done years before at Orta. She, too, like the Virgin's grandmother, is a widow lady, and wears collars of a cut that seems to have prevailed ever since the Virgin was born some twenty years previously. There is a largeness and simplicity of treatment about the figure to which none but an artist of the highest rank can reach, and D'Enrico was not more than a second or third-rate man. The hood is like Handel's Truth sailing upon the broad wings of Time, a prophetic strain that nothing but the old experience of a great poet can reach. The lips of the prophetess are for the moment closed, but she has been prophesying all the morning, and the people round the wall in the background are in ecstasies at the lucidity with which she has explained all sorts of difficulties that they had never been able to understand till now. They are putting their forefingers on their thumbs and their thumbs on their forefingers, and saying how clearly they see it all and what a wonderful woman Anna is. A prophet indeed is not generally without honour save in his own country, but then a country is generally not without honour save with its own prophet, and Anna has been glorifying her country

THE PROPHETESS ANNA

(Chapel of the Circumcision and Purification)

The Sanctuary of Montrigone

rather than reviling it. Besides, the rule may not have applied to prophetesses.

The Death of the Virgin is the last of the six chapels inside the church itself. The Apostles, who of course are present, have all of them real hair, but, if I may say so, they want a wash and a brush-up so very badly that I cannot feel any confidence in writing about them. I should say that, take them all round, they are a good average sample of apostle as apostles generally go. Two or three of them are nervously anxious to find appropriate quotations in books that lie open before them, which they are searching with eager haste; but I do not see one figure about which I should like to say positively that it is either good or bad. There is a good bust of a man, matching the one in the Birth of the Virgin chapel, which is said to be a portrait of Giovanni D'Enrico, but it is not known whom it represents.

Outside the church, in three contiguous cells that form part of the foundations, are:

1. A dead Christ, the head of which is very impressive, while the rest of the figure is poor. I examined the treatment of the hair, which is terra-cotta, and compared it with all other like hair in the chapels above described; I could find nothing like it, and think it most likely that Giacomo Ferro did the figure, and got Tabachetti to do the head, or that they brought the head from some unused figure by Tabachetti at Varallo, for I know no other artist of the time and neighbourhood who could have done it.

2. A Magdalene in the desert. The desert is a little coal-cellar of an arch, containing a skull and a profusion of pink and white paper bouquets, the two largest of which the Magdalene is hugging while she is saying her prayers. She is a very self-sufficient lady, who we may be sure will not stay in the desert a day longer than she can help, and while there will flirt even with the skull if she can find nothing better to flirt with. I cannot think that her repentance is as yet genuine, and as for her praying there is no object in her doing so, for she does not want anything.

3. In the next desert there is a very beautiful figure of St. John the Baptist kneeling and looking upwards. This figure puzzles me more than any other at Montrigone; it appears to be of the fifteenth rather than the sixteenth century; it hardly reminds me of Gaudenzio, and still less of any other Valsesian artist. It is a work of unusual beauty, but I can form no idea as to its authorship.

I wrote the foregoing pages in the church at Montrigone itself, having brought my camp-stool with me. It was Sunday; the church was open all day, but there was no Mass said, and hardly anyone came. The sacristan was a kind, gentle, little old man, who let me do whatever I wanted. He sat on the doorstep of the main door, mending vestments, and to this end was cutting up a fine piece of figured silk from one to two hundred years old, which, if I could have got it for half its value, I should much like to have bought. I sat in the cool of the church while he sat in the doorway, which was still in shadow, snipping and snipping, and then sewing, I am sure with admirable neatness. He made a charming picture, with the arched portico over his head, the green grass and low church wall behind him, and then a lovely landscape of wood and pasture and valleys and hillside. Every now and then he would come and chirrup about Joachim, for he was pained and shocked at my having said that his Joachim was someone else and not Joachim at all. I said I was very sorry, but I was afraid the figure was a woman. He asked me what he was to do. He had known it, man and boy, this sixty years, and had always shown it as St. Joachim; he had never heard anyone but myself question his ascription, and could not suddenly change his mind about it at the bidding of a stranger. At the same time he felt it was a very serious thing to continue showing it as the Virgin's father if it was really her grandmother. I told him I thought this was a case for his spiritual director, and that if he felt uncomfortable about it he should consult his parish priest and do as he was told.

On leaving Montrigone, with a pleasant sense of having

The Sanctuary of Montrigone

made acquaintance with a new and, in many respects, interesting work, I could not get the sacristan and our difference of opinion out of my head. What, I asked myself, are the differences that unhappily divide Christendom, and what are those that divide Christendom from modern schools of thought, but a seeing of Joachims as the Virgin's grandmothers on a larger scale? True, we cannot call figures Joachims when we know perfectly well that they are nothing of the kind; but I registered a vow that henceforward when I called Joachims the Virgin's grandmothers I would bear more in mind than I have perhaps always hitherto done, how hard it is for those who have been taught to see them as Joachims to think of them as something different. I trust that I have not been unfaithful to this vow in the preceding article. If the reader differs from me, let me ask him to remember how hard it is for one who has got a figure well into his head as the Virgin's grandmother to see it as Joachim.

NOTE

This article appeared in *The Universal Review* for November 1889, and is now for the first time reprinted. It had precursors in the shape of:

1. A long Letter to *The Academy* of 23rd October 1886.
2. " Holbein's ' Dance,' " a card dated 28th October 1886, giving photographs of the Berlin and Basle drawings, and a short summary of Butler's views.
3. " Holbein's ' Dance,' " a revised edition of no. 2, with a postscript dated 7th November 1889.

To these three items Butler refers in the course of the article now reprinted, which embodies all the information contained in them.

The Postscript (p. 193) is now printed for the first time from the MS. which Butler pasted into a bound copy of his *Universal Review* articles. This volume is now in the Butler Collection at St. John's College, Cambridge.

The "water-colour painted in body colour" referred to in this essay (p. 174) no longer hangs in the place it occupied when Butler wrote. It is now (August 1925) in the Print Room, and the authorities still maintain that it is a copy "perhaps by Rippel."

The original text-blocks have been used for the Shrewsbury Edition, and for the larger illustrations collotypes now replace the process-blocks of the original issue.

A.T.B.

DESIGN BY HOLBEIN FOR PART OF HIS "HAUS ZUM TANZ"
Now in the Berlin Gallery

L'Affaire Holbein-Rippel[1]

COLLECTORS OFTEN MAINTAIN THE GENUineness of works in their possession against critics who impugn it, but it is less common to find the possessor strenuously declaring his picture to be a copy, while an outsider no less strenuously declares it to be an original. Still rarer is it for the possessor to find an inscription on his work, which he believes to bear out his opinion, and then to see it destroyed with as little apparent compunction as though it had made in favour of his opponent. This, however, is the story which I have now to tell, and my only satisfaction in differing as decidedly as I am compelled to do from the late and present conservators of the collection to which I refer, lies in the fact that I am doing my best, not to rob them of an original but to give them one —and that too an important example of a master of the highest rank. Why they should be so recalcitrant—and they are very recalcitrant—at being told that what they call a copy is an original, and why they should have so effectually obliterated the evidence which they allege confutes me, these are among the curiosities of artistic controversy that I cannot explain. All I know is that they have destroyed the most important piece of evidence on which their case is supposed to rest, and that they have done so, as I firmly believe, in the most absolute good faith.

In the outset I should wish to say that it is with the greatest regret that I differ as pointedly as I shall have to do from Dr. His and Dr. Burckhardt, the late and present conservators of the Basle collection. I have not the honour to be acquainted with Dr. Burckhardt, but am under much obligation to Dr. His, as, indeed, are all students of Holbein. Among the many services which he has rendered them, I would specially mention his very possibly correct ascription to Holbein of a remarkable drawing of some men engaged in quarrying stone, now in the British Museum, among the anonymous German drawings, and never, I believe, ascribed to Holbein till Dr. His saw it. I am convinced that both he and Dr. Burckhardt would as willingly agree with me, as I

[1] From *The Universal Review*, November 1889.

with them, if they felt able to do so, and have much compunction in stating my evidence for their being in error, as conclusively as I hope to do; but Holbein, independently of his greatness, has such an especial claim on Englishmen that I cannot afford to stand on punctilio where a question of a work by him is concerned, nor can I venture to omit any details that may help the reader to form a just conclusion concerning the evidence that I have to put before him.

I ought, perhaps, to explain that some time, probably between the years 1521 and 1525, Holbein decorated the front of a house in Basle, which was commonly called the "Haus zum Tanz," from the string of dancing peasants that formed part of his design. He made several sketches for his decoration—one of which, giving a part of the façade only, is now in the Berlin Gallery. It is in water-colour, and the whole drawing is about eighteen inches by twelve. I have prefaced my article with a reproduction of this drawing, taken from a photograph kindly given me in 1886 by Dr. His, of Basle, who has reproduced it on nearly the same scale as the original, in his valuable work on Holbein published by Boussod Valadon et Cie. (Paris, 1886).

In the Museum at Basle there is a water-colour painted in body colour, about four feet long by nine or ten inches wide, which gives the musicians and dancers of the Berlin drawing, and six more figures which do not come into the part of the design preserved at Berlin. I have given here as many of the figures in the Basle drawing as are common to this and to the Berlin drawing. The work is now in the same room with Holbein's Dead Christ, hangs near it, and is numbered 29. It is described as a copy from Holbein, and the following note concerning it is given on p. 33 of the German edition of the catalogue lately published. The note runs:

"This work has been recently taken by an English amateur (Samuel Butler) for an original drawing by Holbein, but a nearly illegible inscription, on the smaller side of the stone seat to the left, names Nicholas Rippel of Basle, a painter on glass, as the artist, and bears date 1624."

DETAIL FROM A DESIGN BY HOLBEIN FOR PART OF HIS "HAUS ZUM TANZ"
Now in the Berlin Gallery

THE LEFT-HAND FIGURES OF A DRAWING IN THE BASLE MUSEUM

TRACING FROM PHOTOGRAPH OF A FIGURE IN THE BASLE DRAWING

TRACING FROM PHOTOGRAPH OF A FIGURE IN THE BERLIN DRAWING

I take exception to this note, firstly, because there is no longer any inscription on the drawing, legible or illegible, and, secondly, because the inscription, which no doubt existed as lately as last February, cannot be shown to have declared Nicholas Rippel to have been the painter, and did not bear the date 1624, nor, indeed, any date earlier than 1640, by which time Nicholas Rippel, the painter on glass, had been dead nine years. Nevertheless, if the inscription had been allowed to remain—and if it had manifestly borne out the statement of the catalogue, there would have been no wish to meddle with it—I should probably have allowed the note to pass without remark.

I was first struck with the drawing in 1871, when I made a sketch of a part of it. In each of the years 1884, 1885, 1886 I spent a couple of days in trying to copy it, and it was in 1885 while thus engaged that I saw how much more like an original than a copy the work appeared. No copyist, it seemed to me, could have drawn his lines with the freedom and power here displayed. I found this opinion stick by me, and in the following year I enquired into the evidence on which the drawing was held to be a copy. I found this to rest solely on a note in a catalogue, which declared it to be by Jerome Hess, a painter of Basle, who died about 1850. This view was supported with some confidence by Dr. His, who told me that he remembered Hess, and had no doubt about his having made the copy from the house outside which Holbein painted it. This seemed final, and I naturally looked for other work of Hess's in order to make myself better acquainted with so consummate a draughtsman; copies, however, by Hess from Holbein in the vestibule of the Basle Museum presented no analogy to the "Danse des Paysans," either in workmanship or materials employed. They showed all the qualities generally observable in the work of a copyist, and the absence of which had struck me so forcibly in the "Danse." I was about, therefore, to return to the attack, when I was met by a surrender, for it had been discovered on further enquiry that the house on which Holbein had painted his "Danse," had been pulled down some twenty, or from that to forty, years before Hess was born. The note, therefore, in the catalogue was clearly wrong, and there was no external evidence whatever. It was at this point that Dr. His —perhaps a little imprudently—showed me, and then gave me, a photograph of the Berlin drawing.

Turning to internal evidence, I found the drawing to be on very thin paper—three pieces, each about fifteen inches long, with a fourth piece, of about three inches, being pasted neatly side by side before it was begun. I was unable to determine whether or no the paper was of the same make as that used by Holbein for his other extant designs for the "Haus zum Tanz," but I could detect no difference. I would suggest that a paper manufacturer be examined on this point. The joins in the paper are so neatly made that though one falls right across a face it is hardly noticed; but the fact of there being joins at all points to a date when it was not yet easy or even possible to get paper much more than fifteen inches wide. It was perhaps this difficulty which led Holbein to make his other extant designs for the house in question, in separate halves—as Dr. His assures me he did—instead of on single sheets. The paper is so thin that the threads of the canvas lining it show through, and it is worn away in more places than one. The drawing appears to be in good preservation, but the lakes have faded, and I should not like to say how much of the apparent good preservation is due to restoration, without having the work before me; its general appearance is old. Woltmann, indeed (English translation, p. 163), speaks of it as recent, but he cannot have paid much attention to it, and has probably simply followed the note in the catalogue above referred to.

The Hess theory being disposed of, I was required to believe that the drawing was a copy from the work done by Holbein on the house itself by some painter other than Hess, who had painted it from the street; but the Berlin photograph came immediately to my assistance. The closeness of the resemblances between the two drawings forbids the supposition that there can have been at least one and probably two (for Holbein would hardly have painted a work of some forty feet in length from a sketch of only eighteen inches) intermediate versions. The artist himself could not keep so closely to his original lines and to his immediately preceding version in all the cases, that on the dropping out of the intermediate version, or versions, the two extreme forms—that is to say, the original sketch, and the supposed copy from the finished work—should tally as they here do. Much less would they tally as they do if the copy from the finished work was by another hand. I regard it as certain, therefore, that the Basle drawing was done directly from the smaller Berlin version.

And here I am fortunate enough to have an ally in Dr. His himself, who, on consideration, abandoned his previous position (taken, no doubt, provisionally), and in December 1886 wrote to me:

" Je suis parfaitement de votre avis, que notre aquarelle ne peut avoir été exécutée d'après la peinture murale, mais qu'elle est une copie du dessin de Berlin, puisqu'à part de l'addition du chien, l'exactitude des traits et des poses des personnages est extraordinaire, jusque dans les moindres détails, de même que dans les plis des vêtements et dans les objets accessoires."

The closeness, however, of the resemblances in the points of detail was one of the main reasons which led Dr. His to ascribe the work to another hand than Holbein's.

" Cette minutieuse exactitude," he continued, " me parait précisément une preuve du contraire. Jamais un grand artiste ne se répète d'une manière aussi scrupuleusement exacte. On reconnait l'intention de rendre les mêmes physionomies, mais malgré la fidélité apparente de la copie, il lui manque l'esprit du maître. Ce n'est pas le trait caractéristique de Holbein, mais l'œuvre d'un copiste très-habile, peut-être de Hans Bock, peintre Bâlois de la fin du 16me siècle, qui a beaucoup copié Holbein."

L'Affaire Holbein-Rippel

With this conclusion I am unable to agree. I do indeed find the resemblances in many cases astonishingly close, but I find the modifications very considerable also, and to consist of well-considered improvements such as no one but the artist himself would venture to make. At Berlin the musicians are at once too near to, and too much disconnected from, the dancers. The hair of the last dancer almost touches the pipe of the right-hand musician, while below there is an empty space which, if the dancers were at all more drawn to the right, would split the composition into two disconnected groups; at Basle this is corrected by the introduction of a dog, which at once permits the dancers to be all drawn further away from the musicians, and unites the two groups harmoniously. At Berlin the perspective of the stone seat on which the pipers are sitting is not pleasant; at Basle this is concealed in deep shadow. At Berlin the head of the right-hand piper comes a little too low in the composition, and is too large; at Basle it is raised and made a trifle smaller; while any one who compares the manner in which the space above the stone seat is occupied by the feathers in the piper's hat, and the flow of the line from the end of the feathers to the feet of the figure in the two drawings, will find the one at Basle to be much the best. On the ground to the left of the left-hand piper in the Berlin drawing there is a small unoccupied space; at Basle this is filled by an object, that I take to be a wine-cooler; these are modifications which no one but the artist himself would make. It is difficult to believe that if a copy had been wanted of Holbein's " Danse " a copyist would have had recourse to the original sketch, and have enlarged it; he would have gone to the house, where he would have found the most matured conception of the artist, and would have reduced it. If, however, he can be conceived as having preferred to work from the small original sketch, magnifying it four or five times over, and adhering to it for the most part with such marvellous fidelity, he would not have ventured on such important deviations;

he would have been closer or not so close. I deny, moreover, that the resemblances show what Dr. His calls " minutieuse exactitude "; the difference between a timid, scrupulous, slavish line, and a vigorous and free one are easily recognized, and the lines of the Basle drawing are drawn with singular fearlessness. The closeness of resemblance cannot be due to any very sensible effort after exactness, but to similarity of inward mind in each case—to the fact that Holbein knew his own meaning, and was master of it. Great effort would mar the resemblance, instead of making it, as I found to my cost when I tried to copy the work. As it is, the resemblance extends even to the peculiar kind of tremble of the hand adopted to express the flexibility of certain folds. The same character of tremulous line is adopted in each drawing, and not only this, but a character which, as I shall show, Holbein was in the habit of adopting when he wanted to render folds in fine linen, though he does not use it elsewhere. Feeling no doubt, then, that I was right, I wrote a letter that appeared in *The Academy*, 23rd October 1886, and shortly afterwards published a card with photographs from the Basle and Berlin drawings arranged in close juxtaposition, followed by a few sentences of explanation.

In 1887 I again returned to the subject with Dr. His, and found him more inclined to agree with me. He very kindly sent for the drawing into his private room, and took it out of its frame. The canvas on which it was mounted did not look old, but I can form no positive opinion as to its age. The drawing seemed to have been crumpled before mounting, in one or two places.

While we were talking, Dr. His said, " Je commence à être de votre avis," and I thought he was going to come round, when on holding it in a certain light he saw that something was written on the shadow side of the stone seat on which the musicians are resting. Neither of us had suspected that there was an inscription before, and even when Dr. His had found it, it was only with great difficulty that any single letter could be deciphered. My first impression concerning the words is

L'Affaire Holbein-Rippel

best shown by the following extracts, which I take from notes written within an hour of our finding the inscription. I find my words to run:

"The first line was 'Joh' or 'Hans'—no one can say which—followed by 'Hol' and some more letters not legible, running a little over the margin of the seat, but the writer cramped his writing after the 'Hol,' and even so had to run a little over the edge. [Tolerably plain traces of this first line can be seen in the photograph taken by Braun, of Dornach, some few years ago.] Then came something in the next line which Dr. His read as 'Inventor,' but of which I could make nothing; then either in the next line or next but one—I forget which—was something which Dr. His said was an abbreviated 'Nicholas,' and which very well might be; this was followed by 'Rippel' fairly clear. Then there was another line, the end of which to me looked like 'Eher,' but Dr. His read the line as 'Maler' and 'Mar' ('Painter,' and the month of March); then came a very legible 1640, which formed the bottom line. Dr. His is inclined to take the writing as saying that the drawing was a copy from Holbein, made in March 1640 by Nicholas Rippel—and this, provided the writing has been read correctly, is the natural inference to draw from it; but in the first place, though I pass the 'Hans' or 'Joh Holb..n' as doubtless meaning 'Hans Holbein,' and though I pass 'Nicholas Rippel' and '1640,' I cannot allow anything more as certain, and the internal evidence remains where it was. Dr. His and I are agreed that the Basle drawing was done directly from the Berlin sketch; but how about the wine-cooler? How about the dog, and how, again, about the remaining six figures of the Basle drawing, that are not in the Berlin sketch?

"Moreover, I do not believe the writing is contemporaneous with the drawing, and incline to think that Nicholas Rippel found the work in a dilapidated state, had it restored, and commemorated his connection with it by the inscription which we have been trying to read."

The foregoing extracts were written on the 30th September

1887. On the 6th October Dr. His sent me the following reading of the inscription, which I have ventured to reproduce in his own handwriting:

> IOH: HOLB:
> Inventor
> Nic: Rippel
> fecit. aetatis
> S: Creatoris [?]
> 1642..

It may serve to show how little reliance should be placed on this reading if I depart here from chronological order, and give a facsimile of a reading kindly sent me a few days ago by Dr. Burckhardt, and dated 18th October 1889:

> (H. Holbein fecit, Nicolaus Rippel
> .... ? aetatis suae ... pas lisible 1624.
> Il se peut que l'inscription soit
> maintenant un peu effacée par suite
> des manipulations du restaurateur,

After which Dr. Burckhardt continues: "Mais je peux vous faire prouver d'une manière positive qu'au mois de Février passé elle a été parfaitement lisible." Indeed, Dr. Burckhardt had examined it, in the presence of several gentlemen, one of whom should surely be a judge, for he was a restorer

L'Affaire Holbein-Rippel

of pictures—presumably the same who subsequently restored the inscription out of existence. Nevertheless if the inscription was so " perfectly legible," we may express surprise that Dr. Burckhardt did not succeed in reading it more perfectly than by his own showing he appears to have done, and that he did not in at least some one line agree with Dr. His. To return, however, to Dr. His's version; after giving it he continued:

" Le mot ' creatoris ' est assez étrange. On s'attendrait plutôt à lire ' Salvatoris,' ou ' Redemptoris.' Aussi ne suis-je pas sûr des quatre premières lettres du mot, qui sont presque entièrement effacées. Ce mot est du reste d'une importance secondaire. Quant à la date, les deux premiers chiffres sont très distincts. Le troisième paraît être un 4, mais il se pourrait que le trait oblique ne soit qu'accidentel, et dans ce cas il faudrait lire 1612. Nicolas Rippel, peintre sur verre, mourut en 1631, âgé de 68 ans, mais il avait un fils du même nom, né en 1594, et mort en 1666, mais j'ignore si celui s'occupait d'art. Je vous prie de me dire si malgré cette preuve que notre peinture n'est pas de la main de Holbein vous désirez que je vous en fasse faire une photographie."

Bearing in mind how conjectural Dr. His's reading must be, and how obviously anxious he was to face the date as 1612 instead of 1642 or 1640; having reason, moreover, to think, I believe correctly, that the only Nicholas Rippel alive in 1640 or 1642 was not a painter, I saw little approach to " proof " in Dr. His's letter that the drawing was not by Holbein, so I asked for two negatives—one, of the first whole string of dancers reduced in size; and another, of the musicians and stone seat, of the same size as the original—in the hopes to get the inscription. These negatives were taken at the end of October 1887, and Dr. His, in writing to tell me of the fact, added:

" Je ne doute pas que la copie soit exécutée par Nicolas Rippel, né en 1563 et mort en 1631, et non par son fils. Le troisième chiffre, que j'avais pris d'abord pour un 4, doit être un 1. Il n'y a que le premier trait perpendiculaire qui compte. L'autre trait est produit par un fil plus gros dans le tissu de la toile, qui dans toute sa longueur a l'apparence d'un trait plus ou moins interrompu. Le trait horizontal n'existe pas. La date sera donc, selon toute probabilité, 1612."

In due course the negatives with prints from them reached me. Nothing of the inscription was visible, but the one print showed some white spots that are seen on the stone seat in the illustration here given, exactly where the first line of the inscription ran, or perhaps the thirty-second of an inch above it, as though of white paper that had been rubbed. These spots did not show in the print from the other negative, so I supposed they arose from some accidental defect in the one plate, and paid no attention to them; lately, however, I had occasion to print from the other negative, and found the same spots appear; then I washed the print I had received from Basle, and found that the white spots had been touched out on the print, and showed as soon as it was washed. There is no trace of them in Braun's photograph taken some years ago. I do not see, therefore, how I can be mistaken in saying that some time in October 1887 the shadow side of the stone seat was handed over to the " manipulations du restaurateur," though probably with instructions only to manipulate the restoration of the upper part; that this gentleman rubbed it till the paper showed, and that he had not yet restored his manipulations when my negatives were taken. On 3rd February 1888, returning from Varallo, I called on Dr. His. He sent for the picture, and again took it out of the frame. There were no white spots upon it then. I take the following from the notes which I wrote on the afternoon of the same day:

"I found the inscription as illegible now as I did in October last. On the whole, I thought Dr. His right in reading the first line as JOH .. HOLB .., and thought the ' in ' which in some lights may be detected in Braun's photograph as over-running the margin of the seat, to be an accidental stain or grain of the paper. Dr. His reads the

L'Affaire Holbein-Rippel

second line as 'Inventor,' which I should think, perhaps, it probably is, but the word is by no means clear; the third line is legible, and reads 'Nic. Rippel.' The fourth is read by Dr. His as 'Fecit Aetatis'; I thought the 'fecit' probably right, but I could not make out the 'Aetatis' or any other word. The fifth line is illegible. Dr. His reads it 'S. Creatoris,' but this does not make good sense, and with every desire to see 'S. Creatoris,' or, indeed, any words at all, I could make nothing of the few vague stains that alone remain. The last line was read both by Dr. His and myself in October last as 1640 or 1642; we both read the third figure as a four. As far as I could see this morning, the four was a very good four. Going to the Museum this afternoon, and taking the picture to a window with the sun on it, I found the horizontal line of the four visible in the same dull dead colour as the rest of the inscription, and could see no reason for suspecting the cross stroke to be what Dr. His believes it to be. I thought the four to be the clearest figure in the whole date; the only figure about which I was in doubt was the last, and I could not decide whether this should be a 2 or an o. I do not doubt that the date is either 1640 or 1642. As regards the rest of the inscription, we do not know what it says, and until we do, it might as well not exist.

"I was too much engrossed with the inscription, when I first saw the work out of its frame in October last, to pay as much attention as I should have done to the workmanship. This morning the light was good, and I examined it for some time; it did not look so well seen very close in a strong light, with no frame or glass, as it does in the duller light of the Museum, seen at the distance of a yard, and with its frame and glass. No picture or drawing can stand such an ordeal scatheless; at the same time I should admit that I found the work less uniformly good than I had expected. Dr. His pointed to the flowers in the hair of some of the figures, and said that Holbein never did them; here he is very possibly right. When, however, he went on to find fault all over the drawing I was less able to follow him. I went to the Museum on leaving Dr. His, to see Holbein's other drawings, and could parallel the points complained of in most even of Holbein's best authenticated works. Take the drawing of the Madonna's hands in Nos. 55, 71, and 72 of the Basle drawings; or, again, the Bishop's hand in No. 74, and the woman's hand in No. 49: he would be a bold man who would venture to ascribe any of these hands to Holbein, if they were shown to him apart from their known history and context. Dr. His said of some of the heads in the 'Danse,' that they were caricatures, not drawings. So they are to some extent, but there is caricature and caricature, and fine caricature involves fine drawing. Here there is so much admirable drawing, that the fact of Holbein for once in his life having verged on caricature should not weigh against the genuineness of the work.

"I now believe, however, that the drawing has been retouched more largely than I had suspected until I examined it in a strong light and out of its frame. I have since seen it in its usual position, and found it difficult to observe the amount of repainting, which was easily seen when it was so placed that it could be looked closely into. I speak with great diffidence, but I imagined that it might have undergone two restorations, one perhaps at the instance of Nicholas Rippel in the seventeenth century, and another at no very distant date, perhaps shortly before it passed into the Basle collection. If the reader will observe the rotten texture of many of the parts of the drawing that are in shadow, he will not find it easy to doubt that they are of much older date than many of the solidly painted lighter parts. That the work has suffered by this process of restoration, whether single or double, goes without saying, but I deny that it has undergone so much restoration that it should no longer pass as a work by Holbein."

It is plain from the foregoing notes that I saw no difference between the inscription as I had seen it in October 1887, and as I saw it in February 1888, except, it might be, in the first line, and it is not impossible that the restorations of the

L'Affaire Holbein-Rippel

manipulator may have had something to do with my change of opinion here, for that there had been both manipulations and restorations of some kind can hardly, I imagine, be disputed.

In the summer of 1888 I again saw the drawing, but did not examine it minutely, being much engaged with additions to my work upon Varallo. This last summer, on seeing the recently published catalogue, I was surprised to find the date given as 1624, and supposed there had been a printer's error through which the " 2 " and the " 4 " had changed places— a supposition which I maintained until I received Dr. Burckhardt's letter of 18th October last. I obtained permission to take the drawing to a strong light, expecting to read the date plainly enough through the glass, as I had done in February 1888, but, to my surprise, I could see no trace of any part of the inscription, and, as it appeared to me, abundant traces of rubbing. Dr. Burckhardt was not at Basle; I could not therefore obtain permission to take the drawing out of its frame, so I said nothing, but resolved to ask leave to do this as I passed through Basle in September on my way home. In September I found Dr. Burckhardt still away, but Dr. Born, the president of the Museum, was good enough to come, and in his presence, and in that of two other well-known residents of Basle, the picture was taken out of the frame and examined, but we could none of us see one single letter of the inscription.

I submit, then, on leaving this part of my case that even while the inscription was in existence it was so undecipherable that those who had the fullest opportunities and the most eager desire to read it conspicuously failed. Now, however, that it is destroyed it should surely be taken as unread, and no further attention should be paid to it. We are thus left without any evidence concerning the work, of any kind whatsoever, except the internal evidence to be collected from the drawing itself. On this I have touched already. Those who deny that the work is by Holbein must either say it was done from the house, as Dr. Burckhardt elects to do, and in this case they are met with the Berlin drawing, and must account for resemblances inexplicable except on the supposition that the one drawing was taken directly from the other. If, on the other hand, with Dr. His, they admit that the Basle drawing was done directly from the Berlin, they must account for modifications, inexplicable except on the supposition that both sketch and enlarged modification are by the same hand. The resemblances are too great for anything but direct influence of the one drawing on the other; and the points of difference are too great for anything but a modification of his original design by the designer himself. Objectors are thus caught in a dilemma, on one horn or the other of which they must be impaled. Dr. His prefers the one horn, and Dr. Burckhardt the other; but neither of them makes even an attempt to escape from the horn of his adoption, or to find any third on which they can impale myself.

The only serious argument brought forward by Dr. Burckhardt to show that the drawing is not by Holbein is when he says, "Il est constaté en outre que Holbein ne s'est jamais servi pour ses peintures des couleurs à gouache." But surely this is a hazardous statement. It can rarely be established that anybody never did anything, and in the present case Dr. Burckhardt need go no farther than the library of his own museum to find a work in body colour by Holbein —I refer to the armorial bearings of Petrus de Fabrinus, of Augsburg, Rector of the University of Basle in 1523. The work is in the *Registre Matricule de l'Université de Basle*, and is given as plate 5 in Dr. His's collection. I would note that the date of the armorial bearings—about 1523—agrees very well with that usually assigned to the "Haus zum Tanz."

Let us now compare the character of line in the two drawings. I cannot, indeed, pretend that my illustrations are absolutely faithful, for a drawing done with washes can only be reproduced satisfactorily by a photograph, and both the Berlin and Basle drawings are washed, as are also the drawings of the Passion series. The two largest of my

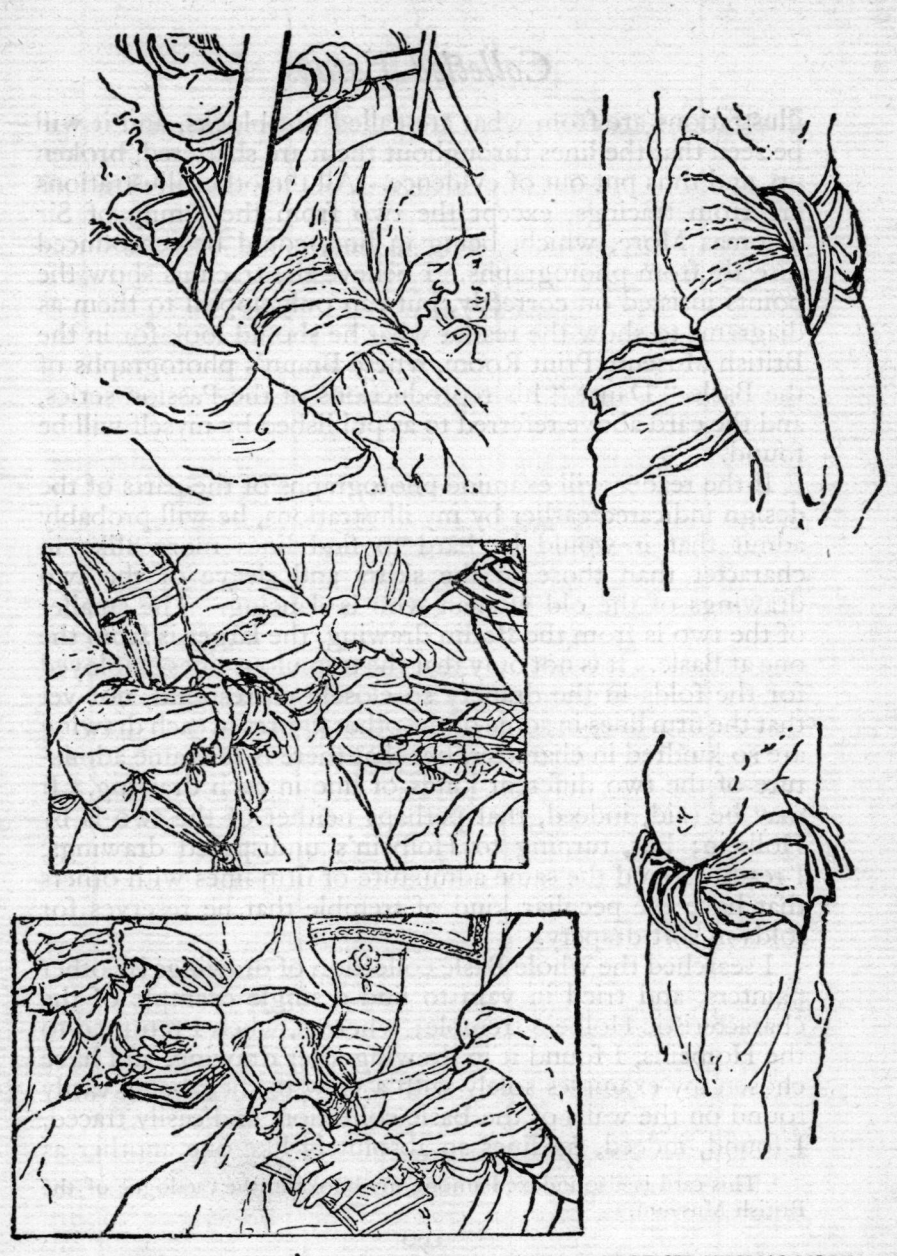

DETAILS FROM HOLBEIN'S PASSION SERIES AND FAMILY OF SIR THOMAS MORE

illustrations are from what are called tint-blocks, and it will be seen that the lines throughout them are shattered, broken up, and thus put out of evidence. All the other illustrations are from tracings, except the two from the family of Sir Thomas More, which, being in line, could be reproduced directly from photographs. I believe the tracings show the points insisted on correctly, but can only appeal to them as diagrams to show the reader what he should look for in the British Museum Print Room, where Braun's photographs of the Basle "Danse," his reproductions of the Passion series, and the card above referred to as published by myself will be found.[1]

If the reader will examine photographs of the parts of the design indicated earlier by my illustrations, he will probably admit that it would be hard to find lines more alike in character than those in the skirts and sleeve of the two drawings of the old woman who is dancing. The smaller of the two is from the Berlin drawing, the larger is from the one at Basle. It is not only that the tremulous lines employed for the folds in the drapery so closely correspond, nor yet that the firm lines in some of the other figures in each drawing are so kindred in character, but that there is the same admixture of the two different kinds of line in each drawing. It may be said, indeed, that perhaps neither of the two is by Holbein; but, turning to Holbein's undisputed drawings, I readily found the same admixture of firm lines with others that have the peculiar kind of tremble that he reserves for folds in soft drapery.

I searched the whole Basle collection of drawings by other painters, and tried in vain to find a single example of the characteristic Holbein tremble; whereas, when I returned to the Holbeins, I found it in drawing after drawing, and have chosen my examples solely with a view to their being easily found on the walls of the Basle collection, and easily traced. I found, indeed, no lines so absolutely like one another as

[1] This card is also indexed among my books in the catalogue of the British Museum.

L'Affaire Holbein-Rippel

those of the Basle and the Berlin drawings of the " Danse," but should attribute the more especially close affinity of these to the fact of their having been perhaps done within only a very few hours of one another, while the artist was still in much the same vein; for the character of a man's line changes with change of health or surroundings as much as that of his handwriting. Signatures written within an hour or a day of one another will, I imagine, generally resemble one another more than those written at intervals of some time, but this is a question of no great importance. It is enough to note the remarkable resemblance between the idiosyncrasies of the lines employed, and this, I confess, is to me as conclusive as a written signature would be, and would make me ascribe the Basle drawing unhesitatingly to Holbein, even if I had none of the collateral evidence derivable from the Berlin drawing.

It only remains to explain how an original drawing—and I venture to say one of the finest and most characteristic that Holbein has left us—should so long have been reputed to be only a copy. The Basle collection is one of the best known in Europe; hundreds of excellent judges must examine the work we have been considering, in every year. Does it not seem a little, to say the least of it, presumptuous to set one's own judgement up against that of so many more competent observers? I assure the reader that this has frequently occurred to myself with as much force as it will probably have done to him. But in the first place I do not believe any one has given nearly as much attention to the work as I have, I do not know of any one else who has tried to copy it, and it was not until I did this and was thus kept hours before it on consecutive days in consecutive years, that I came to suspect the received ascription. Can I wonder that what so long escaped myself should have escaped more competent but more casual observers? If I had not tried to copy it I should have gone on calling it a copy to the end of my days. Moreover, the drawing came from a bad source. M. Birmann, from whom it passed to the Basle Museum, and among whose collection it was hung apart from the other

Holbeins, does not appear to have known much about pictures. There are no other works of much interest among his pictures. He is believed to have made the note above referred to in his catalogue, and it did not occur to those into whose hands his pictures passed to doubt that he was rightly informed. People are naturally shy of supposing that what they find described as a copy in the catalogue of an inferior collection is in reality an original, and it is very natural that having been once set down as a copy it should continue to be held as such.

The main reason, however, why the error was not discovered sooner lies in the impossibility till recently of comparing the work with the Berlin drawing. It was not till Dr. His got a negative taken of this for his work already referred to, that it became possible to put the two drawings practically side by side, and it is not till this is done that surmise can give place to very tolerable certainty. I regard Dr. His, therefore, in spite of his strong opposition to my views, as the real discoverer of Holbein's more finished study for his " Danse des Paysans." Once place a good photograph of the Berlin drawing side by side with another taken from the one at Basle, and it will not be easy henceforth to see this last as anything but an enlarged and more matured colour-study done directly from the first—the last six figures, not here given, of the Basle drawing being done either from a sketch now lost, or without preliminary sketch—and they are certainly slighter than the left-hand eight figures here reproduced. Such a study Holbein doubtless made, and it is not easy to resist the conclusion that we have it fortunately preserved to us in the work we have been now considering.

L'Affaire Holbein-Rippel

POSTSCRIPT

The following memo was written 26th September 1890, but I had left myself no margin, and the MS. *would not bind with the printed matter. I therefore copy it, without alteration.* — S. BUTLER, 27th February 1900.

Basle, 26th September 1890. Hotel National.

I went to the Museum this morning to see Dr. Burckhardt, having been informed by Herr Arnold Refardt that this gentleman still maintained that he could read the inscription as per his statement in the French edition of the Basle Museum Catalogue. Dr. B. was not at the Museum, but Herr Refardt and I went to a place called the Casino, where we found him superintending the removal of objects from an exhibition recently held in connection with the Burckhardt family. Herr Refardt introduced me; I, of course, was extremely civil; so was Dr. B. I said I had heard he believed himself still able to read the inscription, and he replied that he and Dr. His could read it with ease. I said in that case I must be mistaken, and would very gladly reconsider my position; would he allow me, then, to have the drawing again taken out of its frame? He consented, so Herr Refardt and I went back to the Museum.

Standing in front of the drawing, before Mr. Kaufmann came to take it out of its frame, both Herr Refardt and I at first thought we could see a good deal more than we could a year ago. It seemed as though we could see four or five lines, distinctly and regularly written. On examining the work, however, when the glass was removed, and with the help of a magnifying glass, this proved to be an optical illusion, due (I suppose), to some parts of the admitted "restoration" having dried more dead than others, though I know not how or why this should be. There were no letters visible except an R pretty plain, and an i p, or double p, we could not be certain which. There were traces of an N, or M, we could not say which, immediately before the R, and I do not doubt that we have here the wreck of the "Nic. Rippel," which Dr. His and I saw quite plainly on two occasions when we examined the drawing together.

I thought these wrecks of letters were perhaps a little plainer than when I last saw the drawing—in fact, I do not remember then seeing them at all; but my seeing them now is probably due to accidents of light, or manner of holding, and I do not think the drawing has been tampered with since I saw it last.

Dr. Born, President of the Museum, came in while we were examining the drawing. I asked him whether he could see anything, but he declared that he could not find a single undoubtful letter. Mr. Kaufmann could see as I did, N or M or Ni, whatever it may be, which he accepted as probably Ni; and he could make out Rip, but could not be certain about the second p.

Herr Refardt, when I traced the letters for him as nearly as I could without touching the drawing, saw this also. Not one of the four of us, however, turn the drawing which way we would, and though we had a good magnifying glass, could see a single other letter or figure; what looked like lines of writing while the drawing was on the wall, proved to be only a few stronger stains, doubtless following old writing but now void of all significance, and we were as unanimous as we were last year that there is not a legible character in the whole inscription except those mentioned already. Nevertheless, I am free to admit that there is more general appearance of there having once been an inscription than I remember to have seen a year ago. Possibly the admitted "restoration" may have lost colour a little, and allowed the wreck of the old inscription to appear more plainly; but some of these apparent traces are on a part of the seat where there never was any inscription, and it is more likely that they are mere accidents due to the grain of the paper. I have not my Holbein article with me, but see no reason, so far as I remember it, to wish to alter.

In the afternoon we called on Dr. Sieber, who was suffer-

L'Affaire Holbein-Rippel

ing from a recent fall; we told him what had passed and he was much amused, but showed some impatience on hearing that Dr. Burckhardt still stuck to it that he could see the inscription. To Dr. Born in the morning I had said, laughing, " C'est peut être, Monsieur, parce que nos yeux sont un peu vieux, que nous ne pouvons rien distinguer; les yeux de Dr. Burckhardt sont plus jeunes, et naturellement il voit mieux que nous." Dr. Born saw what I meant and laughed.

A MEDIEVAL GIRL SCHOOL (OROPA)

NOTE

THIS article appeared in *The Universal Review* for December 1889, and was reprinted (but without illustrations) in the two collections of Butler's essays brought out by R. A. Streatfeild in 1904 and 1913 respectively. The illustrations have now been restored.

A.T.B.

THE CONVERSATION ROOM
(Dimora Chapel)

A Medieval Girl School (Oropa)[1]

THIS LAST SUMMER I REVISITED OROPA, near Biella, to see what connection I could find between the Oropa chapels and those at Varallo. I will take this opportunity of describing the chapels at Oropa, and more especially the remarkable fossil, or petrified girl school, commonly known as the "Dimora," or Sojourn of the Virgin Mary in the Temple.

If I do not take these works so seriously as the reader may expect, let him look, before he blames me, at the photographs here reproduced. Have the good people of Oropa themselves taken them very seriously? Are we in an atmosphere where we need be at much pains to speak with bated breath? We, as is well known, love to take even our pleasures sadly; the Italians take even their sadness *allegramente*, and combine devotion with amusement in a manner that we shall do well to study if not imitate. For this best agrees with what we gather to have been the custom of Christ himself, who, indeed, never speaks of austerity but to condemn it. If Christianity is to be a living faith, it must penetrate a man's whole life, so that he can no more rid himself of it than he can of his flesh and bones or of his breathing. The Christianity that can be taken up and laid down as if it were a watch or a book is Christianity in name only. The true Christian can no more part from Christ in mirth than in sorrow. And, after all, what is the essence of Christianity? What is the kernel of the nut? Surely common sense and cheerfulness, with unflinching opposition to the charlatanisms and Pharisaisms of a man's own times. The essence of Christianity lies neither in dogma, nor yet in abnormally holy life, but in faith in an unseen world, in doing one's duty, in speaking the truth, in finding the true life rather in others than in oneself, and in the certain hope that he who loses his life on these behalfs finds more than he has lost. What can Agnosticism do against such Christianity as this? I should be shocked if anything I had ever written or shall ever write should seem to make light of these things. I should be shocked also if

[1] From *The Universal Review*, December 1889.

I did not know how to be amused with things that amiable people obviously intended to be amusing.

The reader may need to be reminded that Oropa is among the somewhat infrequent sanctuaries at which the Madonna and infant Christ are not white, but black. I shall return to this peculiarity of Oropa later on, but will leave it for the present. For the general characteristics of the place I must refer the reader to my book *Alps and Sanctuaries*. I propose to confine myself here to the ten or a dozen chapels containing life-sized terra-cotta figures, painted up to nature, that form one of the main features of the place. At a first glance, perhaps, all these chapels will seem uninteresting; I venture to think, however, that some, if not most of them, though falling a good deal short of the best work at Varallo and Crea, are still in their own way of considerable importance. The first chapel with which we need concern ourselves is numbered 4, and shows the Conception of the Virgin Mary. It represents St. Anne as kneeling before a terrific dragon or, as the Italians call it, " insect," about the size of a Crystal Palace pleiosaur. This " insect " is supposed to have just had its head badly crushed by St. Anne, who seems to be begging its pardon. The text " Ipsa conteret caput tuum " is written outside the chapel. The figures have no artistic interest. As regards dragons being called insects, the reader may perhaps remember that the island of S. Giulio, in the Lago d'Orta, was infested with *insetti*, which S. Giulio destroyed, and which appear, in a fresco underneath the church on the island, to have been monstrous and ferocious dragons; but I cannot remember whether their bodies are divided into three sections, and whether or no they have exactly six legs—without which, I am told, they cannot be true insects.

The fifth chapel represents the Birth of the Virgin. Having obtained permission to go inside it, I found the date 1715 cut large and deep on the back of one figure before baking, and I imagine that this date covers the whole. There is a Queen Anne feeling throughout the composition,

A Medieval Girl School (Oropa)

and if we were told that the sculptor and Francis Bird, sculptor of the statue in front of St. Paul's Cathedral, had studied under the same master, we could very well believe it. The apartment in which the Virgin was born is spacious, and in striking contrast to the one in which she herself gave birth to the Redeemer. St. Anne occupies the centre of the composition, in an enormous bed; on her right there is a lady of the George Cruikshank style of beauty, and on the left an older person. Both are gesticulating and impressing upon St. Anne the enormous obligation she has just conferred upon mankind; they seem also to be imploring her not to overtax her strength, but, strange to say, they are giving her neither flowers nor anything to eat and drink. I know no other Birth of the Virgin in which St. Anne wants so little keeping up.

I have explained in my book *Ex Voto*, but should perhaps repeat here, that the distinguishing characteristic of the Birth of the Virgin, as rendered by Valsesian artists, is that St. Anne always has eggs immediately after the infant is born, and usually a good deal more, whereas the Madonna never has anything to eat or drink. The eggs are in accordance with a custom that still prevails among the peasant classes in the Valsesia, where women on giving birth to a child generally are given a *sabaglione*—an egg beaten up with a little wine, or rum, and sugar. East of Milan the Virgin's mother does not have eggs, and I suppose, from the absence of the eggs at Oropa, that the custom above referred to does not prevail in the Biellese district. The Virgin also is invariably washed. St. John the Baptist, when he is born at all, which is not very often, is also washed; but I have not observed that St. Elizabeth has anything like the attention paid her that is given to St. Anne. What, however, is wanting here at Oropa in meat and drink is made up in Cupids; they swarm like flies on the walls, clouds, cornices, and capitals of columns.

Against the right-hand wall are two lady-helps, each warming a towel at a glowing fire, to be ready against the baby should come out of its bath; while in the right-hand foreground we have the *levatrice*, who having discharged her task, and being now so disposed, has removed the bottle from the chimney-piece, and put it near some bread, fruit, and a chicken, over which she is about to discuss the confinement with two other gossips. The *levatrice* is a very characteristic figure, but the best in the chapel is the one here given of the head-nurse, near the middle of the composition; she has now the infant in full charge, and is showing it to St. Joachim, with an expression as though she were telling him that her husband was a merry man. I am afraid Shakespeare was dead before the sculptor was born, otherwise I should have felt certain that he had drawn Juliet's nurse from this figure. As for the little Virgin herself, I believe her to be a fine boy of about ten months old. Viewing the work as a whole, if I only felt more sure what artistic merit really is, I should say that, though the chapel cannot be rated very highly from some standpoints, there are others from which it may be praised warmly enough. It is innocent of anatomy-worship, free from affectation or swagger, and not devoid of a good deal of homely *naïveté*. It can no more be compared with Tabachetti or Donatello than Hogarth can with Rembrandt or Giovanni Bellini; but as it does not transcend the limitations of its age, so neither is it wanting in whatever merits that age possessed; and there is no age without merits of some kind. There is no inscription saying who made the figures, but tradition gives them to Pietro Aureggio Termine, of Biella, commonly called Aureggio. This is confirmed by their strong resemblance to those in the "Dimora" chapel, in which there is an inscription that names Aureggio as the sculptor.

The sixth chapel deals with the Presentation of the Virgin in the Temple. The Virgin is very small, but it must be remembered that she is only seven years old, and she is not nearly so small as she is at Crea, where, though a life-sized figure is intended, the head is hardly bigger than an apple. She is rushing up the steps with open arms towards the High

THE VIRGIN AND HER NURSE
(Chapel of the Birth of the Virgin)

A Medieval Girl School (Oropa)

Priest, who is standing at the top. For her it is nothing alarming; it is the High Priest who appears frightened; but it will all come right in time. The Virgin seems to be saying, "Why, don't you know me? I'm the Virgin Mary." But the High Priest does not feel so sure about that, and will make further inquiries. The scene, which comprises some twenty figures, is animated enough, and though it hardly kindles enthusiasm, still does not fail to please. It looks as though of somewhat older date than the Birth of the Virgin chapel, and I should say shows more signs of direct Valsesian influence. In Marocco's book about Oropa it is ascribed to Aureggio, but I find it difficult to accept this.

The seventh, and in many respects most interesting chapel at Oropa, shows what is in reality a medieval Italian girl school, as nearly like the thing itself as the artist could make it; we are expected, however, to see in this the high-class kind of Girton College for young gentlewomen that was attached to the Temple at Jerusalem, under the direction of the Chief Priest's wife, or some one of his near female relatives. Here all well-to-do Jewish young women completed their education, and here accordingly we find the Virgin, whose parents desired she should shine in every accomplishment, and enjoy all the advantages their ample means commanded.

I have met with no traces of the Virgin during the years between her Presentation in the Temple and her becoming head girl at Temple College. These years, we may be assured, can hardly have been other than eventful; but incidents, or bits of life, are like living forms—it is only here and there, as by rare chance, that one of them gets arrested and fossilized; the greater number disappear like the greater number of antediluvian molluscs, and no one can say why one of these flies, as it were, of life should get preserved in amber more than another. Talk, indeed, about luck and cunning; what a grain of sand as against a hundredweight is cunning's share here as against luck's. What moment could be more humdrum and unworthy of special record than the one chosen by the artist for the chapel we are considering? Why should this one get arrested in its flight and made immortal when so many worthier ones have perished? Yet preserved it assuredly is; it is as though some fairy's wand had struck the medieval Miss Pinkerton, Amelia Sedley, and others who do duty instead of the Hebrew originals. It has locked them up as sleeping beauties, whose charms all may look upon. Surely the hours are like the women grinding at the mill—the one is taken and the other left, and none can give the reason more than he can say why Gallio should have won immortality by caring for " none of these things."

It seems to me, moreover, that fairies have changed their practice now in the matter of sleeping beauties, much as shopkeepers have done in Regent Street. Formerly the shopkeeper used to shut up his goods behind strong shutters, so that no one might see them after closing hours. Now he leaves everything open to the eye and turns the gas on. So the fairies, who used to lock up their sleeping beauties in impenetrable thickets, now leave them in the most public places they can find, as knowing that they will there most certainly escape notice. Look at De Hooghe; look at *The Pilgrim's Progress*, or even Shakespeare himself—how long they slept unawakened, though they were in broad daylight and on the public thoroughfares all the time. Look at Tabachetti, and the masterpieces he left at Varallo. His figures there are exposed to the gaze of every passer-by; yet who heeds them? Who, save a very few, even know of their existence? Look again at Gaudenzio Ferrari, or the " Danse des Paysans," by Holbein, to which I ventured to call attention in *The Universal Review*. No, no; if a thing be in Central Africa, it is the glory of this age to find it out; so the fairies think it safer to conceal their *protégés* under a show of openness; for the schoolmaster is much abroad, and there is no hedge so thick or so thorny as the dulness of culture.

It may be, again, that ever so many years hence, when Mr. Darwin's earth-worms shall have buried Oropa hundreds of feet deep, someone sinking a well or making a railway-cutting will unearth these chapels, and will believe them to

A Medieval Girl School (Oropa)

have been houses, and to contain the *exuviae* of the living forms that tenanted them. In the meantime, however, let us return to a consideration of the chapel as it may now be seen, and as I show it in my three illustrations.

The work consists of about forty figures in all, not counting Cupids, and is divided into four main divisions. First, there is the large public sitting-room or drawing-room of the College, where the elder young ladies are engaged in various elegant employments. Three, at a table to the left, are making a mitre for the Bishop, as may be seen from the model on the table. Some are merely spinning or about to spin. One young lady, whom I have not been able to show, is doing an elaborate piece of needlework at a tambour-frame near the window; others are making lace or slippers, probably for the new curate; another is struggling with a letter, or perhaps a theme, which seems to be giving her a good deal of trouble, but which, when done, will, I am sure, be beautiful. One dear little girl is simply reading *Paul and Virginia* underneath the window, and is so concealed that I hardly think she can be seen from the outside at all, though from inside she is delightful; it was with great regret that I could not get her into any photograph. One most amiable young woman has got a child's head on her lap, the child having played itself to sleep. All are industriously and agreeably employed in some way or other; all are plump; all are nice-looking; there is not one Becky Sharp in the whole school; on the contrary, as in " Pious Orgies," all is pious—or sub-pious—and all, if not great, is at least eminently respectable. One feels that St. Joachim and St. Anne could not have chosen a school more judiciously, and that if one had a daughter oneself this is exactly where one would wish to place her. If there is a fault of any kind in the arrangements, it is that they do not keep cats enough. The place is overrun with mice, though what these can find to eat I know not. It occurs to me also that the young ladies might be kept a little more free of spiders' webs; but in all these chapels, bats, mice, and spiders are troublesome.

Off the main drawing-room on the side facing the window

there is a daïs, which is approached by a large raised semi-circular step, higher than the rest of the floor, but lower than the daïs itself. The daïs is, of course, reserved for the venerable Lady Principal and the under-mistresses, one of whom, by the way, is a little more *mondaine* than might have been expected, and is admiring herself in a looking-glass—unless, indeed, she is only looking to see if there is a spot of ink on her face. The Lady Principal is seated near a table, on which lie some books in expensive bindings, which I imagine to have been presented to her by the parents of pupils who were leaving school. One has given her a photograph album; another a large scrapbook, for illustrations of all kinds; a third volume has red edges, and is presumably of a devotional character. If I dared venture another criticism, I should say it would be better not to keep the ink-pot on the top of these books. The Lady Principal is being read to by the monitress for the week, whose duty it was to recite selected passages from the most approved Hebrew writers; she appears to be a good deal outraged, possibly at the faulty intonation of the reader, which she has long tried vainly to correct; or perhaps she has been hearing of the atrocious way in which her forefathers had treated the prophets, and is explaining to the young ladies how impossible it would be, in their own more enlightened age, for a prophet to fail of recognition.

On the half-daïs, as I suppose the large semicircular step between the main room and the daïs should be called, we find, first, the monitress for the week, who stands up while she recites; and secondly, the Virgin herself, who is the only pupil allowed a seat so near to the august presence of the Lady Principal. She is ostensibly doing a piece of embroidery which is stretched on a cushion on her lap, but I should say that she was chiefly interested in the nearest of four pretty little Cupids, who are all trying to attract her attention, though they pay no court to any other young lady. I have sometimes wondered whether the obviously scandalized gesture of the Lady Principal might not be directed at these

THE BISHOP'S MITRE
(Dimora Chapel)

A Medieval Girl School (Oropa)

Cupids, rather than at anything the monitress may have been reading, for she would surely find them disquieting. Or she may be saying, "Why, bless me! I do declare the Virgin has got another hamper, and St. Anne's cakes are always so terribly rich!" Certainly the hamper is there, close to the Virgin, and the Lady Principal's action may be well directed at it, but it may have been sent to some other young lady, and be put on the sub-daïs for public exhibition. It looks as if it might have come from Fortnum and Mason's, and I half expected to find a label, addressing it to "The Virgin Mary, Temple College, Jerusalem," but if ever there was one the mice have long since eaten it. The Virgin herself does not seem to care much about it, but if she has a fault it is that she is generally a little apathetic.

Whose the hamper was, however, is a point we shall never now certainly determine, for the best fossil is worse than the worst living form. Why, alas! was not Mr. Edison alive when this chapel was made? We might then have had a daily phonographic recital of the conversation, and an announcement might be put outside the chapels, telling us at what hours the figures would speak.

On either side of the main room there are two annexes opening out from it; these are reserved chiefly for the younger children, some of whom, I think, are little boys. In the left annex, behind the ladies who are making a mitre, there is a child who has got a cake, and another has some fruit—possibly given them by the Virgin—and a third child is begging for some of it. The light failed so completely here that I was not able to photograph any of these figures. It was a dull September afternoon, and the clouds had settled thick round the chapel, which is never very light, and is nearly 4000 feet above the sea. I waited till such twilight as made it hopeless that more detail could be got—and a queer ghostly place enough it was to wait in—but after giving the plate an exposure of fifty minutes, I saw I could get no more, and desisted.

These long photographic exposures have the advantage

that one is compelled to study a work in detail through mere lack of other employment, and that one can take one's notes in peace without being tempted to hurry over them; but even so I continually find I have omitted to note, and have clean forgotten, much that I want later on.

In the other annex there are also one or two younger children, but it seems to have been set apart for conversation and relaxation more than any other part of the establishment.

I have already said that the work is signed by an inscription inside the chapel, to the effect that the sculptures are by Pietro Aureggio Termine di Biella. It will be seen that the young ladies are exceedingly like one another, and that the artist aimed at nothing more than a faithful rendering of the life of his own times. Let us be thankful that he aimed at nothing less. Perhaps his wife kept a girls' school; or he may have had a large family of fat, good-natured daughters, whose little ways he had studied attentively; at all events the work is full of spontaneous incident, and cannot fail to become more and more interesting as the age it renders falls farther back into the past. It is to be regretted that many artists, better-known men, have not been satisfied with the humbler ambitions of this most amiable and interesting sculptor. If he has left us no laboured life-studies, he has at least done something for us which we can find nowhere else, which we should be very sorry not to have, and the fidelity of which to Italian life at the beginning of the eighteenth century will not be disputed.

The eighth chapel is that of the "Sposalizio," is certainly not by Aureggio, and I should say was mainly by the same sculptor who did the Presentation in the Temple. On going inside I found the figures had come from more than one source; some of them are constructed so absolutely on Valsesian principles, as regards technique, that it may be assumed they came from Varallo. Each of these last figures is in three pieces, that are baked separately and cemented together afterwards, hence they are more easily transported; no more clay is used than is absolutely necessary; and the off-side of

CENTRAL VIEW OF THE DIMORA CHAPEL

A Medieval Girl School (Oropa)

the figure is neglected; they will be found chiefly, if not entirely, at the top of the steps. The other figures are more solidly built, and do not remind me in their business features of anything in the Valsesia. There was a sculptor, Francesco Sala, of Locarno (doubtless the village a short distance below Varallo, and not the Locarno on the Lago Maggiore), who made designs for some of the Oropa chapels, and some of whose letters are still preserved, but whether the Valsesian figures in this present work are by him or not I cannot say. The statues are twenty-five in number; I could find no date or signature; the work reminds me of Montrigone; several of the figures are not at all bad, and several have horsehair for hair, as at Varallo. The effect of the whole composition is better than we have a right to expect from any sculpture dating from the beginning of the eighteenth century.

The ninth chapel, the Annunciation, presents no feature of interest; nor yet does the tenth, the Visit of Mary to Elizabeth. The eleventh, the Nativity, though rather better, is still not remarkable.

The twelfth, the Purification, is absurdly bad, but I do not know whether the expression of strong personal dislike to the Virgin which the High Priest wears is intended as prophetic, or whether it is the result of incompetence, or whether it is merely a smile gone wrong in the baking. It is amusing to find Marocco, who has not been strict about archaeological accuracy hitherto, complain here that there is an anachronism, inasmuch as some young ecclesiastics are dressed as they would be at present, and one of them actually carries a wax candle. This is not as it should be; in works like those at Oropa, where implicit reliance is justly placed on the earnest endeavours that have been so successfully made to thoroughly and carefully and patiently ensure the accuracy of the minutest details, it is a pity that even a single error should have escaped detection; this, however, has most unfortunately happened here, and Marocco feels it his duty to put us on our guard. He explains that the mistake arose from the sculptor's having taken both his general arrangement and his details from some picture of the fourteenth or fifteenth century, when the value of the strictest historical accuracy was not yet so fully understood.

It seems to me that in the matter of accuracy, priests and men of science whether lay or regular on the one hand, and plain people whether lay or regular on the other, are trying to play a different game, and fail to understand one another because they do not see that their objects are not the same. The cleric and the man of science (who is only the cleric in his latest development) are trying to develop a throat with two distinct passages—one that shall refuse to pass even the smallest gnat, and another that shall gracefully gulp even the largest camel; whereas we men of the street desire but one throat, and are content that this shall swallow nothing bigger than a pony. Everyone knows that there is no such effectual means of developing the power to swallow camels as incessant watchfulness for opportunities of straining at gnats, and this should explain many passages that puzzle us in the work both of our clerics and our scientists. I, not being a man of science, still continue to do what I said I did in *Alps and Sanctuaries*, and make it a rule to earnestly and patiently and carefully swallow a few of the smallest gnats I can find several times a day, as the best astringent for the throat I know of.

The thirteenth chapel is the Marriage Feast at Cana of Galilee. This is the best chapel as a work of art; indeed, it is the only one which can claim to be taken quite seriously. Not that all the figures are very good; those to the left of the composition are commonplace enough; nor are the Christ and the giver of the feast at all remarkable; but the ten or dozen figures of guests and attendants at the right-hand end of the work are as good as anything of their kind can be, and remind me so strongly of Tabachetti that I cannot doubt they were done by someone who was indirectly influenced by that great sculptor's work. It is not likely that Tabachetti was alive long after 1640, by which time he would

A Medieval Girl School (Oropa)

have been about eighty years old;[1] and the foundations of this chapel were not laid till about 1690; the statues are probably a few years later; they can hardly, therefore, be by one who had even studied under Tabachetti; but until I found out the dates, and went inside the chapel to see the way in which the figures had been constructed, I was inclined to think they might be by Tabachetti himself, of whom, indeed, they are not unworthy. On examining the figures I found them more heavily constructed than Tabachetti's are, with smaller holes for taking out superfluous clay, and more finished on the off-sides. Marocco says the sculptor is not known. I looked in vain for any date or signature. Possibly the right-hand figures (for the left-hand ones can hardly be by the same hand) may be by some sculptor from Crea, which is at no very great distance from Oropa, who was penetrated by Tabachetti's influence; but whether as regards action and concert with one another, or as regards excellence in detail, I do not see how anything can be more realistic, and yet more harmoniously composed. The placing of the musicians in a minstrels' gallery helps the effect; these musicians are six in number, and the other figures are twenty-three. Under the table, between Christ and the giver of the feast, there is a cat.

The fourteenth chapel, the Assumption of the Virgin Mary, is without interest.

The fifteenth, the Coronation of the Virgin, contains forty-six angels, twenty-six cherubs, fifty-six saints, the Holy Trinity, the Madonna herself, and twenty-four innocents, making 156 statues in all. Of these I am afraid there is not one of more than ordinary merit; the most interesting is a half-length nude life-study of Disma—the good thief. After what had been promised him it was impossible to exclude him, but it was felt that a half-length nude figure would be as much as he could reasonably expect.

Behind the sanctuary there is a semi-ruinous, and wholly valueless work, which shows the finding of the black image,

[1] Tabachetti died in 1615. Cf. *ante*, p. 159. – A.T.B.

which is now in the church, but is only shown on great festivals.

This leads us to a consideration that I have delayed till now. The black image is the central feature of Oropa; it is the *raison d'être* of the whole place, and all else is a mere incrustation, so to speak, around it. According to this image, then, which was carved by St. Luke himself, and than which nothing can be better authenticated, both the Madonna and the infant Christ were as black as anything can be conceived. It is not likely that they were as black as they have been painted; no one yet ever was so black as that; yet, even allowing for some exaggeration on St. Luke's part, they must have been exceedingly black if the portrait is to be accepted; and uncompromisingly black they accordingly are on most of the wayside chapels for many a mile around Oropa. Yet in the chapels we have been hitherto considering—works in which, as we know, the most punctilious regard has been shown to accuracy—both the Virgin and Christ are uncompromisingly white. As in the shops under the Colonnade where devotional knick-knacks are sold, you can buy a black china image or a white one, whichever you like; so with the pictures—the black and white are placed side by side—*pagando il danaro si può scegliere*. It rests not with history or with the Church to say whether the Madonna and Child were black or white, but you may settle it for yourself, whichever way you please, or rather you are required, with the acquiescence of the Church, to hold that they were both black and white at one and the same time.

It cannot be maintained that the Church leaves the matter undecided, and by tolerating both types proclaims the question an open one, for she acquiesces in the portrait by St. Luke as genuine. How, then, justify the whiteness of the Holy Family in the chapels? If the portrait is not known as genuine, why set such a stumbling-block in our paths as to show us a black Madonna and a white one, both as historically accurate, within a few yards of one another?

I ask this not in mockery, but as knowing that the Church

must have an explanation to give, if she would only give it, and as myself unable to find any, even the most far-fetched, that can bring what we see at Oropa, Loreto, and elsewhere into harmony with modern conscience, either intellectual or ethical.

I see, indeed, from an interesting article in *The Atlantic Monthly* for September 1889, entitled "The Black Madonna of Loreto," that black Madonnas were so frequent in ancient Christian art that "some of the early writers of the Church felt obliged to account for it by explaining that the Virgin was of a very dark complexion, as might be proved by the verse of Canticles which says, 'I am black, but comely, O ye daughters of Jerusalem.' Others maintained that she became black during her sojourn in Egypt.... Priests, of to-day, say that extreme age and exposure to the smoke of countless altar-candles have caused that change in complexion which the more naïve fathers of the Church attributed to the power of an Egyptian sun"; but the writer ruthlessly disposes of this supposition by pointing out that in nearly all the instances of black Madonnas it is the flesh alone that is entirely black, the crimson of the lips, the white of the eyes, and the draperies having preserved their original colour. The authoress of the article (Mrs. Hilliard) goes on to tell us that Pausanias mentions two statues of the black Venus, and says that the oldest statue of Ceres among the Phigalenses was black. She adds that Minerva Aglaurus, the daughter of Cecrops, at Athens, was black; that Corinth had a black Venus, as also the Thespians; that the oracles of Dodona and Delphi were founded by black doves, the emissaries of Venus, and that the Isis Multimammia in the Capitol at Rome is black.

Sometimes I have asked myself whether the Church does not intend to suggest that the whole story falls outside the domain of history, and is to be held as the one great epos, or myth, common to all mankind; adaptable by each nation according to its own several needs; translatable, so to speak, into the facts of each individual nation, as the written word is translatable into its language, but appertaining to the realm of the imagination rather than to that of the understanding, and precious for spiritual rather than literal truths. More briefly, I have wondered whether she may not intend that such details as whether the Virgin was white or black are of very little importance in comparison with the basing of ethics on a story that shall appeal to black races as well as to white ones.

If so, it is time we were made to understand this more clearly. If the Church, whether of Rome or England, would lean to some such view as this—tainted though it be with mysticism—if we could see either great branch of the Church make a frank, authoritative attempt to bring its teaching into greater harmony with the educated understanding and conscience of the time, instead of trying to fetter that understanding with bonds that gall it daily more and more profoundly; then I, for one, in view of the difficulty and graciousness of the task, and in view of the great importance of historical continuity, would gladly sink much of my own private opinion as to the value of the Christian ideal, and would gratefully help either Church or both, according to the best of my very feeble ability. On these terms, indeed, I could swallow not a few camels myself cheerfully enough.

Can we, however, see any signs as though either Rome or England will stir hand or foot to meet us? Can any step be pointed to as though either Church wished to make things easier for men holding the opinions held by the late Mr. Darwin, or by Mr. Herbert Spencer and Professor Huxley? How can those who accept evolution with any thoroughness accept such doctrines as the Incarnation or the Redemption with any but a quasi-allegorical and poetical interpretation? Can we conceivably accept these doctrines in the literal sense in which the Church advances them? And can the leaders of the Church be blind to the resistlessness of the current that has set against those literal interpretations which she seems to hug more and more closely the more religious life is awakened at all? The clergyman is wanted as supplement-

A Medieval Girl School (Oropa)

ing the doctor and the lawyer in all civilized communities; these three keep watch on one another, and prevent one another from becoming too powerful. I, who distrust the doctrinaire in science even more than the doctrinaire in religion, should view with dismay the abolition of the Church of England, as knowing that a blatant bastard science would instantly step into her shoes; but if some such deplorable consummation is to be avoided in England, it can only be through more evident leaning on the part of our clergy to such an interpretation of the Sacred History as the presence of a black and white Madonna almost side by side at Oropa appears to suggest.

I fear that in these last paragraphs I may have trenched on dangerous ground, but it is not possible to go to such places as Oropa without asking oneself what they mean and involve. As for the average Italian pilgrims, they do not appear to give the matter so much as a thought. They love Oropa, and flock to it in thousands during the summer; the President of the Administration assured me that they lodged, after a fashion, as many as ten thousand pilgrims on the 15th of last August. It is astonishing how living the statues are to these people, and how the wicked are upbraided and the good applauded. At Varallo, since I took the photographs I published in my book *Ex Voto*, an angry pilgrim has smashed the nose of the dwarf in Tabachetti's Journey to Calvary, for no other reason than inability to restrain his indignation against one who was helping to inflict pain on Christ. It is the real hair and the painting up to nature that does this. Here at Oropa I found a paper on the floor of the " Sposalizio " Chapel, which ran as follows:

" By the grace of God and the will of the administrative chapter of this sanctuary, there have come here to work —— ——, mason, —— ——, carpenter, and —— ——, plumber, all of Chiavazza, on the twenty-first day of January 1886, full of cold (*pieni di freddo*).

" They write these two lines to record their visit. They pray the Blessed Virgin that she will maintain them safe and sound from everything equivocal that may befall them (*sempre sani e salvi da ogni equivoco li possa accadere*). Oh, farewell! We reverently salute all the present statues, and especially the Blessed Virgin, and the reader."

Through *The Universal Review*, I suppose, all its readers are to consider themselves saluted; at any rate, these good fellows, in the effusiveness of their hearts, actually wrote the above in pencil. I was sorely tempted to steal it, but, after copying it, left it in the Chief Priest's hands instead.

ART IN THE VALLEY OF SAAS

NOTE

This article appeared in *The Universal Review* for November 1890, and was reprinted in the two collections of Butler's essays brought out by R. A. Streatfeild in 1904 and 1913 respectively. The reader will find Butler's corrected views on Tabachetti's life and career in the Shrewsbury Edition of *Ex Voto*.

A.T.B.

Art in the Valley of Saas[1]

HAVING BEEN TOLD BY MR. FORTESCUE, of the British Museum, that there were some chapels at Saas-Fée which bore analogy to those at Varallo, described in my book *Ex Voto*, I went to Saas during this last summer, and venture now to lay my conclusions before the reader.

The chapels are fifteen in number, and lead up to a larger and singularly graceful one, rather more than half-way between Saas and Saas-Fée. This is commonly but wrongly called the chapel of St. Joseph, for it is dedicated to the Virgin, and its situation is of such extreme beauty—the great Fée glaciers showing through the open portico—that it is in itself worth a pilgrimage. It is surrounded by noble larches and overhung by rock; in front of the portico there is a small open space covered with grass, and a huge larch, the stem of which is girt by a rude stone seat. The portico itself contains seats for worshippers, and a pulpit from which the preacher's voice can reach the many who must stand outside. The walls of the inner chapel are hung with votive pictures, some of them very quaint and pleasing, and not overweighted by those qualities that are usually dubbed by the name of artistic merit. Innumerable wooden and waxen representations of arms, legs, eyes, ears, and babies tell of the cures that have been effected during two centuries of devotion, and can hardly fail to awaken a kindly sympathy with the long dead and forgotten folk who placed them where they are.

The main interest, however, despite the extreme loveliness of St. Mary's chapel, centres rather in the small and outwardly unimportant oratories (if they should be so called) that lead up to it. These begin immediately with the ascent from the level ground on which the village of Saas-im-Grund is placed, and contain scenes in the history of the Redemption, represented by rude but spirited wooden figures, each about two feet high, painted, gilt, and rendered as life-like in all respects as circumstances would permit. The figures

[1] From *The Universal Review*, November 1890.

have suffered a good deal from neglect, and are still not a little misplaced. With the assistance, however, of the Rev. E. J. Selwyn, English Chaplain at Saas-im-Grund, I have been able to replace many of them in their original positions, as indicated by the parts of the figures that are left rough-hewn and unpainted. They vary a good deal in interest, and can be easily sneered at by those who make a trade of sneering. Those, on the other hand, who remain unsophisticated by overmuch art-culture will find them full of character in spite of not a little rudeness of execution, and will be surprised at coming across such works in a place so remote from any art-centre as Saas must have been at the time these chapels were made. It will be my business therefore to throw what light I can upon the questions how they came to be made at all, and who was the artist who designed them.

The only documentary evidence consists in a chronicle of the valley of Saas written in the early years of this century by the Rev. Peter Jos. Ruppen, and published at Sion in 1851. This work makes frequent reference to a manuscript by the Rev. Peter Joseph Clemens Lommatter, *curé* of Saas-Fée from 1738 to 1751, which has unfortunately been lost, so that we have no means of knowing how closely it was adhered to. The Rev. Jos. Ant. Ruppen, the present excellent *curé* of Saas-im-Grund, assures me that there is no reference to the Saas-Fée oratories in the " Actes de l'Eglise " at Saas, which I understand go a long way back; but I have not seen these myself. Practically, then, we have no more documentary evidence than is to be found in the published chronicle above referred to.

We there find it stated that the large chapel, commonly, but as above explained, wrongly called St. Joseph's, was built in 1687, and enlarged by subscription in 1747. These dates appear on the building itself, and are no doubt accurate. The writer adds that there was no actual edifice on this site before the one now existing was built, but there was a miraculous picture of the Virgin placed in a mural niche, before which the pious herdsmen and devout inhabitants

Art in the Valley of Saas

of the valley worshipped under the vault of heaven.[1] A miraculous (or miracle-working) picture was always more or less rare and important; the present site, therefore, seems to have been long one of peculiar sanctity. Possibly the name Fée may point to still earlier pagan mysteries on the same site.

As regards the fifteen small chapels, the writer says they illustrate the fifteen mysteries of the Psalter, and were built in 1709, each householder of the Saas-Fée contributing one chapel. He adds that Heinrich Andenmatten, afterwards a brother of the Society of Jesus, was an especial benefactor or promoter of the undertaking. One of the chapels, the Ascension (No. 12 of the series), has the date 1709 painted on it; but there is no date on any other chapel, and there seems no reason why this should be taken as governing the whole series.

Over and above this, there exists in Saas a tradition, as I was told immediately on my arrival, by an English visitor, that the chapels were built in consequence of a flood, but I have vainly endeavoured to trace this story to an indigenous source.

The internal evidence of the wooden figures themselves—nothing analogous to which, it should be remembered, can be found in the chapel of 1687—points to a much earlier date. I have met with no school of sculpture belonging to the early part of the eighteenth century to which they can be plausibly

---

[1] M. Ruppen's words run: "1687 wurde die Kapelle zur hohen Stiege gebaut, 1747 durch Zusatz vergrössert und 1755 mit Orgeln ausgestattet. Anton Ruppen, ein geschickter Steinhauer und Maurermeister leitete den Kapellebau, und machte darin das kleinere Altärlein. Bei der hohen Stiege war früher kein Gebetshäuslein; nur ein wunderthätiges Bildlein der Mutter Gottes stand da in einer Mauer vor dem fromme Hirten und viel andächtiges Volk unter freiem Himmel beteten.

"1709 wurden die kleinen Kapellelein die 15 Geheimnisse des Psalters vorstellend auf dem Wege zur hohen Stiege gebaut. Jeder Haushalter des Viertels Fée übernahm den Bau eines dieser Geheimnisskapellen, und ein besonderer Gutthäter dieser frommen Unternehmung war Heinrich Andenmatten, nachher Bruder der Gesellschaft Jesu."

assigned; and the supposition that they are the work of some unknown local genius who was not led up to and left no successors may be dismissed, for the work is too scholarly to have come from anyone but a trained sculptor. I refer of course to those figures which the artist must be supposed to have executed with his own hand, as, for example, the central figure of the Crucifixion group and those of the Magdalene and St. John. The greater number of the figures were probably, as was suggested to me by Mr. Ranshaw, of Lowth, executed by a local wood-carver from models in clay and wax furnished by the artist himself. Those who examine the play of line in the hair, mantle, and sleeve of the Magdalene in the Crucifixion group, and contrast it with the greater part of the remaining draperies, will find little hesitation in concluding that this was the case, and will ere long readily distinguish the two hands from which the figures have mainly come. I say "mainly," because there is at least one other sculptor who may well have belonged to the year 1709, but who fortunately has left us little. Examples of his work may perhaps be seen in the nearest villain with a big hat in the Flagellation chapel, and in two cherubs in the Assumption of the Virgin.

We may say, then, with some certainty, that the designer was a cultivated and practised artist. We may also not less certainly conclude that he was of Flemish origin, for the horses in the Journey to Calvary and Crucifixion chapels, where alone there are any horses at all, are of Flemish breed, with no trace of the Arab blood adopted by Gaudenzio at Varallo. The character, moreover, of the villains is Northern —of the Quentin Matsys, Martin Schongauer type, rather than Italian; the same sub-Rubensesque feeling which is apparent in more than one chapel at Varallo is not less evident here—especially in the Journey to Calvary and Crucifixion chapels. There can hardly, therefore, be a doubt that the artist was a Fleming who had worked for several years in Italy.

It is also evident that he had Tabachetti's work at Varallo

well in his mind. For not only does he adopt certain details of costume (I refer particularly to the treatment of soldiers' tunics) which are peculiar to Tabachetti at Varallo, but whenever he treats a subject which Tabachetti had treated at Varallo, as in the Flagellation, Crowning with Thorns, and Journey to Calvary chapels, the work at Saas is evidently nothing but a somewhat modified abridgment of that at Varallo. When, however, as in the Annunciation, the Nativity, the Crucifixion, and other chapels, the work at Varallo is by another than Tabachetti, no allusion is made to it. The Saas artist has Tabachetti's Varallo work at his finger-ends, but betrays no acquaintance whatever with Gaudenzio Ferrari, Gio. Ant. Paracca, or Giovanni D'Enrico.

Even, moreover, when Tabachetti's work at Varallo is being most obviously drawn from, as in the Journey to Calvary chapel, the Saas version differs materially from that at Varallo, and is in some respects an improvement on it. The idea of showing other horsemen and followers coming up from behind, whose heads can be seen over the crown of the interposing hill, is singularly effective as suggesting a number of others that are unseen, nor can I conceive that anyone but the original designer would follow Tabachetti's Varallo design with as much closeness as it has been followed here, and yet make such a brilliantly successful modification. The stumbling, again, of one horse (a detail almost hidden, according to Tabachetti's wont) is a touch which Tabachetti himself might add, but which no Saas wood-carver who was merely adapting from a reminiscence of Tabachetti's Varallo chapel would be likely to introduce. These considerations have convinced me that the designer of the chapels at Saas is none other than Tabachetti himself who, as has been now conclusively shown, was a native of Dinant, in Belgium.

The Saas chronicler, indeed, avers that the chapels were not built till 1709 – a statement apparently corroborated by a date now visible on one chapel; but we must remember that the chronicler did not write until a century or so later than 1709, and though indeed, his statement may have been taken from the lost earlier manuscript of 1738, we know nothing about this either one way or the other. The writer may have gone by the still existing 1709 on the Ascension chapel, whereas this date may in fact have referred to a restoration, and not to an original construction. There is nothing, as I have said, in the choice of the chapel on which the date appears, to suggest that it was intended to govern the others. I have explained that the work is isolated and exotic. It is by one in whom Flemish and Italian influences are alike equally predominant; by one who was saturated with Tabachetti's Varallo work, and who can improve upon it, but over whom the other Varallo sculptors have no power. The style of the work is of the sixteenth and not of the eighteenth century—with a few obvious exceptions that suit the year 1709 exceedingly well. Against such considerations as these, a statement made at the beginning of this century referring to a century earlier and a promiscuous date upon one chapel, can carry but little weight. I shall assume, therefore, henceforward, that we have here groups designed in a plastic material by Tabachetti, and reproduced in wood by the best local wood-sculptor available, with the exception of a few figures cut by the artist himself.

We ask, then, at what period in his life did Tabachetti design these chapels, and what led to his coming to such an out-of-the-way place as Saas at all? We should remember that, according both to Fassola and Torrotti (writing in 1671 and 1686 respectively), Tabachetti[1] became insane about the year 1586 or early in 1587, after having just begun the Salutation chapel. I have explained in *Ex Voto* that I do not

[1] The story of Tabachetti's insanity and imprisonment is very doubtful, and it is difficult to make his supposed visit to Saas fit in with the authentic facts of his life. Cavaliere Negri, to whose pamphlet on Tabachetti I have already referred the reader, mentions neither. Tabachetti left his native Dinant in 1585, and from that date until his death he appears to have lived chiefly at Varallo and Crea. In 1588 he was working at Crea; in 1590 he was at Varallo and again in 1594, 1599, and 1602. He died in 1615, possibly during a visit to Varallo, though his home at the time was at Costigliole, near Asti. See also note on p. 159.—R.A.S.

Art in the Valley of Saas

believe this story. I have no doubt that Tabachetti was declared to be mad, but I believe this to have been due to an intrigue, set on foot in order to get a foreign artist out of the way, and to secure the Massacre of the Innocents chapel, at that precise time undertaken, for Gio. Ant. Paracca, who was an Italian.

Or he may have been sacrificed in order to facilitate the return of the workers in stucco whom he had superseded on the Sacro Monte. He may have been goaded into some imprudence which was seized upon as a pretext for shutting him up; at any rate, the fact that when in 1587 he inherited his father's property at Dinant, his trustee (he being expressly stated to be " expatrié ") was " datif," " dativus," appointed not by himself but by the court, lends colour to the statement that he was not his own master at the time; for in later kindred deeds, now at Namur, he appoints his own trustee. I suppose, then, that Tabachetti was shut up in a madhouse at Varallo for a considerable time, during which I can find no trace of him, but that eventually he escaped or was released.

Whether he was a fugitive, or whether he was let out from prison, he would in either case, in all reasonable probability, turn his face homeward. If he was escaping, he would make immediately for the Savoy frontier, within which Saas then lay. He would cross the Baranca above Fobello, coming down on to Ponte Grande in the Val Anzasca. He would go up the Val Anzasca to Macugnaga, and over the Monte Moro, which would bring him immediately to Saas. Saas, therefore, is the nearest and most natural place for him to make for, if he were flying from Varallo, and here I suppose him to have halted.

It so happened that on the 9th September 1589 there was one of the three great outbreaks of the Mattmark See that have from time to time devastated the valley of Saas.[1] It is

---

[1] This is thus chronicled by M. Ruppen: "1589 den 9 September war eine Wassergrösse, die viel Schaden verursachte. Die Thalstrasse, die von den Steinmatten an bis zur Kirche am Ufer der Visp lag, wurde ganz zerstört. Man ward gezwungen eine neue Strasse in einiger Ent-

probable that the chapels were decided upon in consequence of some grace shown by the miraculous picture of the Virgin, which had mitigated a disaster occurring so soon after the anniversary of her own Nativity. Tabachetti, arriving at this juncture, may have offered to undertake them if the Saas people would give him an asylum. Here, at any rate, I suppose him to have stayed till some time in 1590, probably the second half of it; his design of eventually returning home, if he ever entertained it, being then interrupted by a summons to Crea near Casale, where I believe him to have worked with a few brief interruptions thenceforward for little if at all short of half a century, or until about the year 1640. I admit, however, that the evidence for assigning him so long a life rests solely on the supposed identity of the figure known as " Il Vecchietto," in the Varallo Descent from the Cross chapel, with the portrait of Tabachetti himself in the Ecce Homo chapel, also at Varallo.

I find additional reason for thinking the chapels owe their origin to the inundation of 9th September 1589, in the fact that the 8th September is made a day of pilgrimage to the Saas-Fée chapels throughout the whole valley of Saas. It is true the 8th September is the festival of the Nativity of the Virgin Mary, so that under any circumstances this would be a great day, but the fact that not only the people of Saas, but the whole valley down to Visp, flock to this chapel on the 8th September, points to the belief that some special act of grace on the part of the Virgin was vouchsafed on this day in connection with this chapel. A belief that it was owing to the intervention of St. Mary of Fée that the inundation was not attended with loss of life would be very likely to lead to the foundation of a series of chapels leading up to the place where her miraculous picture was placed, and to the more special celebration of her Nativity in connection with this spot throughout the valley of Saas. I have discussed

fernung vom Wasser durch einen alten Fussweg auszuhauen welche vier und einerhalben Viertel der Klafter, oder 6 Schuh und 9 Zoll breit sollte " (p. 43).

Art in the Valley of Saas

the subject with the Rev. Jos. Ant. Ruppen, and he told me he thought the fact that the great *fête* of the year in connection with the Saas-Fée chapels was on the 8th September pointed rather strongly to the supposition that there was a connection between these and the recorded flood of 9th September 1589.

Turning to the individual chapels they are as follows:

1. The Annunciation. The treatment here presents no more analogy to that of the same subject at Varallo than is inevitable in the nature of the subject. The Annunciation figures at Varallo have proved to be mere draped dummies with wooden heads; Tabachetti, even though he did the heads, which he very likely did, would take no interest in the Varallo work with the same subject. The Annunciation, from its very simplicity as well as from the transcendental nature of the subject, is singularly hard to treat, and the work here, whatever it may once have been, is now no longer remarkable.

2. The Salutation of Mary by Elizabeth. This group, again, bears no analogy to the Salutation chapel at Varallo, in which Tabachetti's share was so small that it cannot be considered as in any way his. It is not to be expected, therefore, that the Saas chapel should follow the Varallo one. The figures, four in number, are pleasing and well arranged. St. Joseph, St. Elizabeth, and St. Zacharias are all talking at once. The Virgin is alone silent.

3. The Nativity is much damaged and hard to see. The treatment bears no analogy to that adopted by Gaudenzio Ferrari at Varallo. There is one pleasing young shepherd standing against the wall, but some figures have no doubt (as in others of the chapels) disappeared, and those that remain have been so shifted from their original positions that very little idea can be formed of what the group was like when Tabachetti left it.

4. The Purification. I can hardly say why this chapel should remind me, as it does, of the Circumcision chapel at Varallo, for there are more figures here than space at Varallo

will allow. It cannot be pretended that any single figure is of extraordinary merit, but amongst them they tell their story with excellent effect. Two, those of St. Joseph and St. Anna (?), that doubtless were once more important factors in the drama, are now so much in corners near the window that they can hardly be seen.

5. The Dispute in the Temple. This subject is not treated at Varallo. Here at Saas there are only six doctors now; whether or no there were originally more cannot be determined.

6. The Agony in the Garden. Tabachetti had no chapel with this subject at Varallo, and there is no resemblance between the Saas chapel and that by D'Enrico. The figures are no doubt approximately in their original positions, but I have no confidence that I have rearranged them correctly. They were in such confusion when I first saw them that the Rev. E. J. Selwyn and myself determined to rearrange them. They have doubtless been shifted more than once since Tabachetti left them. The sleeping figures are all good. St. James is perhaps a little prosaic. One Roman soldier who is coming into the garden with a lantern, and motioning silence with his hand, does duty for the others that are to follow him. I should think more than one of these figures is actually carved in wood by Tabachetti, allowance being made for the fact that he was working in a material with which he was not familiar, and which no sculptor of the highest rank has ever found congenial.

7. The Flagellation. Tabachetti has a chapel with this subject at Varallo, and the Saas group is obviously a descent with modification from his work there. The figure of Christ is so like the one at Varallo that I think it must have been carved by Tabachetti himself. The man with the hooked nose, who at Varallo is stooping to bind his rods, is here upright: it was probably the intention to emphasize him in the succeeding scenes as well as this, in the same way as he has been emphasized at Varallo, but his nose got pared down in the cutting of later scenes, and could not easily be

Art in the Valley of Saas

added to. The man binding Christ to the column at Varallo is repeated (*longo intervallo*) here, and the whole work is one inspired by that at Varallo, though no single figure except that of the Christ is adhered to with any very great closeness. I think the nearer malefactor, with a goitre, and wearing a large black hat, is either an addition of the year 1709, or was done by the journeyman of the local sculptor who carved the greater number of the figures. The man stooping down to bind his rods can hardly be by the same hand as either of the two black-hatted malefactors, but it is impossible to speak with certainty. The general effect of the chapel is excellent, if we consider the material in which it is executed, and the rudeness of the audience to whom it addresses itself.

8. The Crowning with Thorns. Here again the inspiration is derived from Tabachetti's Crowning with Thorns at Varallo. The Christs in the two chapels are strikingly alike, and the general effect is that of a residuary impression left in the mind of one who had known the Varallo Flagellation exceedingly well.

9. St. Veronica. This and the next succeeding chapels are the most important of the series. Tabachetti's Journey to Calvary at Varallo is again the source from which the present work was taken, but, as I have already said, it has been modified in reproduction. Mount Calvary is still shown, as at Varallo, towards the left-hand corner of the work, but at Saas it is more towards the middle than at Varallo, so that horsemen and soldiers may be seen coming up behind it—a stroke that deserves the name of genius none the less for the manifest imperfection with which it has been carried into execution. There are only three horses fully shown, and one partly shown. They are all of the heavy Flemish type adopted by Tabachetti at Varallo. The man kicking the fallen Christ and the goitred man (with the same teeth missing), who are so conspicuous in the Varallo Journey to Calvary, reappear here, only the kicking man has much less nose than at Varallo, probably because (as explained)

the nose got whittled away and could not be whittled back again. I observe that the kind of lapelled tunic which Tabachetti, and only Tabachetti, adopts at Varallo, is adopted for the centurion in this chapel, and indeed throughout the Saas chapels this particular form of tunic is the most usual for a Roman soldier. The work is still a very striking one, notwithstanding its translation into wood and the decay into which it has been allowed to fall; nor can it fail to impress the visitor who is familiar with this class of art as coming from a man of extraordinary dramatic power and command over the almost impossible art of composing many figures together effectively in all-round sculpture. Whether all the figures are even now as Tabachetti left them I cannot determine, but Mr. Selwyn has restored Simon the Cyrenian to the position in which he obviously ought to stand, and between us we have got the chapel into something more like order.

10. *The Crucifixion.* This subject was treated at Varallo not by Tabachetti but by Gaudenzio Ferrari. It confirms therefore my opinion as to the designer of the Saas chapels to find in them no trace of the Varallo Crucifixion, while the kind of tunic which at Varallo is only found in chapels wherein Tabachetti worked again appears here. The work is in a deplorable state of decay. Mr. Selwyn has greatly improved the arrangement of the figures, but even now they are not, I imagine, quite as Tabachetti left them. The figure of Christ is greatly better in technical execution than that of either of the two thieves; the folds of the drapery alone will show this even to an unpractised eye. I do not think there can be a doubt but that Tabachetti cut this figure himself, as also those of the Magdalene and St. John, who stand at the foot of the cross. The thieves are coarsely executed, with no very obvious distinction between the penitent and the impenitent one, except that there is a fiend painted on the ceiling over the impenitent thief. The one horse introduced into the composition is again of the heavy Flemish type adopted by Tabachetti at Varallo. There is

Art in the Valley of Saas

great difference in the care with which the folds on the several draperies have been cut, some being stiff and poor enough, while others are done very sufficiently. In spite of smallness of scale, ignoble material, disarrangement and decay, the work is still striking.

11. The Resurrection. There being no chapel at Varallo with any of the remaining subjects treated at Saas, the sculptor has struck out a line for himself. The Christ in the Resurrection chapel is a carefully modelled figure, and if better painted might not be ineffective. Three soldiers, one sleeping, alone remain. There were probably other figures that have been lost. The sleeping soldier is very pleasing.

12. The Ascension is not remarkably interesting; the Christ appears to be, but perhaps is not, a much more modern figure than the rest.

13. The Descent of the Holy Ghost. Some of the figures along the end wall are very good, and were, I should imagine, cut by Tabachetti himself. Those against the two side walls are not so well cut.

14. The Assumption of the Virgin Mary. The two large cherubs here are obviously by a later hand, and the small ones are not good. The figure of the Virgin herself is unexceptionable. There were doubtless once other figures of the Apostles which have disappeared; of these a single St. Peter (?), so hidden away in a corner near the window that it can only be seen with difficulty, is the sole survivor.

15. The Coronation of the Virgin is of later date, and has probably superseded an earlier work. It can hardly be by the designer of the other chapels of the series. Perhaps Tabachetti had to leave for Crea before all the chapels at Saas were finished.

Lastly, we have the larger chapel dedicated to St. Mary, which crowns the series. Here there is nothing of more than common artistic interest, unless we except the stone altar mentioned in Ruppen's chronicle. This is of course classical in style, and is, I should think, very good.

Once more I must caution the reader against expecting to

find highly finished gems of art in the chapels I have been describing. A wooden figure not more than two feet high clogged with many coats of paint can hardly claim to be taken very seriously, and even those few that were cut by Tabachetti himself were not meant to have attention concentrated on themselves alone. As mere wood-carving the Saas-Fée chapels will not stand comparison, for example, with the triptych of unknown authorship in the Church of St. Anne at Gliss, close to Brieg. But, in the first place, the work at Gliss is worthy of Holbein himself; I know no wood-carving that can so rivet the attention; moreover, it is coloured with water-colour and not oil, so that it is tinted, not painted; and, in the second place, the Gliss triptych belongs to a date (1519) when artists held neither time nor impressionism as objects, and hence, though greatly better than the Saas-Fée chapels as regards a certain Japanese curiousness of finish and *naïveté* of literal transcription, it cannot even enter the lists with the Saas work as regards *élan* and dramatic effectiveness. The difference between the two classes of work is much that between, say, John Van Eyck or Memling and Rubens or Rembrandt, or, again, between Giovanni Bellini and Tintoretto; the aims of the one class of work are incompatible with those of the other. Moreover, in the Gliss triptych the intention of the designer is carried out (whether by himself or no) with admirable skill; whereas at Saas the wisdom of the workman is rather of Ober-Ammergau than of the Egyptians, and the voice of the poet is not a little drowned in that of his mouthpiece. If, however, the reader will bear in mind these somewhat obvious considerations, and will also remember the pathetic circumstances under which the chapels were designed—for Tabachetti when he reached Saas was no doubt shattered in body and mind by his four years' imprisonment—he will probably be not less attracted to them than I observed were many of the visitors both at Saas-Grund and Saas-Fée with whom I had the pleasure of examining them.

I will now run briefly through the other principal works

Art in the Valley of Saas

in the neighbourhood to which I think the reader would be glad to have his attention directed.

At Saas-Fée itself the main altar-piece is without interest, as also one with a figure of St. Sebastian. The Virgin and Child above the remaining altar are, so far as I remember them, very good, and greatly superior to the smaller figures of the same altar-piece.

At Almagel, an hour's walk or so above Saas-Grund—a village, the name of which, like those of the Alphubel, the Monte Moro, and more than one other neighbouring site, is supposed to be of Saracenic origin—the main altar-piece represents a female saint with folded arms being beheaded by a vigorous man to the left. These two figures are very good. There are two somewhat inferior elders to the right, and the composition is crowned by the Assumption of the Virgin. I like the work, but have no idea who did it. Two bishops flanking the composition are not so good. There are two other altars in the church: the right-hand one has some pleasing figures, not so the left-hand.

In St. Joseph's chapel, on the mule-road between Saas-Grund and Saas-Fée, the St. Joseph and the two children are rather nice. In the churches and chapels which I looked into between Saas and Stalden, I saw many florid extravagant altar-pieces, but nothing that impressed me favourably.

In the parish church at Saas-Grund there are two altar-pieces which deserve attention. In the one over the main altar the arrangement of the Last Supper in a deep recess half-way up the composition is very pleasing and effective; in that above the right-hand altar of the two that stand in the body of the church there are a number of round lunettes, about eight inches in diameter, each containing a small but spirited group of wooden figures. I have lost my notes on these altar-pieces and can only remember that the main one has been restored, and now belongs to two different dates, the earlier date being, I should imagine, about 1670. A similar treatment of the Last Supper may be found near Brieg in the church of Naters, and no doubt the two altar-pieces are by the same man. There are, by the way, two very ambitious altars on either side the main arch leading to the chancel in the church at Naters, of which the one on the south side contains obvious reminiscences of Gaudenzio Ferrari's Sta. Maria frescoes at Varallo; but none of the four altar-pieces in the two transepts tempted me to give them much attention. As regards the smaller altar-piece at Saas-Grund, analogous work may be found at Cravagliana, half-way between Varallo and Fobello, but this last has suffered through the inveterate habit which Italians have of showing their hatred towards the enemies of Christ by mutilating the figures that represent them. Whether the Saas work is by a Valsesian artist who came over to Switzerland, or whether the Cravagliana work is by a Swiss who had come to Italy, I cannot say without further consideration and closer examination than I have been able to give. The altar-pieces of Mairengo, Chiggiogna, and, I am told, Lavertezzo, all in the Canton Ticino, are by a Swiss or German artist who has migrated southward; but the reverse migration was equally common.

Being in the neighbourhood, and wishing to assure myself whether the sculptor of the Saas-Fée chapels had or had not come lower down the valley, I examined every church and village which I could hear of as containing anything that might throw light on this point. I was thus led to Visperti-menen, a village some three hours above either Visp or Stalden. It stands very high, and is an almost untouched example of a medieval village. The altar-piece of the main church is even more floridly ambitious in its abundance of carving and gilding than the many other ambitious altar-pieces with which the Canton Valais abounds. The Apostles are receiving the Holy Ghost on the first storey of the composition, and they certainly are receiving it with an overjoyed alacrity and hilarious ecstasy of *allegria spirituale* which it would not be easy to surpass. Above the village, reaching almost to the limits beyond which there is no culti-vation, there stands a series of chapels like those I have been

Art in the Valley of Saas

describing at Saas-Fée, only much larger and more ambitious. They are twelve in number, including the church that crowns the series. The figures they contain are of wood (so I was assured, but I did not go inside the chapels): they are life-size, and in some chapels there are as many as a dozen figures. I should think they belonged to the later half of the eighteenth century, and here, one would say, sculpture touches the ground; at least, it is not easy to see how cheap exaggeration can sink an art more deeply. The only things that at all pleased me were a smiling donkey and an ecstatic cow in the Nativity chapel. Those who are not allured by the prospect of seeing perhaps the very worst that can be done in its own line, need not be at the pains of climbing up to Vispertimenen. Those, on the other hand, who may find this sufficient inducement will not be disappointed, and they will enjoy magnificent views of the Weisshorn and the mountains near the Dom.

I have already referred to the triptych at Gliss. This is figured in Wolf's work on Chamonix and the Canton Valais, but a larger and clearer reproduction of such an extraordinary work is greatly to be desired. The small wooden statues above the triptych, as also those above its modern companion in the south transept, are not less admirable than the triptych itself. I know of no other like work in wood, and have no clue whatever as to who the author can have been beyond the fact that the work is purely German and eminently Holbeinesque in character.

I was told of some chapels at Rarogne, five or six miles lower down the valley than Visp. I examined them, and found they had been stripped of their figures. The few that remained satisfied me that we have had no loss. Above Brieg there are two other like series of chapels. I examined the higher and more promising of the two, but found not one single figure left. I was told by my driver that the other series, close to the Pont Napoléon on the Simplon road, had been also stripped of its figures, and, there being a heavy storm at the time, have taken his word for it that this was so.

NOTE

THIS Lecture was given at the Working Men's College, Great Ormond Street, 30th January 1892. It was published in *The Eagle*, vol. xvii, no. 97, and "reprinted, with preface and additional matter," as a pamphlet soon afterwards. The preface is dated 22nd March 1892; and the additional matter consists of two communications to *The Athenaeum*:

1. The Localization of Scheria, 30th January 1892.
2. The Topography of the Odyssey, 20th February 1892.

The Lecture was reprinted by R. A. Streatfeild in *The Humour of Homer, and other Essays* (1913); but he omitted both preface and additional matter as having been incorporated into *The Authoress of the Odyssey* (published 1897), and both are again omitted in the Shrewsbury Edition, as well as Butler's other Odyssean pamphlets and communications, of which the more important are mentioned on p. xxxv of the Shrewsbury Edition of *The Authoress*. An exception has, however, been made in favour of the previously unprinted Lecture which follows in the present volume (pp. 273-306).

A few corrections which Butler made in his own copies of the pamphlet (now in the Library of St. John's College, Cambridge) are incorporated.

A.T.B.

The Humour of Homer

THE FIRST OF THE TWO GREAT POEMS COMmonly ascribed to Homer is called the Iliad—a title which we may be sure was not given it by the author.

It professes to treat of a quarrel between Agamemnon and Achilles that broke out while the Greeks were besieging the city of Troy, and it does, indeed, deal largely with the consequences of this quarrel; whether, however, the ostensible subject did not conceal another that was nearer the poet's heart[1]—I mean the last days, death, and burial of Hector—is a point that I cannot determine. Nor yet can I determine how much of the Iliad as we now have it is by Homer, and how much by a later writer or writers. This is a very vexed question, but I myself believe the Iliad to be entirely by a single poet.

The second poem commonly ascribed to the same author is called the Odyssey. It deals with the adventures of Ulysses during his ten years of wandering after Troy had fallen. These two works have of late years been believed to be by different authors. The Iliad is now generally held to be the older work by some one or two hundred years.

The leading ideas of the Iliad are love, war, and plunder, though this last is less insisted on than the other two. The key-note is struck with a woman's charms, and a quarrel among men for their possession. It is a woman who is at the bottom of the Trojan war itself. Woman throughout the Iliad is a being to be loved, teased, laughed at, and if necessary carried off. We are told in one place of a fine bronze cauldron for heating water which was worth twenty oxen, whereas a few lines lower down a good serviceable maid-of-all-work is valued at four oxen. I think there is a spice of malicious humour in this valuation, and am confirmed in this opinion by noting that though woman in the Iliad is on one occasion depicted as a wife so faithful and affectionate that nothing more perfect can be found either in real life or fiction, yet as a general rule she is drawn as teasing, scolding, thwarting, contradicting, and hoodwinking the sex that has

---

[1] I do not now think so.—S.B.

the effrontery to deem itself her lord and master. Whether or no this view may have arisen from any domestic difficulties between Homer and his wife is a point which again I find it impossible to determine.

We cannot refrain from contemplating such possibilities. If we are to be at home with Homer there must be no sitting on the edge of one's chair dazzled by the splendour of his reputation. He was after all only a literary man, and those who occupy themselves with letters must approach him as a very honoured member of their own fraternity, but still as one who must have felt, thought, and acted much as themselves. He struck oil, while we for the most part succeed in boring only; still we are his literary brethren, and if we would read his lines intelligently we must also read between them. That one so shrewd, and yet a dreamer of such dreams as have been vouchsafed to few indeed besides himself—that one so genially sceptical, and so given to looking into the heart of a matter, should have been in such perfect harmony with his surroundings as to think himself in the best of all possible worlds—this is not believable. The world is always more or less out of joint to the poet—generally more so; and unfortunately he always thinks it more or less his business to set it right—generally more so. We are all of us more or less poets—generally, indeed, less so; still we feel and think, and to think at all is to be out of harmony with much that we think about. We may be sure, then, that Homer had his full share of troubles, and also that traces of these abound up and down his work if we could only identify them, for anything that everyone does is in some measure a portrait of himself; but here comes the difficulty—not to read between the lines, not to try and detect the hidden features of the writer—this is to be a dull, unsympathetic, incurious reader; and on the other hand to try and read between them is to be in danger of running after every will o' the wisp that conceit may raise for our delusion.

I believe it will help you better to understand the broad humour of the Iliad, which we shall presently reach, if you

The Humour of Homer

will allow me to say a little more about the general characteristics of the poem. Over and above the love and war that are his main themes, there is another which the author never loses sight of—I mean distrust and dislike of the ideas of his time as regards the gods and omens. No poet ever made gods in his own image more defiantly than the author of the Iliad. In the likeness of man created he them, and the only excuse for him is that he obviously desired his readers not to take them seriously. This at least is the impression he leaves upon his reader, and when so great a man as Homer leaves an impression it must be presumed that he does so intentionally. It may be almost said that he has made the gods take the worse, not the better, side of man's nature upon them, and to be in all respects as we ourselves—yet without virtue. It should be noted, however, that the gods on the Trojan side are treated far more leniently than those who help the Greeks.

The chief gods on the Grecian side are Juno, Minerva, and Neptune. Juno, as you will shortly see, is a scolding wife, who in spite of all Jove's bluster wears the breeches, or tries exceedingly hard to do so. Minerva is an angry termagant—mean, mischief-making, and vindictive. She begins by pulling Achilles' hair, and later on she knocks the helmet from off the head of Mars. She hates Venus, and tells the Grecian hero Diomede that he had better not wound any of the other gods, but that he is to hit Venus if he can, which he presently does " because he sees that she is feeble and not like Minerva or Bellona." Neptune is a bitter hater.

Apollo, Mars, Venus, Diana, and Jove, so far as his wife will let him, are on the Trojan side. These, as I have said, meet with better, though still somewhat contemptuous, treatment at the poet's hand. Jove, however, is being mocked and laughed at from first to last, and if one moral can be drawn from the Iliad more clearly than another, it is that he is only to be trusted to a very limited extent. Homer's position, in fact, as regards divine interference is the very opposite of David's. David writes, " Put not your trust in princes nor in any child of man; there is no sure help but from the Lord." With Homer it is, " Put not your trust in Jove neither in any omen from heaven; there is but one good omen—to fight for one's country. Fortune favours the brave; heaven helps those who help themselves."

The god who comes off best is Vulcan, the lame, hobbling, old blacksmith, who is the laughing-stock of all the others, and whose exquisitely graceful skilful workmanship forms such an effective contrast to the uncouth exterior of the workman. Him, as a man of genius and an artist, and furthermore as a somewhat despised artist, Homer treats, if with playfulness, still with respect, in spite of the fact that circumstances have thrown him more on the side of the Greeks than of the Trojans, with whom I understand Homer's sympathies mainly to lie.

The poet either dislikes music or is at best insensible to it. Great poets very commonly are so. Achilles, indeed, does on one occasion sing to his own accompaniment on the lyre, but we are not told that it was any pleasure to hear him, and Patroclus, who was in the tent at the time, was not enjoying it; he was only waiting for Achilles to leave off. But though not fond of music, Homer has a very keen sense of the beauties of nature, and is constantly referring both in and out of season to all manner of homely incidents that are as familiar to us as to himself. Sparks in the train of a shooting-star; a cloud of dust upon a high road; foresters going out to cut wood in a forest; the shrill cry of the cicale; children making walls of sand on the sea-shore, or teasing wasps when they have found a wasps' nest; a poor but very honest woman who gains a pittance for her children by selling wool, and weighs it very carefully; a child clinging to its mother's dress and crying to be taken up and carried—none of these things escape him. Neither in the Iliad nor the Odyssey do we ever receive so much as a hint as to the time of year at which any of the events described are happening; but on one occasion the author of the Iliad really has told us that it was a very fine day, and this not from a business

The Humour of Homer

point of view, but out of pure regard to the weather for its own sake.

With one more observation I will conclude my preliminary remarks about the Iliad. I cannot find its author within the four corners of the work itself. I believe the writer of the Odyssey to appear in the poem as a prominent and very fascinating character whom we shall presently meet, but there is no one in the Iliad on whom I can put my finger with even a passing idea that he may be the author. Still, if under some severe penalty I were compelled to find him, I should say it was just possible that he might consider his own lot to have been more or less like that which he forecasts for Astyanax, the infant son of Hector. At any rate his intimate acquaintance with the topography of Troy, which is now well ascertained, and still more his obvious attempt to excuse the non-existence of a great wall which, according to his story, ought to be there and which he knew had never existed, so that no trace could remain, while there were abundant traces of all the other features he describes — these facts convince me that he was in all probability a native of the Troad, or country round Troy. His plausibly concealed Trojan sympathies, and more particularly the aggravated exaggeration with which the flight of Hector is described, suggest to me, coming as they do from an astute and humorous writer, that he may have been a Trojan, at any rate by the mother's side, made captive, enslaved, compelled to sing the glories of his captors, and determined so to overdo them that if his masters cannot see through the irony others sooner or later shall. This, however, is highly speculative, and there are other views that are perhaps more true, but which I cannot now consider.

I will now ask you to form your own opinions as to whether Homer is or is not a shrewd and humorous writer.

Achilles, whose quarrel with Agamemnon is the ostensible subject of the poem, is son to a marine goddess named Thetis, who had rendered Jove an important service at a time when he was in great difficulties. Achilles, therefore, begs his mother Thetis to go up to Jove and ask him to let the Trojans discomfit the Greeks for a time, so that Agamemnon may find he cannot get on without Achilles' help, and may thus be brought to reason.

Thetis tells her son that for the moment there is nothing to be done, inasmuch as the gods are all of them away from home. They are gone to pay a visit to Oceanus in Central Africa, and will not be back for another ten or twelve days; she will see what can be done, however, as soon as ever they return. This in due course she does, going up to Olympus and laying hold of Jove by the knee and by the chin. I may say in passing that it is still a common Italian form of salutation to catch people by the chin. Twice during the last summer I have been so seized in token of affectionate greeting, once by a lady and once by a gentleman.

Thetis tells her tale to Jove, and concludes by saying that he is to say straight out " yes " or " no " whether he will do what she asks. Of course he can please himself, but she should like to know how she stands.

" It will be a plaguy business," answers Jove, " for me to offend Juno and put up with all the bitter tongue she will give me. As it is, she is always nagging at me and saying I help the Trojans. Still, go away now at once before she finds out that you have been here, and leave the rest to me. See, I nod my head to you, and this is the most solemn form of covenant into which I can enter. I never go back upon it, nor shilly-shally with anybody when I have once nodded my head." Which, by the way, amounts to an admission that he does shilly-shally sometimes.

Then he frowns and nods, shaking the hair on his immortal head till Olympus rocks again. Thetis goes off under the sea and Jove returns to his own palace. All the other gods stand up when they see him coming, for they do not dare to remain sitting while he passes, but Juno knows he has been hatching mischief against the Greeks with Thetis, so she attacks him in the following words:

" You traitorous scoundrel," she exclaims, " which of the

The Humour of Homer

gods have you been taking into your counsel now? You are always trying to settle matters behind my back, and never tell me, if you can help it, a single word about your designs."

"'Juno,' replied the father of gods and men, 'you must not expect to be told everything that I am thinking about: you are my wife, it is true, but you might not be able always to understand my meaning; in so far as it is proper for you to know of my intentions you are the first person to whom I communicate them either among the gods or among mankind, but there are certain points which I reserve entirely for myself, and the less you try to pry into these, or meddle with them, the better for you.'

"'Dread son of Saturn,' answered Juno, 'what in the world are you talking about? *I* meddle and pry? No one, I am sure, can have his own way in everything more absolutely than you have. Still I have a strong misgiving that the old merman's daughter Thetis has been talking you over. I saw her hugging your knees this very self-same morning, and I suspect you have been promising her to kill any number of people down at the Grecian ships, in order to gratify Achilles.'

"'Wife,' replied Jove, 'I can do nothing but you suspect me. You will not do yourself any good, for the more you go on like that the more I dislike you, and it may fare badly with you. If I mean to have it so, I mean to have it so; you had better therefore sit still and hold your tongue as I tell you, for if I once begin to lay my hands about you, there is not a god in heaven who will be of the smallest use to you.'

"When Juno heard this she thought it better to submit, so she sat down without a word, but all the gods throughout Jove's mansion were very much perturbed. Presently the cunning workman Vulcan tried to pacify his mother Juno, and said, 'It will never do for you two to go on quarrelling and setting heaven in an uproar about a pack of mortals. The thing will not bear talking about. If such counsels are to prevail a god will not be able to get his dinner in peace. Let me then advise my mother (and I am sure it is her own opinion) to make her peace with my dear father, lest he should scold her still further, and spoil our banquet; for if he does wish to turn us all out there can be no question about his being perfectly able to do so. Say something civil to him, therefore, and then perhaps he will not hurt us.'

"As he spoke he took a large cup of nectar and put it into his mother's hands, saying, 'Bear it, my dear mother, and make the best of it. I love you dearly and should be very sorry to see you get a thrashing. I should not be able to help you, for my father Jove is not a safe person to differ from. You know once before when I was trying to help you he caught me by the foot and chucked me from the heavenly threshold. I was all day long falling from morn to eve, but at sunset I came to ground on the island of Lemnos, and there was very little life left in me, till the Sintians came and tended me.'

"On this Juno smiled, and with a laugh took the cup from her son's hand. Then Vulcan went about among all other gods drawing nectar for them from his goblet, and they laughed immoderately as they saw him bustling about the heavenly mansion."

Then presently the gods go home to bed, each one in his own house that Vulcan had cunningly built for him or her. Finally Jove himself went to the bed which he generally occupied; and Jove his wife went with him.

There is another quarrel between Jove and Juno at the beginning of the fourth book.

The gods are sitting on the golden floor of Jove's palace and drinking one another's health in the nectar with which Hebe from time to time supplies them. Jove begins to tease Juno, and to provoke her with some sarcastic remarks that are pointed at her though not addressed to her directly.

"'Menelaus,' he exclaimed, 'has two good friends among the goddesses, Juno and Minerva, but they only sit still and look on, while Venus on the other hand takes much better care of Paris, and defends him when he is in danger. She has only just this moment been rescuing him when he made sure he was at death's door, for the victory really did lie with Menelaus. We must think what we are to do about all this. Shall we renew strife between the combatants or shall we make them friends again? I think the best plan would be for the city of Priam to remain unpillaged, but for Menelaus to have his wife Helen sent back to him.'

"Minerva and Juno groaned in spirit when they heard this. They were sitting side by side, and thinking what mischief they could do to the Trojans. Minerva for her part said not one word, but sat scowling at her father, for she was in a furious passion with him, but Juno could not contain herself, so she said:

"'What, pray, son of Saturn, is all this about? Is my trouble then to go for nothing, and all the pains that I have taken, to say nothing of my horses, and the way we have sweated and toiled to get the people together against Priam and his children? You can do as you please, but you must not expect all of us to agree with you.'

"And Jove answered, 'Wife, what harm have Priam and Priam's children done you that you rage so furiously against them, and want to sack their city? Will nothing do for you but you must eat Priam with his sons and all the Trojans into the bargain? Have it your own way then, for I will not quarrel with you—only remember what I tell you: if at any time I want to sack a city that belongs to any friend of yours, it will be no use your trying to hinder me, you will have to let me do it, for I only yield to you now with the greatest reluctance. If there was one city under the sun which I respected more than another it was Troy with its king and people. My altars there have never been without the savour of fat or of burnt sacrifice and all my dues were paid.'

"'My own favourite cities,' answered Juno, 'are Argos, Sparta, and Mycenae. Sack them whenever you may be displeased with them. I shall not make the smallest protest against your doing so. It would be no use if I did, for you are much stronger than I am, only I will not submit to seeing my own work wasted. I am a goddess of the same race as yourself. I am Saturn's eldest daughter and am not only nearly related to you in blood, but I am wife to yourself, and you are king over the gods. Let it be a case, then, of give and take between us, and the other gods will follow our lead. Tell Minerva, therefore, to go down at once and set the Greeks and Trojans by the ears again, and let her so manage it that the Trojans shall break their oaths and be the aggressors.'"

This is the very thing to suit Minerva, so she goes at once and persuades the Trojans to break their oath.

In a later book we are told that Jove has positively forbidden the gods to interfere further in the struggle. Juno therefore determines to hoodwink him. First she bolted herself inside her own room on the top of Mount Ida and had a thorough good wash. Then she scented herself, brushed her golden hair, put on her very best dress and all her jewels. When she had done this, she went to Venus and besought her for the loan of her charms.

"'You must not be angry with me, Venus,' she began, 'for being on the Grecian side while you are yourself on the Trojan; but you know every one falls in love with you at once, and I want you to lend me some of your attractions. I have to pay a visit at the world's end to Oceanus and Mother Tethys. They took me in and were very good to me when Jove turned Saturn out of heaven and shut him up under the sea. They have been quarrelling this long time past and will not speak to one another. So I must go and see them, for if I can only make them friends again I am sure that they will be grateful to me for ever afterwards.'"

Venus thought this reasonable, so she took off her girdle and lent it to Juno, an act by the way which argues more good nature than prudence on her part. Then Juno goes down to Thrace, and in search of Sleep the brother of Death. She finds him and shakes hands with him. Then she tells him she is going up to Olympus to make love to Jove, and that while she is occupying his attention Sleep is to send him off into a deep slumber.

The Humour of Homer

Sleep says he dares not do it. He would lull any of the other gods, but Juno must remember that she had got him into a great scrape once before in this way, and Jove hurled the gods about all over the palace, and would have made an end of him once for all, if he had not fled under the protection of Night, whom Jove did not venture to offend.

Juno bribes him, however, with a promise that if he will consent she will marry him to the youngest of the Graces, Pasithea. On this he yields; the pair then go up to the top of Mount Ida, and Sleep gets into a high pine tree just in front of Jove.

As soon as Jove sees Juno, armed as she for the moment is with all the attractions of Venus, he falls desperately in love with her, and says she is the only goddess he ever really loved. True, there had been the wife of Ixion and Danae, and Europa and Semele, and Alcmena, and Latona, not to mention herself in days gone by, but he never loved any of these as he now loves her, in spite of his having been married to her for so many years. What then does she want?

Juno tells him the same rigmarole about Oceanus and Mother Tethys that she had told Venus, and when she has done Jove tries to embrace her.

"What," exclaims Juno, "kiss me in such a public place as the top of Mount Ida! Impossible! I could never show my face in Olympus again, but I have a private room of my own and—" "What nonsense, my love!" exclaims the sire of gods and men as he catches her in his arms. On this Sleep sends him into a deep slumber, and Juno then sends Sleep to bid Neptune go off to help the Greeks at once.

When Jove awakes and finds the trick that has been played upon him, he is very angry and blusters a good deal as usual, but somehow or another it turns out that he has got to stand it and make the best of it.

In an earlier book he has said that he is not surprised at anything Juno may do, for she always has crossed him and always will; but he cannot put up with such disobedience from his own daughter Minerva. Somehow or another, however, here too as usual it turns out that he has got to stand it. "And then," Minerva exclaims in yet another place (VIII, 373), "I suppose he will be calling me his grey-eyed darling again, presently."

Towards the end of the poem the gods have a set-to among themselves. Minerva sends Mars sprawling, Venus comes to his assistance, but Minerva knocks her down and leaves her. Neptune challenges Apollo, but Apollo says it is not proper for a god to fight his own uncle, and declines the contest. His sister Diana taunts him with cowardice, so Juno grips her by the wrist and boxes her ears till she writhes again. Latona, the mother of Apollo and Diana, then challenges Mercury, but Mercury says that he is not going to fight with any of Jove's wives, so if she chooses to say she has beaten him she is welcome to do so. Then Latona picks up poor Diana's bow and arrows that have fallen from her during her encounter with Juno, and Diana meanwhile flies up to the knees of her father Jove, sobbing and sighing till her ambrosial robe trembles all around her.

"Jove drew her towards him, and smiling pleasantly exclaimed, 'My dear child, which of the heavenly beings has been wicked enough to behave in this way to you, as though you had been doing something naughty?'

"'Your wife, Juno,' answered Diana, 'has been ill-treating me; all our quarrels always begin with her.'"

The above extracts must suffice as examples of the kind of divine comedy in which Homer brings the gods and goddesses upon the scene. Among mortals the humour, what there is of it, is confined mainly to the grim taunts which the heroes fling at one another when they are fighting, and more especially to crowing over a fallen foe. The most subtle passage is the one in which Briseis, the captive woman about whom Achilles and Agamemnon have quarrelled, is restored by Agamemnon to Achilles. Briseis on her return to the tent of Achilles finds that while she has been with Agamemnon, Patroclus has been killed by Hector, and his dead body is

The Humour of Homer

now lying in state. She flings herself upon the corpse and exclaims:

"How one misfortune does keep falling upon me after another! I saw the man to whom my father and mother had married me killed before my eyes, and my three own dear brothers perished along with him; but you, Patroclus, even when Achilles was sacking our city and killing my husband, told me that I was not to cry; for you said that Achilles himself should marry me, and take me back with him to Phthia, where we should have a wedding feast among the Myrmidons. You were always kind to me, and I shall never cease to grieve for you."

This may of course be seriously intended, but Homer was an acute writer, and if we had met with such a passage in Thackeray we should have taken him to mean that so long as a woman can get a new husband, she does not much care about losing the old one—a sentiment which I hope no one will imagine that I for one moment endorse or approve of, and which I can only explain as a piece of sarcasm aimed possibly at Mrs. Homer.

And now let us turn to the Odyssey, a work which I myself think of as the Iliad's better half or wife. Here we have a poem of more varied interest, instinct with not less genius, and on the whole I should say, if less robust, nevertheless of still greater fascination—one, moreover, the irony of which is pointed neither at gods nor woman, but with one single and perhaps intercalated exception, at man. Gods and women may sometimes do wrong things, but, except as regards the intrigue between Mars and Venus just referred to, they are never laughed at. The scepticism of the Iliad is that of Hume or Gibbon; that of the Odyssey (if any) is like the occasional mild irreverence of the Vicar's daughter. When Jove says he will do a thing, there is no uncertainty about his doing it. Juno hardly appears at all, and when she does she never quarrels with her husband. Minerva has more to do than any of the other gods or goddesses, but she has nothing in common with the Minerva whom we have already seen in the Iliad. In the Odyssey she is the fairy godmother who seems to have no object in life but to protect Ulysses and Telemachus, and keep them straight at any touch and turn of difficulty. If she has any other function, it is to be patroness of the arts and of all intellectual development. The Minerva of the Odyssey may indeed sit on a rafter like a swallow and hold up her aegis to strike panic into the suitors while Ulysses kills them; but she is a perfect lady, and would no more knock Mars and Venus down one after the other than she would stand on her head. She is, in fact, a distinct person in all respects from the Minerva of the Iliad. Of the remaining gods Neptune, as the persecutor of the hero, comes worst off; but even he is treated as though he were a very important person.

In the Odyssey the gods no longer live in houses and sleep in four-post bedsteads, but the conception of their abode, like that of their existence altogether, is far more spiritual. Nobody knows exactly where they live, but they say it is in Olympus, where there is neither rain nor hail nor snow, and the wind never beats roughly; but it abides in everlasting sunshine, and in great peacefulness of light wherein the blessed gods are illumined for ever and ever. It is hardly possible to conceive anything more different from the Olympus of the Iliad.

Another very material point of difference between the Iliad and the Odyssey lies in the fact that the Homer of the Iliad always knows what he is talking about, while the supposed Homer of the Odyssey often makes mistakes that betray an almost incredible ignorance of detail. Thus the giant Polyphemus drives in his ewes home from their pasture, and milks them. The lambs of course have not been running with them; they have been left in the yards, so they have had nothing to eat. When he has milked the ewes, the giant lets each one of them have her lamb—to get, I suppose, what strippings it can, and beyond this what milk the ewe may yield during the night. In the morning, however, Polyphemus milks the ewes again. Hence it is plain either that he expected his lambs to thrive on one pull *per diem* at a milked ewe, and to be kind enough not to suck their mothers, though left with them all night through, or else that the writer of the Odyssey had very hazy notions about the relations between lambs and ewes, and of the ordinary methods of procedure on an upland dairy-farm.

In nautical matters the same inexperience is betrayed. The writer knows all about the corn and wine that must be put on board; the store-room in which these are kept and the getting of them are described inimitably, but there the knowledge ends; the other things put on board are "the things that are generally taken on board ships." So on a voyage we are told that the sailors do whatever is wanted doing, but we have no details. There is a shipwreck, which does duty more than once without the alteration of a word. I have seen such a shipwreck at Drury Lane. Anyone, moreover, who reads any authentic account of actual adventures will perceive at once that those of the Odyssey are the creation of one who has had no history. Ulysses has to make a raft; he makes it about as broad as they generally make a good big ship, but we do not seem to have been at the pains to measure a good big ship.

I will add no more however on this head. The leading characteristics of the Iliad, as we saw, were love, war, and plunder. The leading idea of the Odyssey is the infatuation of man, and the keynote is struck in the opening paragraph, where we are told how the sailors of Ulysses must needs, in spite of every warning, kill and eat the cattle of the sun-god, and perished accordingly.

A few lines lower down the same note is struck with even greater emphasis. The gods have met in council, and Jove happens at the moment to be thinking of Aegisthus, who had met his death at the hand of Agamemnon's son Orestes, in spite of the solemn warning that Jove had sent him through the mouth of Mercury. It does not seem necessary for Jove to turn his attention to Clytemnestra, the partner of Aegisthus's guilt. Of this lady we are presently told that she was naturally of an excellent disposition, and would never have gone wrong but for the loss of the protector in whose charge Agamemnon had left her. When she was left alone without an adviser—well, if a base designing man took to flattering and misleading her—what else could be expected? The infatuation of man, with its corollary, the superior excellence of woman, is the leading theme; next to this come art, religion, and, I am almost ashamed to add, money. There is no love-business in the Odyssey except the return of a bald elderly married man to his elderly wife and grown-up son after an absence of twenty years, and furious at having been robbed of so much money in the meantime. But this can hardly be called love-business; it is at the utmost domesticity. There is a charming young princess, Nausicaa, but though she affects a passing tenderness for the elderly hero of her creation as soon as Minerva has curled his bald old hair for him and titivated him up all over, she makes it abundantly plain that she will not look at a single one of her actual flesh and blood admirers. There is a leading young gentleman, Telemachus, who is nothing if he is not πεπνυμένος, or canny, well-principled, and discreet; he has an amiable and most sensible young male friend who says that he does not like crying at meal times—he will cry in the forenoon on an empty stomach as much as anyone pleases, but he cannot attend properly to his dinner and cry at the same time. Well, there is no lady provided either for this nice young man or for Telemachus. They are left high and dry as bachelors. Two goddesses indeed, Circe and Calypso, do one after the other take possession of Ulysses, but the way in which he accepts a situation which after all was none of his seeking, and which it is plain he does not care two straws about, is, I believe, dictated solely by a desire to exhibit the easy infidelity of Ulysses himself in contrast with the unswerving constancy and fidelity of his wife Penelope. Throughout the Odyssey the men do not really care for women, nor the women for men; they have to pretend to do so now and

The Humour of Homer

again, but it is a got-up thing, and the general attitude of the sexes towards one another is very much that of Helen, who says that her husband Menelaus is really not deficient in person or understanding: or again of Penelope herself, who, on being asked by Ulysses on his return what she thought of him, said that she did not think very much of him nor very little of him; in fact, she did not think much about him one way or the other. True, later on she relents and becomes more effusive; in fact, when she and Ulysses sat up talking in bed and Ulysses told her the story of his adventures, she never went to sleep once. Ulysses never had to nudge her with his elbow and say, "Come, wake up, Penelope, you are not listening"; but, in spite of the devotion exhibited here, the love-business in the Odyssey is artificial and described by one who had never felt it, whereas in the Iliad it is spontaneous and obviously genuine, as by one who knows all about it perfectly well. The love-business in fact of the Odyssey is turned on as we turn on the gas—when we cannot get on without it, but not otherwise.

A fascinating brilliant girl, who naturally adopts for her patroness the blue-stocking Minerva; a man-hatress, as clever girls so often are, and determined to pay the author of the Iliad out for his treatment of her sex by insisting on its superior moral, not to say intellectual, capacity, and on the self-sufficient imbecility of man unless he has a woman always at his elbow to keep him tolerably straight and in his proper place—this, and not the musty fusty old bust we see in libraries, is the kind of person who I believe wrote the Odyssey. Of course in reality the work must be written by a man, because they say so at Oxford and Cambridge, and they know everything down in Oxford and Cambridge; but I venture to say that if the Odyssey were to appear anonymously for the first time now, and to be sent round to the papers for review, there is not even a professional critic who would not see that it is a woman's writing and not a man's. But letting this pass, I can hardly doubt, for reasons which I gave in *The Athenaeum*, and for others that I cannot now insist upon, that the poem was written by a native of Trapani on the coast of Sicily, near Marsala. Fancy what the position of a young, ardent, brilliant woman must have been in a small Sicilian sea-port, say some eight or nine hundred years before the birth of Christ. It makes one shudder to think of it. Night after night she hears the dreary blind old bard Demodocus drawl out his interminable recitals taken from our present Iliad, or from some other of the many poems now lost that dealt with the adventures of the Greeks before Troy or on their homeward journey. Man and his doings! always the same old story, and woman always to be treated either as a toy or as a beast of burden, or at any rate as an incubus. Why not sing of woman also as she is when she is unattached and free from the trammels and persecutions of this tiresome tyrant, this insufferably self-conceited bore and booby, man?

"I wish, my dear," exclaims her mother Arete, after one of these little outbreaks, "that you would do it yourself. I am sure you could do it beautifully if you would only give your mind to it."

"Very well, mother," she replies, "and I will bring in all about you and father, and how I go out for a washing-day with the maids,"—and she kept her word, as I will presently show you.

I should tell you that Ulysses, having got away from the goddess Calypso, with whom he had been living for some seven or eight years on a lonely and very distant island in mid-ocean, is shipwrecked on the coast of Phaeacia, the chief town of which is Scheria. After swimming some forty-eight hours in the water he effects a landing at the mouth of a stream, and, not having a rag of clothes on his back, covers himself up under a heap of dried leaves and goes to sleep. I will now translate from the Odyssey itself.

" So here Ulysses slept, worn out with labour and sorrow; but Minerva went off to the chief town of the Phaeacians, a people who used to live in Hypereia near the wicked Cyclopes.

The Humour of Homer

Now the Cyclopes were stronger than they and plundered them, so Nausithous settled them in Scheria far from those who would loot them. He ran a wall round about the city, built houses and temples, and allotted the lands among his people; but he was gathered to his fathers, and the good king Alcinous was now reigning. To his palace then Minerva hastened that she might help Ulysses to get home.

"She went straight to the painted bedroom of Nausicaa, who was daughter to King Alcinous, and lovely as a goddess. Near her there slept two maids-in-waiting, both very pretty, one on either side of the doorway, which was closed with a beautifully made door. She took the form of the famous Captain Dumas's daughter, who was a bosom friend of Nausicaa and just her own age; then coming into the room like a breath of wind she stood near the head of the bed and said:

"'Nausicaa, what could your mother have been about to have such a lazy daughter? Here are your clothes all lying in disorder, yet you are going to be married almost directly, and should not only be well-dressed yourself, but should see that those about you look clean and tidy also. This is the way to make people speak well of you, and it will please your father and mother, so suppose we make to-morrow a washing day, and begin the first thing in the morning. I will come and help you, for all the best young men among your own people are courting you, and you are not going to remain a maid much longer. Ask your father, then, to have a horse and cart ready for us at daybreak to take the linen and baskets, and you can ride too, which will be much pleasanter for you than walking, for the washing ground is a long way out of the town.'

"When she had thus spoken Minerva went back to Olympus. By and by morning came, and as soon as Nausicaa woke she began thinking about her dream. She went to the other end of the house to tell her father and mother all about it, and found them in their own room. Her mother was sitting by the fireside spinning with her maids-in-waiting all around her, and she happened to catch her father just as he was going out to attend a meeting of the Town Council which the Phaeacian aldermen had convened. So she stopped him and said, ' Papa, dear, could you manage to let me have a good big waggon? I want to take all our dirty clothes to the river and wash them. You are the chief man here, so you ought to have a clean shirt on when you attend meetings of the Council. Moreover, you have five sons at home, two of them married and the other three are good-looking young bachelors; you know they always like to have clean linen when they go out to a dance, and I have been thinking about all this.'"

You will observe that though Nausicaa dreams that she is going to be married shortly, and that all the best young men of Scheria are in love with her, she does not dream that she has fallen in love with any one of them in particular, and that thus every preparation is made for her getting married except the selection of the bridegroom.

You will also note that Nausicaa has to keep her father up to putting a clean shirt on when he ought to have one, whereas her young brothers appear to keep herself up to having a clean shirt ready for them when they want one. These little touches are so lifelike and so feminine that they suggest drawing from life by a female member of Alcinous's own family who knew his character from behind the scenes.

I would also say before proceeding further that in some parts of France and Germany it is still the custom to have but one or at most two great washing days in the year. Each household is provided with an enormous quantity of linen, which when dirty is just soaked and rinsed, and then put aside till the great washing day of the year. This is why Nausicaa wants a waggon, and has to go so far afield. If it was only a few collars and a pocket-handkerchief or two she could no doubt have found water enough near at hand. The big spring or autumn wash, however, is evidently intended.

Returning now to the Odyssey, when he had heard what Nausicaa wanted Alcinous said:

The Humour of Homer

"'You shall have the mules, my love, and whatever else you have a mind for, so be off with you.'

"Then he told the servants, and they got the waggon out and harnessed the mules, while the princess brought the clothes down from the linen room and placed them on the waggon. Her mother got ready a nice basket of provisions with all sorts of good things, and a goatskin full of wine. The princess now got into the waggon, and her mother gave her a golden cruse of oil that she and her maids might anoint themselves.

"Then Nausicaa took the whip and reins and gave the mules a touch which sent them off at a good pace. They pulled without flagging, and carried not only Nausicaa and her wash of clothes, but the women also who were with her.

"When they got to the river they went to the washing pools, through which even in summer there ran enough pure water to wash any quantity of linen, no matter how dirty. Here they unharnessed the mules and turned them out to feed in the sweet juicy grass that grew by the river-side. They got the clothes out of the waggon, brought them to the water, and vied with one another in treading upon them and banging them about to get the dirt out of them. When they had got them quite clean, they laid them out by the seaside where the waves had raised a high beach of shingle, and set about washing and anointing themselves with olive oil. Then they got their dinner by the side of the river, and waited for the sun to finish drying the clothes. By and by, after dinner, they took off their head-dresses and began to play at ball, and Nausicaa sang to them."

I think you will agree with me that there is no haziness—no milking of ewes that have had a lamb with them all night—here. The writer is at home and on her own ground.

"When they had done folding the clothes and were putting the mules to the waggon before starting home again, Minerva thought it was time Ulysses should wake up and see the handsome girl who was to take him to the city of the Phaeacians. So the princess threw a ball at one of the maids, which missed the maid and fell into the water. On this they all shouted, and the noise they made woke up Ulysses, who sat up in his bed of leaves and wondered where in the world he could have got to.

"Then he crept from under the bush beneath which he had slept, broke off a thick bough so as to cover his nakedness, and advanced towards Nausicaa and her maids; these last all ran away, but Nausicaa stood her ground, for Minerva had put courage into her heart, so she kept quite still, and Ulysses could not make up his mind whether it would be better to go up to her, throw himself at her feet, and embrace her knees as a suppliant—[in which case, of course, he would have to drop the bough] or whether it would be better for him to make an apology to her at a reasonable distance, and ask her to be good enough to give him some clothes and show him the way to the town. On the whole he thought it would be better to keep at arm's length, in case the princess should take offence at his coming too near her."

Let me say in passing that this is one of many passages which have led me to conclude that the Odyssey is written by a woman. A girl, such as Nausicaa describes herself, young, unmarried, unattached, and hence, after all, knowing little of what men feel on these matters, having by a cruel freak of inspiration got her hero into such an awkward predicament, might conceivably imagine that he would argue as she represents him, but no man, except such a woman's tailor as could never have written such a masterpiece as the Odyssey, would ever get his hero into such an undignified scrape at all, much less represent him as arguing as Ulysses does. I suppose Minerva was so busy making Nausicaa brave that she had no time to put a little sense into Ulysses' head, and remind him that he was nothing if not full of sagacity and resource. To return:

Ulysses now begins with the most judicious apology that his unaided imagination can suggest. "I beg your ladyship's pardon," he exclaims, "but are you goddess or are you a mortal woman? If you are a goddess and live in

The Humour of Homer

heaven, there can be no doubt but you are Jove's daughter Diana, for your face and figure are exactly like hers," and so on in a long speech which I need not further quote from.

"Stranger," replied Nausicaa, as soon as the speech was ended, "you seem to be a very sensible well-disposed person. There is no accounting for luck; Jove gives good or ill to every man, just as he chooses, so you must take your lot, and make the best of it." She then tells him she will give him clothes and everything else that a foreigner in distress can reasonably expect. She calls back her maids, scolds them for running away, and tells them to take Ulysses and wash him in the river after giving him something to eat and drink. So the maids give him the little gold cruse of oil and tell him to go and wash himself, and as they seem to have completely recovered from their alarm, Ulysses is compelled to say, "Young ladies, please stand a little on one side, that I may wash the brine from off my shoulders and anoint myself with oil; for it is long enough since my skin has had a drop of oil upon it. I cannot wash as long as you keep standing there. I have no clothes on, and it makes me very uncomfortable."

So they stood aside and went and told Nausicaa. Meanwhile (I am translating closely), "Minerva made him look taller and stronger than before; she gave him some more hair on the top of his head, and made it flow down in curls most beautifully; in fact she glorified him about the head and shoulders as a cunning workman who has studied under Vulcan or Minerva enriches a fine piece of plate by gilding it."

Again I argue that I am reading a description of as it were a prehistoric Mr. Knightley by a not less prehistoric Jane Austen—with this difference that I believe Nausicaa is quietly laughing at her hero and sees through him, whereas Jane Austen takes Mr. Knightley seriously.

"Hush, my pretty maids," exclaimed Nausicaa as soon as she saw Ulysses coming back with his hair curled, "hush, for I want to say something. I believe the gods in heaven have sent this man here. There is something very remarkable about him. When I first saw him I thought him quite plain and commonplace, and now I consider him one of the handsomest men I ever saw in my life. I should like my future husband [who, it is plain, then, is not yet decided upon] to be just such another as he is, if he would only stay here, and not want to go away. However, give him something to eat and drink."

Nausicaa now says they must be starting homeward; so she tells Ulysses that she will drive on first herself, but that he is to follow after her with the maids. She does not want to be seen coming into the town with him; and then follows another passage which clearly shows that for all the talk she has made about getting married she has no present intention of changing her name.

" ' I am afraid,' she says, ' of the gossip and scandal which may be set on foot about me behind my back, for there are some very ill-natured people in the town, and some low fellow, if he met us, might say, ' Who is this fine-looking stranger who is going about with Nausicaa? Where did she pick him up? I suppose she is going to marry him, or perhaps he is some shipwrecked sailor from foreign parts; or has some god come down from heaven in answer to her prayers, and she is going to live with him? It would be a good thing if she would take herself off and find a husband somewhere else, for she will not look at one of the many excellent young Phaeacians who are in love with her '; and I could not complain, for I should myself think ill of any girl whom I saw going about with men unknown to her father and mother, and without having been married to him in the face of all the world.' "

This passage could never have been written by the local bard, who was in great measure dependent on Nausicaa's family; he would never speak thus of his patron's daughter; either the passage is Nausicaa's apology for herself, written by herself, or it is pure invention, and this last, considering the close adherence to the actual topography of Trapani on the Sicilian Coast, and a great deal else that I cannot lay before you here, appears to me improbable.

Nausicaa then gives Ulysses directions by which he can find her father's house. "When you have got past the courtyard," she says, "go straight through the main hall, till you come to my mother's room. You will find her sitting by the fire and spinning her purple wool by firelight. She will make a lovely picture as she leans back against a column with her maids ranged behind her. Facing her stands my father's seat in which he sits and topes like an immortal god. Never mind him, but go up to my mother and lay your hands upon her knees, if you would be forwarded on your homeward voyage." From which I conclude that Arete ruled Alcinous, and Nausicaa ruled Arete.

Ulysses follows his instructions aided by Minerva, who makes him invisible as he passes through the town and through the crowds of Phaeacian guests who are feasting in the king's palace. When he has reached the queen, the cloak of thick darkness falls off, and he is revealed to all present, kneeling at the feet of Queen Arete, to whom he makes his appeal. It has already been made apparent in a passage extolling her virtue at some length, but which I have not been able to quote, that Queen Arete is, in the eyes of the writer, a much more important person that her husband Alcinous.

Every one, of course, is very much surprised at seeing Ulysses, but after a little discussion, from which it appears that the writer considers Alcinous to be a person who requires a good deal of keeping straight in other matters besides clean linen, it is settled that Ulysses shall be fêted on the following day and then escorted home. Ulysses now has supper and remains with Alcinous and Arete after the other guests are gone away for the night. So the three sit by the fire while the servants take away the things, and Arete is the first to speak. She has been uneasy for some time about Ulysses' clothes, which she recognized as her own make, and at last she says, "Stranger, there is a question or two that

I should like to put to you myself. Who in the world are you? And who gave you those clothes? Did you not say you had come here from beyond the seas?"

Ulysses explains matters, but still withholds his name, nevertheless Alcinous (who seems to have shared in the general opinion that it was high time his daughter got married, and that, provided she married soembody, it did not much matter who the bridegroom might be) exclaimed, "By Father Jove, Minerva, and Apollo, now that I see what kind of a person you are and how exactly our opinions coincide upon every subject, I should so like it if you would stay with us always, marry Nausicaa, and become my son-in-law."

Ulysses turns the conversation immediately, and meanwhile Queen Arete told her maids to put a bed in the corridor, and make it with red blankets, and it was to have at least one counterpane. They were also to put a woollen nightgown for Ulysses. "The maids took a torch, and made the bed as fast as they could: when they had done so they came up to Ulysses and said, 'This way, sir, if you please, your room is quite ready'; and Ulysses was very glad to hear them say so."

On the following day Alcinous holds a meeting of the Phaeacians and proposes that Ulysses should have a ship got ready to take him home at once: this being settled he invites all the leading people, and the fifty-two sailors who are to man Ulysses' ship, to come up to his own house, and he will give them a banquet—for which he kills a dozen sheep, eight pigs, and two oxen. Immediately after gorging themselves at the banquet they have a series of athletic competitions, and from this I gather the poem to have been written by one who saw nothing very odd in letting people compete in sports requiring very violent exercise immediately after a heavy meal. Such a course may have been usual in those days, but certainly is not generally adopted in our own.

At the games Alcinous makes himself as ridiculous as he

always does, and Ulysses behaves much as the hero of the preceding afternoon might be expected to do—but on his praising the Phaeacians towards the close of the proceedings Alcinous says he is a person of such singular judgement that they really must all of them make him a very handsome present. "Twelve of you," he exclaims, "are magistrates, and there is myself—that makes thirteen; suppose we give him each one of us a clean cloak, a tunic, and a talent of gold," —which in those days was worth about two hundred and fifty pounds.

This is unanimously agreed to, and in the evening, towards sundown, the presents began to make their appearance at the palace of King Alcinous, and the king's sons, perhaps prudently as you will presently see, place them in the keeping of their mother Arete.

When the presents have all arrived, Alcinous says to Arete, "Wife, go and fetch the best chest we have, and put a clean cloak and a tunic in it. In the meantime Ulysses will take a bath."

Arete orders the maids to heat a bath, brings the chest, packs up the raiment and gold which the Phaeacians have brought, and adds a cloak and a good tunic as King Alcinous's own contribution.

Yes, but where—and that is what we are never told—is the £250 which he ought to have contributed as well as the cloak and tunic? And where is the beautiful gold goblet which he had also promised?

"See to the fastening yourself," says Queen Arete to Ulysses, "for fear anyone should rob you while you are asleep in the ship."

Ulysses, we may be sure, was well aware that Alcinous's £250 was not in the box, nor yet the goblet, but he took the hint at once and made the chest fast without the delay of a moment, with a bond which the cunning goddess Circe had taught him.

He does not seem to have thought his chance of getting the £250 and the goblet, and having to unpack his box again, was so great as his chance of having his box tampered with before he got it away, if he neglected to double-lock it at once and put the key in his pocket. He has always a keen eye to money; indeed the whole Odyssey turns on what is substantially a money quarrel, so this time without the prompting of Minerva he does one of the very few sensible things which he does, on his own account, throughout the whole poem.

Supper is now served, and when it is over, Ulysses, pressed by Alcinous, announces his name and begins the story of his adventures.

It is with profound regret that I find myself unable to quote any of the fascinating episodes with which his narrative abounds, but I have said I was going to lecture on the humour of Homer—that is to say of the Iliad and the Odyssey—and must not be diverted from my subject. I cannot, however, resist the account which Ulysses gives of his meeting with his mother in Hades, the place of departed spirits, which he has visited by the advice of Circe. His mother comes up to him and asks him how he managed to get into Hades, being still alive. I will translate freely, but quite closely, from Ulysses' own words, as spoken to the Phaeacians.

"And I said, 'Mother, I had to come here to consult the ghost of the old Theban prophet Teiresias, I have never yet been near Greece, nor set foot on my native land, and have had nothing but one long run of ill luck from the day I set out with Agamemnon to fight at Troy. But tell me how you came here yourself? Did you have a long and painful illness or did heaven vouchsafe you a gentle easy passage to eternity? Tell me also about my father and my son? Is my property still in their hands, or has someone else got hold of it who thinks that I shall not return to claim it? How, again, is my wife conducting herself? Does she live with her son and make a home for him, or has she married again?'

"My mother answered, 'Your wife is still mistress of your house, but she is in very great straits and spends the greater part of her time in tears. No one has actually taken possession of your property, and Telemachus still holds it. He has to accept a great many invitations, and gives much the sort of entertainments in return that may be expected from one in his position. Your father remains in the old place, and never goes near the town; he is very badly off, and has neither bed nor bedding, nor a stick of furniture of any kind. In winter he sleeps on the floor in front of the fire with the men, and his clothes are in a shocking state, but in summer, when the warm weather comes on again, he sleeps out in the vineyard on a bed of vine leaves. He takes on very much about your not having returned, and suffers more and more as he grows older: as for me I died of nothing whatever in the world but grief about yourself. There was not a thing the matter with me, but my prolonged anxiety on your account was too much for me, and in the end it just wore me out.'"

In the course of time Ulysses comes to a pause in his narrative and Queen Arete makes a little speech.

"'What do you think,' she said to the Phaeacians, 'of such a guest as this? Did you ever see anyone at once so good-looking and so clever? It is true, indeed, that his visit is paid more particularly to myself, but you all participate in the honour conferred upon us by a visitor of such distinction. Do not be in a hurry to send him off, nor stingy in the presents you make to one in so great need; for you are all of you very well off.'"

You will note that the queen does not say "*we* are all of *us* very well off."

"Then the hero Echeneus, who was the oldest man among them, added a few words of his own. 'My friends,' he said, 'there cannot be two opinions about the graciousness and sagacity of the remarks that have just fallen from Her Majesty; nevertheless it is with His Majesty King Alcinous that the decision must ultimately rest.'

"'The thing shall be done,' exclaimed Alcinous, 'if I am still king over the Phaeacians. As for our guest, I know he is anxious to resume his journey, still we must persuade him if we can to stay with us until to-morrow, by which time I shall be able to get together the balance of the sum which I mean to press on his acceptance.'"

So here we have it straight out that the monarch knew he had only contributed the coat and waistcoat, and did not know exactly how he was to lay his hands on the £250. What with piracy—for we have been told of at least one case in which Alcinous had looted a town and stolen his housemaid Eurymedusa—what with insufficient changes of linen, toping like an immortal god, swaggering at large, and openhanded hospitality, it is plain and by no means surprising that Alcinous is out at elbows; nor can there be a better example of the difference between the occasional broad comedy of the Iliad and the delicate but very bitter satire of the Odyssey than the way in which the fact that Alcinous is in money difficulties is allowed to steal upon us, as contrasted with the obvious humour of the quarrels between Jove and Juno. At any rate we can hardly wonder at Ulysses having felt that to a monarch of such mixed character the unfastened box might prove a temptation greater than he could resist. To return, however, to the story:

"If it please your Majesty," said he, in answer to King Alcinous, "I should be delighted to stay here for another twelve months, and to accept from your hands the vast treasures and the escort which you are so generous as to promise me. I should obviously gain by doing so, for I should return fuller-handed to my own people and should thus be both more respected and more loved by my acquaintance. Still to receive such presents——"

The king perceived his embarrassment, and at once relieved him. "No one," he exclaimed, "who looks at you can for one moment take you for a charlatan or a swindler. I know there are many of these unscrupulous persons going about just now with such plausible stories that it is very hard to disbelieve them; there is, however, a finish about your style which convinces me of your good disposition," and

The Humour of Homer

so on for more than I have space to quote; after which Ulysses again proceeds with his adventures.

When he had finished them Alcinous insists that the leading Phaeacians should each one of them give Ulysses a still further present of a large kitchen copper and a three-legged stand to set it on, " but," he continues, " as the expense of all these presents is really too heavy for the purse of any private individual, I shall charge the whole of them on the rates ": literally, " We will repay ourselves by getting it in from among the people, for this is too heavy a present for the purse of a private individual." And what this can mean except charging it on the rates I do not know.

Of course everyone else sends up his tripod and his cauldron, but we hear nothing about any, either tripod or cauldron, from King Alcinous. He is very fussy next morning stowing them under the ship's benches, but his time and trouble seem to be the extent of his contribution. It is hardly necessary to say that Ulysses had to go away without the £250, and that we never hear of the promised goblet being presented. Still he had done pretty well.

I have not quoted anything like all the absurd remarks made by Alcinous, nor shown you nearly as completely as I could do if I had more time how obviously the writer is quietly laughing at him in her sleeve. She understands his little ways as she understands those of Menelaus, who tells Telemachus and Pisistratus that if they like he will take them a personally conducted tour round the Peloponnese, and that they can make a good thing out of it, for everyone will give them something—fancy Helen or Queen Arete making such a proposal as this. They are never laughed at, but then they are women, whereas Alcinous and Menelaus are men, and this makes all the difference.

And now in conclusion let me point out the irony of literature in connection with this astonishing work. Here is a poem in which the hero and heroine have already been married many years before it begins: it is marked by a total absence of love-business in such sense as we understand it:

its interest centres mainly in the fact of a bald elderly gentleman, whose little remaining hair is red, being eaten out of house and home during his absence by a number of young men who are courting the supposed widow—a widow who, if she be fair and fat, can hardly also be less than forty. Can any subject seem more hopeless? Moreover, this subject so initially faulty is treated with a carelessness in respect of consistency, ignorance of commonly known details, and disregard of ordinary canons, that can hardly be surpassed, and yet I cannot think that in the whole range of literature there is a work which can be decisively placed above it. I am afraid you will hardly accept this; I do not see how you can be expected to do so, for in the first place there is no even tolerable prose translation, and in the second, the Odyssey, like the Iliad, has been a school book for over two thousand five hundred years, and what more cruel revenge than this can dullness take on genius? The Iliad and Odyssey have been used as text-books for education during at least two thousand five hundred years, and yet it is only during the last forty or fifty that people have begun to see that they are by different authors. There was, indeed, so I learn from Colonel Mure's valuable work, a band of scholars some few hundreds of years before the birth of Christ, who refused to see the Iliad and Odyssey as by the same author, but they were snubbed and snuffed out, and for more than two thousand years were considered to have been finally refuted. Can there be any more scathing satire upon the value of literary criticism? It would seem as though Minerva had shed the same thick darkness over both the poems as she shed over Ulysses, so that they might go in and out among the dons of Oxford and Cambridge from generation to generation, and none should see them. If I am right, as I believe I am, in holding the Odyssey to have been written by a young woman, was ever sleeping beauty more effectually concealed behind a more impenetrable hedge of dullness? —and she will have to sleep a good many years yet before anyone wakes her effectually. But what else can one expect

The Humour of Homer

from people, not one of whom has been at the very slight exertion of noting a few of the writer's main topographical indications, and then looking for them in an Admiralty chart or two? Can any step be more obvious and easy—indeed, it is so simple that I am ashamed of myself for not having taken it forty years ago. Students of the Odyssey for the most part are so engrossed with the force of the zeugma, and of the enclitic particle γε; they take so much more interest in the digamma and in the Aeolic dialect, than they do in the living spirit that sits behind all these things and alone gives them their importance, that, naturally enough, not caring about the personality, it remains and always must remain invisible to them.

If I have helped to make it any less invisible to yourselves, let me ask you to pardon the somewhat querulous tone of my concluding remarks.

WAS THE ODYSSEY WRITTEN BY A WOMAN?

NOTE

This Lecture is now for the first time printed from Butler's MS. It was delivered at the Somerville Club, 7th March 1893; and is dated at the end, 3rd March 1893. On the title-page Butler made the following note: "I have added about 5 pp and read it at Mrs. Bovill's, 9 St. Andrew's Place, on Sunday Mar. 26 [1893]." He means that he extended the lecture after reading it at the Somerville Club and before reading it at the house of his friend Mrs. Bovill (now the Hon. Mrs. R. C. Grosvenor), who in 1893 was living in St. Andrew's Place, Regent's Park.

An Italian version, with modifications, by Capitano Giuseppe Messina-Manzo, was completed about 1895 and eventually appeared in *Quo Vadis?* 4th October 1901. Two copies, with corrections in Butler's hand, are in the Butler Collection at St. John's College, Cambridge.

The argument of the Lecture is developed more fully in *The Authoress of the Odyssey*; but no apology is necessary for making public so characteristic a specimen of Butler's lighter method.

A.T.B.

Was the Odyssey written by a Woman?

However much those who theorize about the Iliad and the Odyssey may deserve stoning, there is no one who can stone them with a clear conscience; for those who hold, as most people in England and Germany now do, that the Iliad and Odyssey belong to ages separated from each other by several generations, must be haunted by the reflection that though the diversity of authorship was prominently insisted on more than two thousand years ago, not one single Homeric student from that day till recent times could be brought to acknowledge what in our own generation is held self-evident. Truly, as has been said by Mr. Gladstone, if Homer is old, the systematic and comprehensive study of him is still young.

If, on the other hand, we keep to the older view and ascribe both Iliad and Odyssey to the same writer, what becomes of by far the most authoritative part of modern Odyssean criticism? Stones, indeed, thrown by those who have not yet got beyond this view may fall thick as hail, but they will make no bruises; nevertheless, when I look back upon the long, dull, dreary record of Iliadic and Odyssean criticism during the last nearly 3000 years, and when I reflect upon the complexity of the interests vested in so-called education, I am appalled at the magnitude, not to say hopelessness, of the task that I have undertaken. People complain of me for, as they say, poking fun at the Odyssey; I have not done so—not yet—but if I had, would not even this be better than poking Oxford and Cambridge at it? or than making it a parade-ground for the display of long-winded pedantry from century to century without apparently so much as a wish to stand face to face and heart to heart with the writer?

It will be my endeavour to convince you that the Odyssey is not, as is commonly supposed, the work of an old man, but of a young woman, who though doubtless much older by the time she had finished her work, was, when she began it, a brilliant, high-spirited girl, hardly more than seventeen or eighteen years old.

She did not deliberately set herself to write an epic poem—

this would be inconceivable. The work grew under her hands, piecemeal, from small beginnings, each additional effort pointing to a fresh possible development, till at last there the Odyssey was—a spontaneous growth rather than a thing done by observation. Such kingdoms of heaven as the Odyssey never do come by observation. Moreover, like all " native wood-notes," the work abounds in the anomalies and inconsistencies that are inseparable from a gradual development of any sort. I cannot detail the evidence on which I rely, but will briefly indicate my conclusions as regards the growth of the poem.

I suppose the famous washing-day episode at the beginning of what is now Book vi to have been the germ from which the whole poem sprang. This consisted originally of about 100 lines, written as a mere girlish *jeu d'esprit*, to introduce herself and her surroundings, and to make fun of the Epic Cycle, much as the mock-heroic Battle of the Frogs and Mice made fun of it centuries later. The success of this attempt prompted the writer to take a bolder flight, and she introduced Ulysses, possibly at the instance of her brothers, still continuing the description of those surroundings of all kinds with which she was most familiar, and still maintaining the same mock-heroic style. By the time she had done describing her father's house, and the people among whom she lived, the poem consisted of what are now Books vi, vii, viii. There was as yet no intention of saying a syllable about Penelope or the suitors, nor any plot beyond the mere fact that Ulysses wanted to get back to Ithaca.

But by this time the writer had begun to feel her own strength and resolved on giving a detailed account of the wanderings of Ulysses. This led to the addition of what are now Books ix, x, xi, xii, and the first 187 lines of Book xiii. Book v was also written as an introduction to Book vi which, as I have said, was already composed. This statement, though not strictly accurate, is near enough for my present purpose. With increased sense of power on the writer's part we also find increased dignity and seriousness in the poem; comedy is not indeed entirely dropped, but it is more rare. In all the eight books, however, which we have now got, that is to say Books v to line 187 of Book xiii, there was still, as they originally stood, hardly any mention of Penelope and none whatever of the suitors. Finally, and, as far as I can gather, after a considerable interval, the writer resolved on facing the scandalous stories then current about Penelope and on putting another construction upon them; whereon Books i-iv and xiii-xxiv were added. For a somewhat more detailed and more precise statement I must refer you to the pamphlet which I have just published " On the Trapanese Origin of the Odyssey."[1] The point we have now to consider is how far I am justified in speaking of the writer as " she."

Let me begin by dealing with the supposed improbability of there having been any Greek poetesses at the date assignable to the Odyssey, which can hardly be later than 1000 B.C. Those who turn to the article " Sappho," in Smith's *Dictionary of Classical Biography*, will find that poetesses abounded as early as 600 B.C., before which date we have hardly any Greek literature except the Iliad, Odyssey, Hesiod, and some, perhaps, of the Homeric Hymns. We find Gorgo and Andromeda mentioned as Sappho's rivals; among her fellows were Anactoria of Miletus, Gongyle of Colophon, Eunica of Salamis, Gyrinna, Atthis, and Mnasidica. "Those," says the writer, " who attained the highest celebrity for their works were Damophylia the Pamphylian and Erinna of Telos." This last-named poetess wrote a long poem upon the distaff, which was considered equal to Homer himself.

Again, there was Baucis, who wrote Erinna's epitaph. In Müller's work on the Dorians I find reference made to the amatory poetesses of Lesbos. He tells us also of Corinna, who is said to have competed successfully for a prize with Pindar, and to Myrto, who certainly competed against him, but with what success we know not. There was also Diotima the Arcadian, and looking through Bergk's *Poetae*

[1] See *The Authoress of the Odyssey*, Shrewsbury Edition, p. xxxv.—A.T.B.

Lyrici I find other names of women. Among the Hebrews again, we find Miriam, Deborah, and Hannah, all of them believed to be much older than the Odyssey. As early as 1500 B.C., and how much earlier we know not, the Greeks were an important and independent people, extending over a large, but unknown area. They are called in an Egyptian inscription of this date the princes of the north. If then Greek poetesses were as abundant as we know them to have been 600 B.C. in the islands of the Aegean, and also in both Greece itself and Asia Minor, there is no ground for surprise at finding one in Sicily 1000 B.C.; especially in a part of Sicily which, according to Thucydides, was colonized by Greek-speaking peoples centuries before the close of what is commonly called the Homeric age. The civilization depicted in the Odyssey is as advanced as any that is likely to have existed in Melos or Mitylene 400 years later, and the position of man seems to have been one of as complete subjection as it has been at any time from that day to this—certainly far more so than in that Athenian civilization with which we are best acquainted. What, for example, can be more masterful than the status of Helen, Calypso, Penelope, Queen Arete, and Circe, to say nothing of the omnipresent ascendancy of Minerva? In all the scenes where these women are introduced, it is they, not the men, who lead.

Furthermore, the fact that the recognized heads of poetry were the nine Muses—for it is always these, or " The Muse," that is invoked, and never Minerva or Apollo—throws back the suggestion of female authorship to a very remote period, when to be an author at all was to be a poet—for prose-writing is a comparatively late development. It is absurd to suppose that women would be made to preside over literature if this was an art which they rarely practised; and when we come to think of it, in an age in which men were mostly occupied with either fighting or hunting, the arts of peace, and among them all kinds of literary accomplishment, would be more naturally woman's province than man's. If the truth were known, we might very likely find that it is man,

Was the Odyssey written by a Woman?

not woman, who has been the interloper in the domain of literature.

Having thus met the only *a priori* objection to my view that has yet presented itself to me, I turn to the internal evidence to be found in the Odyssey itself. What then, let me ask, is the most unerring test of female authorship? Surely a preponderance of female interest, and a fuller knowledge of those things which a woman naturally knows, than of those which fall more commonly to man's business. People always write by preference of what they know best, and they know best what they most are, and have most to do with. This extends itself to ways of thought even more than to mere material actions. If the women are invariably well drawn in any work while the men are comparatively speaking mechanical, it will be almost always safe to infer that the writer is a woman; and the converse holds good with men. Man and woman never fully understand one another; and, as a man understands men better than a woman can do, so does a woman, women. It is our delight as well as duty to understand each other as completely as ever we can, and the more we do so the happier and better we are; but do what we can to break down the barriers between us, they can never be broken down completely, except as between man and wife, and each sex will dwell mainly, though of course not exclusively, within its own separate world.

Now, it is admitted on all hands that the preponderance of interest in the Iliad lies with men, and in the Odyssey with women. The women in the Iliad are few in number and seldom occupy the stage. True, the goddesses play important parts, but they are almost invariably laughed at. Men seem to be forced to caricature women before they can draw them at all, and so perhaps a woman never draws a man with such perfect felicity as when she is laughing at him. Either sex, in fact, can caricature the other most delightfully, and certainly no one has ever shown more clearly that she considered the noblest study for womankind to be man's little ways and weaknesses than the authoress of the Odyssey has done. But returning to the preponderance of male or female interest in the Iliad and Odyssey, it is a mere truism to say that whereas man dominates the Iliad, woman does so as regards the Odyssey, in which we find Minerva, Penelope, Euryclea, Helen, Idothea, Calypso, Nausicaa, Queen Arete, Circe, and who can say how many more? Nor is there one of these who is not faultlessly drawn, each in her own way. When Ulysses goes down into Hades it is a dream of fair women that is presented to us. First we have Ulysses' own mother, then Teiresias as a pure matter of business; then a bevy of celebrated women one after another, nor is it till these have been all of them disposed of that a few members of the baser sex are allowed to come upon the scene. When again, at the beginning of Book iv, Menelaus is celebrating the marriages of his son and of his daughter, it is the daughter's and not the son's marriage with which the writer first deals, and it is the daughter and not the son in whom she takes the greater interest. Of course she does. What woman does not find the bride more interesting than the bridegroom, unless he happens to be her own? Granted that in this case there was no time to be lost, for the engagement had been going on for over ten years, and Hermione was turned thirty, still I venture to think that if the writer had been a man, he would have married Megapenthes first and Hermione afterwards.

Moreover, though the men in the Odyssey are being constantly laughed at and made to do things that no reasonable man would do, the women are never laughed at. Venus, indeed, is made a little ridiculous in one passage, but she was a goddess, so it did not matter. Besides, the brunt of the ridicule was borne by Mars, and Venus is instantly rehabilitated. Women are sometimes spoken of, and dealt with, severely in the Odyssey, but they are always taken seriously and never from first to last do anything which a woman could not do without loss of dignity.

It was this contrast between the way in which the men and the women behave in the Odyssey which led me finally to

Was the Odyssey written by a Woman?

conclude that I was reading the work of a woman, and not of a man. I was continually aghast at the manner in which the men were made to speak and act, and believing, with true male conceit, that the poem was written as a matter of course by a man, I conjectured that he must have been some bard who lived in the servants' hall, much as the chaplain did in a great house a couple of hundred years ago among ourselves, and who, though he saw great people, did not mix with them. This quieted me for a time, but by and by it struck me that though the men were so frequently both foolish and snobbish, the women were always ladies when the writer meant to make them so. Could a servants' hall bard go so hopelessly wrong with almost all his men, and yet be so exquisitely right with every single one of his women—each in her own degree? Impossible; yet, even so, I was too stupid to catch that it was a woman and not a man who was drawing them, till at last I suppose Minerva saw what a muddle I was in and told me. Then, of course, the whole thing was plain, and I saw more quiet malice than innocence in the drawing of King Menelaus, Alcinous, and Ulysses. Truly man is not always quick to know when he is being laughed at.

I am aware how dangerous all this is, and how easy it is to find irony and humour in places where the writer was writing all the time in the most absolute good faith. Take the Prayer Book for example as an extreme case. I mean no irreverence, but take it as the severest test that I can think of. " Give peace in our time, O Lord, because there is none other that fightest for us, but *only thou*, O God "; or again, " Almighty and everlasting God, *who alone workest great marvels*; send down upon our Bishops and Curates, and all Congregations committed to their charge, the healthful Spirit of thy grace "; or again, " *One* day in thy courts is better than a thousand." People find what they bring. Granted; but is it not possible that people have found so much seriousness in the more humorous books of the Odyssey because they brought it there? To the serious all things are serious—and if they are not, they ought to be. Besides, when people are simply unfortunate, as we all at times are, they are not persistently unfortunate, and there is too much method in the misfortunes of the authoress of the Odyssey throughout the Phaeacian episode to admit of our accepting them as unintentional.

I ought to quote enough to make my meaning more clear. I say nothing about the absurd way in which Ulysses behaves when he meets Nausicaa. I have dealt with this elsewhere, as also with the way in which Alcinous forgets to pay the talent of gold and to give the gold cup which he had promised Ulysses. Let me then take the speeches of Ulysses and of King Alcinous at the Phaeacian games. Ulysses has been asked to enter himself for some one or other of the competitions, but has declined on the score of having suffered so much recently as to feel unable to do so. On this Euryalus, a young Phaeacian nobleman, insults him.

"I gather then," he exclaims, "that you are unskilled in any of those many sports that we take delight in. I suppose you are one of those grasping traders who go about in ships, and think of nothing but of their outward freights and homeward cargoes, there does not seem to be much of the athlete about you."

"For shame, sir," answered Ulysses fiercely, "you are an insolent fellow, so true is it that the gods do not grace all men neither in person nor understanding. One man may be of weak presence, but heaven has adorned this with such a good conversation that he charms every one who sees him: his honeyed moderation carries his hearers with him so that he is leader in every assembly of his fellows, and wherever he goes he is looked up to. Another may be as handsome as a god, but his good looks are not crowned with discretion. This is your case. No god could make a finer-looking fellow than you are, but you are a fool. Your ill-judged remarks have made me exceedingly angry, and you are quite mistaken, for I excel in a great many athletic exercises; indeed, so long as I had youth and strength I was

Was the Odyssey written by a Woman?

among the first athletes of the age. Now, however, I am worn out with labour and sorrow, for I have gone through much both on the field of battle and by sea; still, in spite of all this I shall compete, for your taunts have stung me to the quick."

On this Ulysses throws a disc much heavier than any which the Phaeacians were in the habit of throwing (so that one does not quite see how it happened to be there at all) and, of course, sends it far beyond any disc yet thrown. Pleased with the success of his throw he addresses the bystanders in what the writer tells us is a more agreeable manner.

"Young men," said he, "come up to that throw if you can, and I will throw another disc as heavy or even heavier. If any one wants to have a bout with me let him come on, for I am exceedingly angry. I will box, wrestle, or run, I do not care what it is, with any man among you except Laodamas, but not with him because I am his guest, and one cannot compete with one's own personal friends. At least, I do not think it a prudent or sensible thing for a guest to challenge his host's family at any game, especially when he is in a foreign country. He will cut the ground from under his own feet if he does, but I make no exception as regards any one else, for I want to have the matter out and know who is the best man. I am a good hand at every kind of athletic exercise known among mankind. I am an excellent archer. In battle I am always the first to bring a man down with my arrow, no matter how many more are taking aim at him alongside of me. Philoctetes was the only man who could shoot better than I could, when we Greeks were before Troy, and were in practice. . . . I can throw a dart as far as another man can shoot an arrow. Running is the only thing in respect of which I am afraid some one of the Phaeacians might beat me, for I have been brought down very low at sea. My provisions ran short, and I am still exceedingly weak."

The others said nothing in reply to all this, and King Alcinous was the only one to speak.

"Sir," said he, "we have had much pleasure in hearing all that you have told us, from which I understand that you are willing to show your prowess as having been displeased with some insolent remarks that have been made to you by one of our athletes, and which could never have been uttered by any one who knew how to behave himself. I hope you will apprehend my meaning and will explain to any of your chief men who may be dining with yourself and your family when you get home that we have a hereditary aptitude for accomplishments of every kind. We are not particularly remarkable for our boxing, nor yet for wrestling, but we are singularly fleet of foot, and are excellent sailors. We are extremely fond of good dinners, music, and dancing: we also like frequent changes of linen, warm baths, and good beds; so now, please, some of you who are the best dancers set about dancing that our guest on his return home may be able to tell his friends how much we surpass all other nations as sailors, runners, dancers, and minstrels" (Od. viii, 202-252).

Is this innocence? Why, Alcinous, when the games began, claimed boxing and wrestling as special accomplishments of the Phaeacians, and it was about these and not about the running that the guest was to tell his friends on his return home; but now when Ulysses says he will box or wrestle with any of them, but had rather not run, Alcinous immediately declines the boxing and wrestling, and falls back on running. The famous dialogue in *Box and Cox* is not more barefaced: "Can you fight?" "No." "Then come on."

Colonel Mure,[1] it is true, failed *chercher la femme*, but he was fully alive to the satire that pervades the whole Phaeacian episode. "There can," he writes, "be little doubt from the distinctive peculiarities with which the poet has invested the Phaeacians and the precision and force of the sarcasm dis-

---

[1] William Mure (1799-1860), author of *A Critical History of the Language and Literature of Ancient Greece*, from which work Butler proceeds to quote.—A.T.B.

played in his portrait of their character, that the episode is intended as a satire on the habits of some real people, with which he was familiar."

Of Alcinous Colonel Mure says: "The characteristics of his eloquence are egotism and self-laudatory bombast, balanced by an equal share of hyperbolical compliments to his guest, good-humoured diffuseness, and incoherent wandering from subject to subject, as vanity prompts the one, or levity dismisses the other.... Nor can there be a better proof how completely the spirit of this portion of the poem has been misapprehended, than the pompous solemnity with which the whole humour of the dialogue is treated in the popular modern paraphrases."

Colonel Mure then proceeds to the Phaeacian game scene, a part of which I have just read you, and he sees it in exactly the same light as I do. He continues with regard to the name "Alcinous" which means "strong of intellect," "that the satirical allusion to the levity and frivolity of its owner is sufficiently apparent," but he does not draw attention to the fact that there is not a pin to choose between the eloquence of Alcinous and that of Ulysses. It is hard to say which of them makes the greater fool of himself. Menelaus, again, is treated in exactly the same way—conceit and swagger is the dominant note in each character, until as a matter of literary exigency Ulysses has to be pulled through this or that feat with Minerva, or Calypso, or Circe, or some other woman at his elbow to keep him straight. A middle-aged or elderly gentleman of position must, according to the writer of the Odyssey, be inevitably a fool—as indeed he generally is—and she was not going to make him out anything else; but as she has repeatedly used the same spot in the neighbourhood of Trapani for different scenes, making it do double and sometimes even treble duty, so, I take it, she has made the same person sit for two or three different characters, and whenever she wanted an extra special middle-aged gentleman she turned, instinctively, to her own parent. I believe that what I have said is substantially correct, but it must be remembered that the Ulysses of the Phaeacian episode was modified in a more serious direction as the work grew under the hands of its writer. Moreover, though I do not hesitate to believe that the poem was composed as a written work, yet it is probable that alterations in what had been already written were more difficult to effect than they are in our own time, and hence the traces of the original scheme have been allowed to remain.

I find I am wandering from the point upon which I was insisting, namely that the preponderance of interest in the Odyssey is about matters that concern women rather than men. Mr. Gladstone, in his work on Homer, has observed this and says: " It is but rarely in the Iliad that grandeur or force give way to allow the exhibition of domestic affection. Conversely in the Odyssey the family life supplies the tissue into which is woven the thread of the poem." I find again from Professor Jebb's *Introduction to Homer* that Bentley said Homer wrote the Iliad for men and the Odyssey for women, and in his *Bentley* he speaks of this as an ancient saying. We may be sure that if Bentley were living now he would have said, not: " Homer wrote the Iliad for men and the Odyssey for women," but: " The Iliad was written for men, and the Odyssey for women "; and in this case surely, considering how old a matter female authorship appears to be, the most reasonable inference is that the writer of the Iliad gives man the foremost place in his work because he was himself a man, but that the work in which woman preponderates was more probably written by a woman.

Over and above the general predominance of woman and the domesticities, we should consider the more special characteristics that distinguish a woman's work from a man's. I am speaking of those women who stand in the foremost rank. Distrusting my own judgement, I asked a literary friend of great experience, what he considered to be the most conclusive evidence of a work's having been written by a woman. He answered: " Jealousy for the honour of her sex, and severity against those who have done anything to lower its dignity." I should say that this is true, and I do not know any work in which these characteristics are more omnipresent than they are in the Odyssey. A goddess, indeed, may please herself, but death is the only punishment for mortal women who misconduct themselves. Hence, when Ulysses has killed the suitors, the maidservants who had misbehaved with them are first made to clean up all the blood and are then hanged. The Phoenician woman who stole little Eumaeus, and also otherwise misbehaved, meets a violent death almost immediately afterwards. The writer does indeed try to throw the blame of Clytemnestra's guilt on Aegisthus; Clytemnestra, she says, was naturally a woman of excellent disposition and remained so as long as she was in good hands, but it was felt that her case was too black for more extenuation, and she is abandoned to her fate. These three cases—all lightly touched upon—are the only ones in point which occur, for the poem is essentially purist. On the other hand the little indications of respect for women generally are so unfailing that I should have to give them a lecture to themselves if I were to deal with them in any adequate manner.

But perhaps, seeing how limited our time is, I shall employ it best in dwelling on a point on which I touched in my preface to "The Humour of Homer"[1]—I mean the obvious manner in which Penelope is being, if I may say so, whitewashed. I need not tell you what the version of Penelope's conduct given in Apollonius Rhodius, Lycophron, and other later classical writers was; you can find it in Smith's *Dictionary* under "Penelope." But if I can show reason for thinking that these stories were current in the Odyssean age, and that the writer is engaged in a hopeless struggle to put another face upon them, I shall have gone far to prove that the writer was herself a woman; for in those days a male poet would have been little likely to go much out of his way in order to whitewash either Penelope or anyone else. I think that only a woman, justly indignant at what she considered

[1] [See p. 238, *ante*.]

as an insult to her sex, would be inclined to undertake the impossible task of making Penelope at the same time both plausible and virtuous.

I have already said that this task was no part of the original scheme. Let us see, then, what it is that the writer asks us to believe, or rather swallow, as soon as she has determined to undertake it. We are told that more than 100 young men fall violently in love, all at the same time, with a supposed widow who, before the suit was ended must have been getting on towards forty, and that they pester her for several years with addresses that are most distasteful to her. They are so madly in love with her that they cannot think of proposing to any one else (ii, 205-207) till she has made her choice; when she has done this they will go, till then they will pay her out for her cruel treatment of them by eating her son Telemachus out of house and home. This, therefore, they proceed to do, and Penelope, who is a model both wife and mother, suffers agonies of grief, partly for the loss of her husband, and partly because she cannot get the suitors out of the house.

Nevertheless, the suitors do not sleep at the castle; they sleep at various places in the town, in the middle of which Ulysses' castle evidently stands (ii, 397, and elsewhere). Not one of them ever sees Penelope alone. When she comes into their presence she is attended by two of her maidens, who stand on either side of her (i, 331-335), and she holds a screen or fan modestly before her face. The suitors were not men of scrupulous delicacy, and in spite of their devotion to herself they carry on shamelessly with her maids. It is a little strange that not one of those who came from long distances should have insisted in having bed as well as board at the castle, but we gather that Penelope had succeeded in drawing the line at board; and so much care is taken that not one breath of scandal shall attach to her, that we are tempted to infer a sense on the writer's part that it was necessary to put this care well in evidence.

Still stranger, however, is the fact that these ardent,

Was the Odyssey written by a Woman?

passionate lovers never quarrel among themselves for the possession of their middle-aged paragon. The survival of the fittest does not seem to have been yet invented. They show no signs of jealousy, but get on together as a very happy family, playing draughts in the forecourt, flaying goats and singeing pigs in the yard, drinking an untold quantity of wine, and generally keeping high feast. They insist that Penelope should marry somebody, but who the happy somebody is to be seems a matter of very secondary importance. No one appears to think it essential that she should marry himself in particular. Not one of them ever finds out that his own case is hopeless and takes his leave. And so matters jog on year after year—during all which time Penelope is not getting any younger—the suitors dying of love for Penelope, and Penelope all the time dying only to be rid of them.

True, the suitors are not less in love with the good cheer they enjoy at Telemachus's expense than they are with his mother; but, as I pointed out in my preface to "The Humour of Homer,"[1] this mixture of perfect lover and perfect sponger is so impossible that no one would have recourse to it unless aware that he or she was in extreme difficulty. If men are in love they will not sponge, and if they sponge they are not in love; we may take it either way, but not both. When, therefore, the writer of the Odyssey not only attributes such impossible conduct to the suitors, but also wants us to believe that a clever woman could not get at any rate some few of her hundred lovers out of her house, though she did her very utmost to do so for many years, we may know that we are being hoodwinked as far as the writer can hoodwink us, and will conclude that the suitors were not so black, nor Penelope so white, as we are given to understand. We see also that the writer who tells us such a story with a grave face can know nothing of what men feel towards women, and not much of what women commonly feel towards men. We conclude her, therefore, to be as yet very young and un-

[1] [See p. 238, *ante*.]

married. At any rate, if it was an old man who wrote all this it must have been one who had either known less in his youth or forgotten more in his old age than the writer of the Iliad is at all likely to have done. If he remembered enough to be able to write the Odyssey he would have remembered more than he has.

We have above seen the story as told from Penelope's point of view. Let us now hear what the suitors urged when put upon their defence. We find this in Book ii, where Telemachus convenes the people of Ithaca and gives the suitors formal notice to go. He states his case. Two great misfortunes have fallen upon his house. The first of these is the loss of his excellent father: the second, which he says is "much more serious," is that the suitors are playing ducks and drakes with his estate. And the worst of it is, he continues, that they are all young men without means, so that there is nothing to be got by suing them. They would not be worth powder and shot. If he is to be eaten out of house and home at all he would rather their fathers did it, for in this case if he got judgement, there would be some chance of seeing his money, whereas he is now practically without a remedy.

To this Antinous, the leading suitor, replies that it is all Penelope's own doing. She is an incorrigible flirt. For years past she has been encouraging every single one of them, and sending him flattering messages without meaning one word of what she says. And then he adds: "There was that other trick she played on us. She set up a great tambour-frame in her room and began to work on an enormous piece of fine needlework. 'Sweethearts,' said she, 'I know my poor husband is dead and gone; still, I hope you will not press me to marry again immediately. I wish to leave behind me some monumental record of my skill in embroidery, and propose making a pall for the funeral of my father-in-law, Laertes. He will die some day, and the women of the place will gossip about me if so rich a man is buried without a pall.' On this she set to work, and we could see her keeping

Was the Odyssey written by a Woman?

to it all day long, but at night she used to pick it out again by torchlight. She fooled us in this way for over three years; but in the fourth, one of her women, who knew what she was doing, told us all about it, so we caught her, and she had to finish it whether she would or no."

Antinous continues that the suitors refuse to be plagued any longer with the airs she gives herself on the score of the accomplishments Minerva has taught her, and because she is so clever. " We never yet heard," he concludes, " of any such woman as she is. We know all about Tyro, Alcmena, Mycene, and the famous women of old, but they were a mere nothing to your mother—any one of them. It was not right of her to treat us in that way, and as long as she continues in her present mind, so long shall we continue to eat you out of house and home; and I do not see why she should change, for she gets all the honour and glory, and it is you, not she, that pays. As for us we will not go about our business, nor elsewhere, until she has made her choice and married somebody."

Roughly, then, the authoress's version is that Penelope is an injured innocent, and the suitors' that she is a heartless flirt, who likes a hundred lovers better than one husband. Which comes nearest—not to the truth, for we may be sure the suitors could have said a great deal more than the writer chooses to say they said—but to the original story which she was sophisticating and retelling in her own way?

We cannot forget that when Telemachus first told Minerva about the suitors he admitted that his mother had not point blank refused at once (i, 245-251). " She does not," he says, " refuse the hateful marriage." Hateful to whom? Not to Telemachus, unless here as elsewhere he is affecting a dislike to his mother's marriage which he is far from feeling. At times, indeed, he does profess unbounded indignation at the idea of his mother's marrying again, but from other passages it is clear that he would have been only too thankful to get her out of the house if she would go of her own accord. He would not insist on her doing so, partly because, as he tells the suitors, it would come hard upon him to have to repay to his grandfather, Icarius, the dowry that Ulysses had had when he married Penelope, and partly because he was afraid of the Furies and of men's evil speeches (ii, 130-136); but Penelope herself says that he was continually urging her to marry and go, on the score of the expense he was incurring through the protracted attentions that were being paid to her (xix, 530-534). We must conclude, therefore, that Telemachus intends the word " hateful " to apply to his mother, not to himself; nevertheless, he continues, " Nor does she bring the matter to an end." Apparently not, but if not, why not? Not to refuse at once is to court courtship, and if she had not meant to court it she would have soon found some means of bringing the matter to an end. Did she ever try snubbing? Nothing of the kind is placed on record. Did she ever say, " Well, Antinous, whoever else I may marry, you may make your mind quite easy that it will not be you "? Then there was boring—did she never try that? Did she never read them any of her own poetry, or some of the beautiful themes she had written when at the College which was attached to the Temple of Minerva? Did she sing them her own songs, or play them music of her own composition? I have always found this successful when I wanted to get rid of people. There are, indeed, signs as though something had been done in this direction, for the suitors say they cannot stand her high-art nonsense and aesthetic rhodomontade any longer, but it is more likely she had been trying to attract than to repel. Did she ever set them by the ears by repeating, with due embellishment, what they had said to her about one another? Did she insist that they should attend family prayers and go to church on Sundays? Did she ever ask Antinous or Eurymachus to sit to her for the web, give them a good stiff pose, and make them stick to it? Did she find errands for them to run, and then scold them, or say she did not want them? Or make them do commissions for her, and forget to pay them? Or keep on sending them back to the shop to change

Was the Odyssey written by a Woman?

things, and they had given ever so much too much money, and she wished she had gone and done it herself? In a word did she ever do a single one of the thousand things so clever a matron would have been at no loss to hit upon if she had been in earnest about not wishing to be courted?

Telemachus in his rejoinder to the suitors does not so much as hint that his mother had taken any of the infinite courses that were open to her. He denies none of their facts. He never says that Penelope had not encouraged them by sending them, man by man, messages to raise their hopes, nor does he attempt to explain his mother's conduct about the web. This, then, being admitted, and it being also transparent that Penelope had used no due diligence in getting rid of the suitors, can we avoid suspecting that there is a screw loose somewhere, and that some story of a very different character is being manipulated to meet the exigencies of the writer? And shall we be so very far wrong if we conclude that according to the original version Penelope picked out her web not so much in order to delay the marriage as to prolong the courtship?

It was no doubt because Laertes saw what was going on that he went to live in the country, as we are told in Book i, and Penelope probably chose the particular form her work assumed in order to get him out of the house the quicker. Why could she not have set about making a pall for somebody else? No wonder the poor old gentleman never came to town now. As for his being so very badly off as we are given to understand he was in the eleventh book, there is not one grain of truth in that story. The writer had to make him out poor in order to explain his not having interfered to protect Penelope; but Penelope's own excuse for making her web was that he was a man of large property and ought to have a large shroud. It is just the same with the suitors. When they are wanted to be poor they are so very, very poor that it would not be of the smallest use for Telemachus to go to law with them; but when it is desired that Penelope should show her astuteness by getting presents out of them, just before Ulysses kills them, they have any amount of money. I do not for a moment imply that this determination to have things both ways—which, if time allowed, I could abundantly illustrate from the Odyssey—is any argument in favour of the writer's having been a woman; nothing could be farther from my thoughts; but I do claim it as showing that the writer knew she was in a mess, and was not going to stick at trifles when she meant having her own way.

She never does stick at trifles, and I cannot think that she cared two straws whether she was in a mess or no. There the thing was and the reader might take it or leave it. From first to last she shows herself fond of flimsy disguises and of mystifications that stultify themselves and mystify nobody. She obviously intends her disguises to be thin, and repeatedly seems to take a kind of art-for-art's-sake pleasure in a literary falsehood. To go no further than Books i and iii, Minerva in each of these tells plausible circumstantial stories about herself without one grain of truth in them, and then, before the lies she had been at such pains to concoct were well out of her mouth, reveals herself by flying off into the air in the form of an eagle. There is a flavour of consecutive fifths [1] about these flights, and I cannot but think the authoress would have found a smoother progression open to her if she had been at much trouble in looking out for one; but however this may be, nothing has more tended to convince me of the homogeneousness of the work—and, let me add, of the instinctive truthfulness of the writer—than the way in which white lies pervade it from first to last, coupled with a not less omnipresent insistence on the punctilious performance of all religious observances.

To let this pass, however, Laertes must have had money or how could Ulysses have been so rich himself? He left for Troy when he was very young, and could not have made much money before he went. He certainly sent nothing back from Troy, and though he seems to have had a dowry

[1] In music it is forbidden to have consecutive fifths between the same parts.

Was the Odyssey written by a Woman?

of some kind with Penelope, the greater part of his enormous wealth must have been given him by his father who, we may be sure, kept more for himself than he gave his son. What, then, had become of all this vast property—unless, indeed, it had gone in paying Penelope's debts? But as a matter of fact it had not gone at all, and Laertes never came near his daughter-in-law now, not because he was poor, but because the writer did not know how to explain his non-interference unless on some pretext or another she got him away from the town.

The account, again, which Ulysses' mother in Hades gives him of affairs in Ithaca shows a sense that there is something to be concealed. She says nothing about the suitors. All she says is that Telemachus has to see a good deal of company, but she supposes he cannot well help it as he is asked out everywhere himself. Nothing can be more coldly euphemistic nor show fuller knowledge that there was a good deal more going on than the speaker chose to say. If Anticlea had believed her daughter-in-law innocent she would have laid the whole situation before Ulysses, and implored him to get home as fast as ever he could. It may, indeed, be maintained that the suitors were not yet come to Ithaca in force, for the visit to Hades came early in the wanderings of Ulysses and before his seven years in the island of Calypso; but in this case Telemachus could at the utmost be only twelve or thirteen years old, and a children's party would be all the entertainment he need either give or receive. It is plain that the writer has made a slip in her chronology, for throughout the poem Telemachus is only just arriving at man's estate in the twentieth year of Ulysses' absence from home; the writer, therefore, has in her mind the state of things existing just before Ulysses returned, and has forgotten that she is making it out to have happened some seven years too soon. This is even more evident lower down when Agamemnon says that Telemachus, who was a baby in arms at the beginning of the Trojan war, must have now reached man's estate (xi, 449). The suitors had been at the castle several years before Telemachus was old enough to entertain. They were there, as Telemachus himself tells us, while he was himself but a child. The silence, therefore, of Ulysses' mother is wilful, and is irreconcilable with the facts as conveyed to us in Books i-iv and xiii-xxiv. I can only explain it by supposing, as I have already said, that at the time Book xi was written the intention still was, neither to whitewash Penelope nor to kill the suitors, but to ignore these last altogether, and to say as little as possible about Penelope herself.

Minerva, indeed, with quick womanly instinct, took in the situation at a glance and goes straight to the point. "If your mother's mind," she says (i, 275), "is set on marrying again," and this implies that the speaker had no doubt that it was so set, "send her back to her father who will find her both husband and dowry." From which we infer Minerva's opinion to have been not only, as I have said, that Penelope did mean marrying again, but also that she meant to take her time about the courtship, and was not likely to be brought to the point by any measure less decisive than sending her back to live with her father.

We know, moreover, what Minerva thought of Penelope from another source. Minerva appears to Telemachus in a dream at the beginning of Book xv, when he is staying with King Menelaus, and gives him to understand that his mother is on the point of marrying Eurymachus, one of the suitors—which, by the way, we are intended to suppose was a wanton and unjustifiable falsehood on Minerva's part. Nevertheless, if the matter had rested there nothing probably would have pleased Telemachus better, but Minerva adds that in this case Penelope will probably steal some of his family plate. "You know," she exclaims, "what women are; they always want to do the best they can for the man who is married to them at the moment; they forget all about their former husband and the children that they had by him. Go home, therefore, at once and put every thing in charge of the most respectable housekeeper you can find until it shall please heaven to send you a wife of your own."

Was the Odyssey written by a Woman?

This passage not only betrays a want of confidence in Penelope that is out of keeping with her ostensible antecedents, but it goes far to show that Minerva, or rather the authoress, had read the Cypria in which poem (now lost) we know that Helen did exactly what is here represented as likely to be done by Penelope; and I may also say in passing that it helps those who, like myself, insist on the unity of the poem, by showing a few lines lower down that the writer of Book xv knows neither more nor less about Ionian topography than the writer of Book iv does, inasmuch as both suppose that Telemachus on his way home to Ithaca from Pylos would pass through the strait between Ithaca and Same, which he would not have done.

Returning, however, to the libellous dream sent by Minerva to Telemachus, if Penelope's antecedents had been such as the writer wishes us to accept, Telemachus would have exclaimed: "My dear Minerva, what a word has escaped the boundary of your teeth. My mother steal the plate, and go off with an unprincipled scoundrel like Eurymachus? Monstrous! She is the last woman in the whole world to do anything of the kind." And then he should wake up as from a hideous dream. But what happens in reality? Telemachus does indeed wake up in great distress of mind, but it is about the plate and not about his mother. "Who steals my mother steals trash, but whoso filches from me my family plate, etc." He kicks poor Pisistratus, who was in bed with him, to wake him up, and says they must harness the horses and be off home at once. Pisistratus remonstrates and says it is pitch dark—plate or no plate they really must wait till morning. Besides they ought to say good-bye to Menelaus, and get a present out of him—he will be sure to give them one if Telemachus will only not be in such an unconscionable hurry. Can anything show more decisively what was the writer's inner mind about Penelope, or at any rate that such conduct would be consistent with the ideas the audience had formed about her?

I may remark that Minerva and Telemachus regard the

stealing from two different points of view. Telemachus regards it in so far as it affects himself; Minerva takes it much more as a matter of course—but then the plate was not hers. The authoress of the Odyssey is never very severe against mere theft. It was not nice of Penelope to want to marry again—still she had a right to please herself—and so long as she was *bona fide* going to be married she might steal as much plate as she pleased without loss of dignity or character. It would be Telemachus's affair, not hers. This, indeed, is what Telemachus himself seems rather to feel, and hence no doubt his eagerness to be off without the delay of a moment. Nor can we forget that Penelope in Book xviii is made to think it perfectly right to get as many presents as she can out of the suitors and to be delighted with the gifts though detesting the givers. The mere stealing, of course, is part and parcel of the times, and has nothing to do with the question of the writer's sex; still there is sense of enjoyment on the writer's part at the way in which Penelope gets the presents, which I confess suggests to me the hand of one who looked on men as fair game—and this, man seldom or never does when it is himself that pays.

But throughout the poem the author shows herself keenly alive to the value of money. Tears, money, and religion dominate it from the first page to the last. If she has for a time been profuse of splendour, as she sometimes is, she soon gets tired of it. Even on such a grand occasion as the weddings of Hermione and Megapenthes[1] a couple of mountebanks and a man to play the lyre seem to have been all the professional talent engaged, and by Book xv the writer's nerve has failed her and the gorgeousness of King Menelaus's establishment has collapsed. In that Book Menelaus insists that Telemachus and Pisistratus shall have something to eat before they start on their homeward journey. The king explains that they will have to take pot-luck,

[1] True, Book ii, lines 3-21 are, beyond all question, interpolated after the work had been perhaps for some time completed, but I can hardly doubt that it was the authoress herself who interpolated them.

Was the Odyssey written by a Woman?

but says he will tell the women to see that there is enough for them " of what there may be in the house." This is just like Menelaus's (or Alcinous's, for, as I have explained, they are the same person) usual fussiness. Why could he not leave it all to Helen? Helen said patronizingly of him in Book iv that he was really not deficient in person or understanding, but after reading Books iv and xv it is not easy to agree with her; one can quite understand her having run away with Paris, and the only wonder was that a second war on Helen's account did not become necessary after she had been got back safely to Lacedaemon. We learn from the Iliad (vii, 467-469) that Menelaus and Agamemnon had been in the wine trade. There is a frank *bourgeoisie* about him in the Odyssey which confirms this. Surely the fact that two young bachelors were staying to lunch was not such a frightful discord but it might have been taken unprepared! " Of what there may be in the house," indeed! If there did not happen to be anything good in the house at the moment, Menelaus might have sent out and got something before lunch time. But there ought to have been no sending out about it. Menelaus and Helen ought never to have had a meal without celery salt, tarragon butter, and all the rest of it.

What a come-down, again, do we not find as regards the butler Eteoneus! He was not a real butler at all; he was only a kind of char-butler, he did not sleep in the house (xv, 96), and for aught we know his wife may have kept a greengrocer's shop round the corner. Worse than this, he had no footman—not even a boy—under him, for Menelaus tells him to light the fire and set about cooking dinner (xv, 96, 97), and he does so as a matter of course without one word of remonstrance. Is it possible not to be reminded of a certain memorable " swarry " at Bath some sixty years ago? What has become of Asphalion? What of Adraste, Alcippe, and Phylo? What of all the numerous servants, both men and women, who waited on Telemachus and Pisistratus in Book iv? Books iv and xv are separated in point of time by a very few days, yet in the last-named book we have only this one melancholy char-butler, who is kitchen-maid, cook, and parlour-maid all in one. Telemachus and Pisistratus have to yoke their horses themselves. The stock upper and under female servants who do duty at all Odyssean meals are turned on as usual, but there are none others. True, we are told in lines 3-19 of Book iv that there were great festivities when Telemachus and Pisistratus first reached Menelaus's palace, but there is not a trace of these festivities in the three hundred lines that follow the announcement that they were going on, and the context proves that there were no festivities at all; in fact, it is obvious that the lines just referred to are an afterthought inserted to explain the non-appearance of Hermione in Book xv. Having, however, married Hermione, the writer cannot keep her hands off poor Megapenthes, so he has to be married at the same time with his sister; nevertheless, when we meet him again a fortnight later there is no sign of the existence of the lady who had been sent for, for him, from Sparta—to Lacedaemon! Dr. Butler had not, indeed, as yet written his *Ancient Geography*, so the writer may be excused for supposing that Sparta and Lacedaemon were two different places; still, I think that if Megapenthes had been really as much married as we are told he was in Book iv the bride would not have dropped out so completely as she has done in Book xv.

When Menelaus has invited his guests to a lunch which we can see is going to be scrappy, he points out to them that it will not only be more comfortable for them and more becoming on every ground that they should stay, but that it will also be cheaper for them to have their dinner with him (xv, 77, 78) before they start than to get it on the road later on. "And if," he continues, "you have a fancy for taking a trip in Hellas or Middle Argos, wait till I can yoke my horses and I will personally conduct you through all our principal cities. No one will send us away empty-handed; everyone will make us a present of some kind—a copper-stand, or a copper, or a couple of mules, or a gold cup" (xv, 80-85).

Was the Odyssey written by a Woman?

And what again, is meant by calling the Peloponnese "Middle Argos"? Middle between what and what? Is it possible that it means the Peloponnese that lies between the two great Greek-speaking countries of Asia Minor on the one hand, and Italy (with Sicily) on the other? By the time, however, that the Odyssey was written it would seem as though the old Greek-speaking Pelasgi were being already ousted from Italy, for the people of Tmesa, on the toe of Italy, are described as speaking a non-Greek language.

As I have touched upon the visit of Telemachus to King Menelaus, let me point out, without, however, for a moment suggesting that it is an argument in favour of female authorship, the very singular nature of the arrangements made by Minerva for her *protégé* in respect of his whole voyage to Pylos and Lacedaemon. When she first suggested it to him, she knew that Mercury had been sent to Calypso to insist on her letting Ulysses come home at once. It was on her own urgent suit to Jove that he had been so sent; she perfectly well knew, therefore, that Ulysses would be back in Ithaca almost immediately, yet she must needs choose this particular moment of all others for despatching Telemachus on a long voyage in quest of him. She preaches to him on the seashore about his duty in a style with which every young person who has ever had a grandmother or a maiden aunt must be perfectly familiar, and which has earned for poor Mentor (whose shape she had assumed) a certain grandmotherly reputation which he can never hope to lose. She tells Telemachus how very careful he ought to be, and how unlikely it is that he will ever be so good a man as his father. Sons, she says, next to never are, though she does not seem to think that daughters may not make as good women as their mothers were; nevertheless, she concludes, that as he does not seem to be without some share of his father's good sense there is yet a chance of his succeeding in the search which he is about to undertake—a search which his counsellor was stultifying and frustrating to the utmost of her power. Besides, he was to be away, if necessary, for a twelvemonth;

yet here, before he has been gone three weeks, she fills him with an agony of apprehension about the plate, and sends him back post-haste to Ithaca. No doubt the trip had been a very pleasant change for him, and he had got some presents; but nothing could be more fruitless as far as news of his father was concerned, and Ulysses actually returned before his son did.

The authoress herself seems to have felt the force of what I have just been saying, for at the end of Book xiii she makes Ulysses remonstrate with Minerva in this very sense. He complains of her having let Telemachus go. "Why," he says, " did you not tell him that I was coming back, for you knew all about it? Did you want him, too, to suffer all kinds of hardship upon the sea, while people here were eating up his estate?" "Never mind him," replied Minerva, " I sent him that he might get himself a good name by having gone there. He is taking no sort of harm, but is quite comfortable with Menelaus, and is surrounded by abundance of every kind." Of course, what she ought to have said was, " How, you stupid man, can you ask me such a question? Can you not see that I sent him because my authoress had set her heart on getting Helen of Troy into her poem, and did not know how to do it without sending Telemachus to Sparta?"

In another place Penelope herself shows a like tendency to remonstrate against the manner in which Minerva keeps back information which she could have imparted if she chose. The goddess disguised as Penelope's sister Iphthime has come to her bedside and told her that her son Telemachus shall come safely home again. " If then," exclaims Penelope, " you are a goddess, or have heard news from heaven, tell me about that other poor fellow. Is he dead? or is he still living?" Whereon Minerva says that the conversation must close at once, and vanishes through the latch hole of the door.

Now, however, time is beginning to press. I have dwelt so long with the question whether or no the writer was trying to put a face more honourable to her sex on certain

Was the Odyssey written by a Woman?

gross man's stories that were current in her own day about Penelope, because I believe that an affirmative answer to this question, when coupled with the predominance of woman throughout the poem, goes far to warrant the presumption that the writer was herself a woman. Assuredly there is nothing to show that the writer was a man, and as the work must have been written either by a man or by a woman, we are left to decide the sex of the writer by the internal evidence only. But surely this ought to be sufficient. The problem whether a literary work is by a man or by a woman is one which our reviewers set themselves without hesitation week by week—indeed, it is generally the first question they ask themselves about any anonymous book that is presented to them—and they seldom fail to answer it correctly. For myself, I have explained that I approached the Odyssey with so strong a preconception in favour of its having been written by a man, that it took me some months to see how hopelessly impossible this opinion in reality is. I did not seek the conclusion I arrived at, but was driven to it in spite of all the obstacles that my own stupidity could raise.

I am aware that the view I have taken represents the authoress as a very phenomenal person, but surely the Odyssey is a very phenomenal work. There is none more so in the whole range of literature, and nothing but a phenomenal person can explain many of the anomalies with which it abounds. When the phenomenal person happens to be a young woman, there is no knowing what she will or will not do till she has actually done it; but no such masterpiece as the Odyssey could have been written in imitation of the Iliad or the other poems of the Epic Cycle. The Odyssey, like all other living works, has a deep undercurrent of melancholy. He who does not feel this may as well put the poem down, for it does not speak to him. If a work is to live the ink in which it is written must be enriched and vivified with the tears and life's blood of the writer, though he or she, perhaps, hardly knows it and will certainly do his or her utmost to conceal the fact. I do not mean to say that the authoress was always, or even generally, unhappy; she was often, at any rate let us hope so, supremely happy. Nevertheless, there is throughout her work a sense as though the world with all its joyousness was yet more or less out of joint, an inarticulate, indefinable pathos which, even when for a time lost sight of, soon reasserts itself. Now that I know the poem to have been written by a woman I am ashamed of myself for not having been guided to my conclusion by the recognition of its exquisitely subtle tenderness rather than by the considerations that actually led me to it.

And what, let me ask, have those who oppose my view got to say against it? I shall be very glad to take notes of anything that any of you may be good enough to urge, but I have so far seen nothing brought forward that deserves the name of argument. The few experts with whom I am acquainted show themselves mysterious and give me to understand that they could easily demolish me if they chose to try, but they have none of them shown any indecent haste in trying, and I should be sorry to think that I could have done more to provoke them than I have done. It has been my endeavour to challenge them as directly as possible, and if any of you are kind enough to take an interest in the question, let me beg you either to join issue with me yourselves or to persuade somebody else to do so in such manner as I can properly reply to. The only approach to argument with which my academic friends have met me, beyond the more ordinary " I smell heresy," is in the matter of the death of the suitors; they say that no woman could have written the scene in which Ulysses takes his revenge. I cannot see this; for the whole scene, except the delightful episode in which Ulysses spares the lives of Phemius and of Medon, consists of little else than, " And then Ulysses killed so and so." A woman can kill a man on paper as well as a man can, and this scene, I confess, appears to me the most mechanical and least satisfactory in the whole poem. The real obstacle, however, to a general belief that the Odyssey was written by a woman is not anything that can be found

Was the Odyssey written by a Woman?

in the poem itself, but the long prevalence of an opinion that the Odyssey was written by the same person who wrote the Iliad. The age and respectability of this opinion has engendered a certain invincible scholasticism that prevents us from being able to take in what we should see at a glance, if we would only remember how much so-called Homeric critics have misled us in the past. If people would read the poem slowly, intelligently, and without commentary, forgetting all past criticism until they have looked at the matter with their own eyes, I cannot think they would have much doubt that they were reading a woman's masterpiece, not a man's.

This, however, is not an easy thing to do. I know very well that I should never have done it myself if I had not passed some five-and-thirty rebellious years without giving the Odyssey so much as a thought. The poem is so august, it is hallowed by the well deserved veneration of so many ages; it is like the work called " La Musa " in the Museum at Cortona, so mysterious as well as so divinely lovely; it has been so long associated with the epic poem that stands supreme, for if the Iliad is the Mont Blanc of ancient literature the Odyssey is assuredly its Monte Rosa—who can lightly vivisect a work of such ineffable prestige, as though it were an overlooked *parvenu* book picked up for fourpence at a second-hand bookstall? Lightly, no; but inflexibly, yes, if its natural health and beauty are to be restored by doing so. One of our most accomplished living scholars a few months ago chided with me for reading the Odyssey as it seemed to him too ruthlessly. " I confess," he said to me, " I do not give much thought to all these details. I read the poem not to theorize about it, but to revel in its amazing beauty." It would shock me to think I had done anything to impair his sense of that beauty, which I trust I share in even measure with himself; but surely if the Odyssey has charmed us as a man's work, the charm and wonder of it are infinitely increased when we see it as a woman's.

Still more must it charm us when we find we have long

known and loved the writer herself, and see so considerable a part of the Odyssey as a reflection of her own surroundings. This, however, is not argument, and my present business is rather to clear away the cobwebs of criticism than to dwell on the beauty of the work itself. I have shown you that in the earliest known ages of Greek literature poetesses abounded and gained a very high reputation. I have shown you that by universal consent the domestic and female interest of the poem predominates over the male. I have shown that the writer was one extremely jealous for the honour of woman, so much so as to be daunted by no impossibilities when trying to get rid of a story that she considered to be an insult to her sex. Is it much to ask you to believe that, these things being so, we should accept the poem, not as written by a man for women, but as written for both men and women by one who was herself a woman?

THE "WORKS AND DAYS" OF HESIOD TRANSLATED

NOTE

THIS TRANSLATION IS A BY-PRODUCT OF Butler's work on the Odyssey and the Iliad. The following passage about it occurs in the postscript, dated 27th May 1919, to the Preface of *Samuel Butler: A Memoir* (pp. xiv*b, c*):

" It is stated in chapter 43 (ii, 434) that Butler's translation of Hesiod's *Works and Days* has not yet been published. This is still the fact, but I ought to add that in 1912, or thereabouts, the London County Council Technical Schools applied for permission to print Butler's ' Seven Sonnets and a Psalm of Montreal,' which Streatfeild had had privately printed. They only proposed to use Butler's work as material for printing lessons, not to publish the result; but Streatfeild and I did not wish the sonnets to be printed under any other authority than his or mine just at that moment, because they were to be included in *The Note-Books of Samuel Butler*, then about to be published. But he offered them Butler's translation of the *Works and Days*, and handed them a copy of it which he made in his own handwriting. They began to print it, and in April 1919 the secretary showed me what progress had been made and told me he hoped the work would soon be completed. It is not to be published by them; they propose to turn out only a few copies and they are not to be for sale."

When they had printed it the Technical Schools used Butler's work also as a lesson in bookbinding; and in June 1924 I received from them a copy of the translation beautifully printed and bound in whole Niger morocco, with a note at the end saying, among other things:

" The production of this book has been hindered by War and post-War conditions; it is due to the efforts of the Principal, F. V. Burridge, that book-work is again possible in the school. Finished April 1924."

Butler's original MS. and also the copy made by Streatfeild are now in my possession.

For the purpose of the translation here printed Butler's MS. was submitted to Mr. Donald S. Robertson, Fellow of

Trinity College, Cambridge, son of Butler's old friend and fellow art-student, Mr. H. R. Robertson. He has very kindly been through it and made corrections and alterations, suggested to him by his classical learning, as he did with Butler's translations of the Iliad and the Odyssey. The editors offer him their cordial thanks for the skill and knowledge which he has expended upon the work.

In the *Memoir* (ii, 363) is reproduced a letter written by Butler to my sister Lilian, 9th January 1902, wherein he says that he has been editing my letters to him.

"If he has any of mine, and if they contain as much treasonable matter as his to me, I trust he will allow me, when he gets better, to edit them by writing over those parts that give my true opinion of those most near and dear to me as follows:

"'Hail, holy Light, offspring of Heaven first-born!
Or of the Eternal co-eternal beam
May I express thee unblamed? Since God is light,
And never but in unapproached light
Dwelt from eternity,' etc.—

lines which, I take it, no one will credit me with knowing, and which assuredly I should not know if I had not had to write them and the next forty-five and a half lines of the third book of *Paradise Lost* many a hundred times over when I was a boy at school."

And in his next letter to my sister, writing again of my letters, he says: "Treated with a moderate application of 'Hail, holy Light,' etc., they are quite safe—in all cases of doubt I apply the Milton."

There are two passages in the *Works and Days* which Butler hoped to make "safe" by treating them also with a moderate application of the Milton. Streatfeild, in his copy, left them blank and the Technical Schools filled up the blanks by inserting the original Greek. The ingenious Donald Robertson found that Butler's *lucus-a-non-lucendo*

The "Works and Days" of Hesiod

method had failed to make these passages so "safe" that their obscurity was impenetrable. Also he and we came to the conclusion that many things which might properly have been considered risky more than a quarter of a century ago, when Butler wrote, and even so recently as just before the War, when Streatfeild copied, are not in these modern days, open to objection. The passages (lines 727 to 737 and lines 757 to 759) are therefore here printed as Butler originally wrote them.

This version differs from Streatfeild's copy in several other small particulars; the most interesting to the general reader will probably be that on p. 323. Here Butler wrote and the Technical Schools have printed: "The wheel for a plough-carriage should be three spans across, if the carriage be ten palms long." This in our version appears thus: "The wheel for a waggon should be three spans across, if the waggon be ten palms long." In a letter, about his having made as few alterations as possible, Mr. Robertson wrote: "I felt that I must alter the 'plough-wheel' business. Wheeled ploughs were a novelty in Pliny's time, and it is absolutely certain that Hesiod's plough had no wheel. Of course, the meaning of *all* the technical terms in these passages is very disputable. On the other hand, Butler certainly *meant what he wrote*, and if you think it should be kept, I daresay you are right."

It is also interesting to know that between lines 564 and 571 Butler's MS. reads: "the star Arcturus leaves the streams of Ocean and begins to show brightly in the twilight. Next after him the swallow, plaintive daughter of Pandion, will rise and show her light to mortals at the very beginning of spring." On this Donald Robertson wrote: "It looks as though he thought (wrongly) that the swallow was a constellation. Of course it refers to the coming of the bird. The Greek is ambiguous, but could not have misled a Greek reader. It means literally: 'And after him the swallow . . . appears into light for men.'" And this view of the meaning has been preserved in the translation we are printing.

Collected Essays

Donald Robertson was particularly pleased with Butler's mistaking the bird for the constellation because it seemed to justify his boast " that he resembled the Emperor Marcus Aurelius Antoninus in that he was thankful to say he had never troubled himself about the appearance of things in the heavens " (*Memoir*, i, 282). He used to say that he knew the sun and the moon and there his astronomy ended.

H.F.J.

The "Works and Days" of Hesiod

O MUSES, YOU WHO FROM PIERIA NOISE forth great deeds in song, hymn to me Jove your father through whom are all men, famous and unknown alike. At will he can strengthen and at will he can subdue the strong; at will he can put down the proud and set up the man of low degree; at will he can make the crooked straight and chastise the overbearing—even he, Jove, the Lord of thunder, whose mansion is in the highest. Hear me, then, thou; behold, understand, and give righteous judgement; now, therefore, O Perses, I will speak words of truth.

There are two kinds of strife on earth, the one praiseworthy, and the other not to be commended. They are quite different; the one breeds wicked wars and discord—this is the bad one; men do not love it, nevertheless they give it honour as perforce and by the will of heaven; the other, which is far better, was elder born out of the womb of night, and Jove who dwells on high stablished it in the roots of earth and among men. This kind of strife will set even the idle man a-working, for on seeing a rich man he makes haste to plough and plant and put his house in order; thus neighbour strives with neighbour in the race for riches, and the striving is good. So again potter vies with potter, builder with builder, beggar with beggar, and bard with bard.

Lay, then, these things to heart, O Perses, lest the mischief-making kind of strife keep you from work and set you hanging about places of assembly and listening to law suits. A man can have little time for suits and meetings unless he has laid by a yearly seasonable store of the grain which Ceres grows out of the ground. If he is a man of substance he may foment wrangling and contention about other people's property, but you will have no chance of being able to do this henceforward; let us then settle matters between us with that righteousness which is the best gift of heaven. We have already divided our heritage, and you took much more than your share, for you bribed the judges largely and they gave you judgement accordingly—fools for not knowing how much greater the half is than the whole, and how much content a dinner of herbs may offer.¹

42 The gods have hidden the ways of money from mankind; otherwise you might get enough in a day to keep you idle for a twelvemonth. You might hang up your rudder in the chimney corner, and it would be lost labour to plough with oxen or mules. Jove concealed this knowledge from us because Prometheus had overreached him and in punishment he hid fire from mankind; but the noble son of Iapetus outwitted him, and stole it back for us in a hollow fennel stalk, whereon Jove spoke to him in anger saying:

54 "Son of Iapetus, excellent in all cunning, you are proud of having stolen fire and beguiled me, but bitterly shall you rue it—you and all future generations; I will give them for their fire a foe which all men shall be fain to hug to their own hearts."

59 The sire of gods and men laughed out as he spoke, and at once bade the famed workman Vulcan mix earth and water, fashioning it with human strength and speech into the likeness of a maiden, fair as the gods to see. He bade Minerva teach her to work and weave, and golden Venus to give her a face that should set men wasting with desire, and he bade Mercury, guide of the dead, endow her with a shifty shameless soul.

69 Thus did he command, and they obeyed. Famed Vulcan kneaded earth as Jove had bidden him into the likeness of a modest maiden, Minerva girded and arranged her; the Graces and the great goddess Winsome hung golden chains

75 about her neck, while the Hours so sweet and fair decked her with garlands of spring flowers. Then the slayer of Argus, guardian of the dead, filled her with lies and shiftiness and cunning, according to the counsel of Jove; and the herald of the gods endowed her with the power of speech, calling her by name Pandora, because all the gods in Olympus had given her some gift that should be the bane of man.

83 When he had finished this piece of sheer and unutterable falsehood Jove sent the famed slayer of Argus, messenger of

¹ Literally, "What a boon there is in mallow and asphodel."

The "Works and Days" of Hesiod

the gods, to take her to Epimetheus, and Epimetheus forgot how Prometheus had warned him never to accept any gift from Jove, but to send it back lest it should be something that might bane mankind, so he took it to his much ruing.

Now the men of old dwelt on earth free from all ill and without either war or diseases such as kill men nowadays (for men age fast when they are in trouble) but the woman lifted the lid from the jar in which all the ills were kept, and let them fly forth, thus bringing toil and trouble upon mankind. Hope alone did not break out, and remained shut up inside the jar—for such was the counsel of Jove—but thousands of other ills are going about among us, and both earth and sea are full of them. Disease haunts us night and day unbidden, baning us without saying a word, for Jove has robbed it of the power of speech, and when Jove wills a thing there is no help for it.

And now if you will listen I will touch well and truly on another matter which I would have you mark, for it shows how gods and men spring from one common source.

In the beginning the gods who dwell in heaven made the men of the golden age. These were they who lived in the time of Saturn when he was king of heaven; they were as happy as the gods, and as free from all care or sickness; cruel age had no power against them, but sound in hand and foot alike at all times they held high feast untouched by any kind of harm. When they died they fell, as it were, asleep; all good things were theirs, the earth yielded them its fruits unbidden, without stint or grudge, and at their own will and pleasure they held their lands and other goods, being rich also in sheep; for they were dear to the immortal gods. Now that they are dead and underground, Jove has ordained that they should become good spirits, haunting the earth as guardians of mortal men, noting good and evil, and going everywhere about the world cloaked in a cloud that hides them—and they bring good fortune with them. Such, then, is their royal office.

The gods who dwell in heaven then made the men of the silver age, who were like those of the golden neither in person nor understanding. The mothers of that age kept their children at home for a hundred years, they being still mere infants; but when they were grown up and had reached their full stature they did not live long, and suffered much, mainly through their own folly. For they laid violent hands upon one another, neither would they serve the gods, nor do sacrifice upon their holy altars, as men should do according to the custom of their country; Jove, therefore, was angry and made away with them because they would not give due honour to the blessed gods that hold Olympus. When this race also had passed away to their dwelling under the earth they took rank as mortals blessed in the second degree, and are held in not a little honour.

143 Father Jove then made a third race—the men of bronze—nothing like the men of the silver age, but redoubtable spearmen and given to war and lawlessness. They did not eat bread and had hearts as hard as adamant, so that none dared go near them; they were men of prodigious strength with huge arms growing from their shoulders and the mighty framework of their bodies. The armour of these men was of bronze, so also were their houses; the tools, moreover, with which they worked were of bronze, for as yet there was no iron. These men fell by one another's hands and went down into the chill house of Hades leaving no name behind them. Mighty though they were dark death laid hold upon them and they looked upon the sun's light no longer.

156 When this race, too, was dead and underground, Jove sent yet a fourth into the world, a better and a juster people; these were the mighty heroes whom our fathers reckoned as demigods over the whole earth, these fell in battle amid the din of war, some before seven-gated Thebes the land of Cadmus, fighting for the flocks of Oedipus, while others set sail over the sea and fell before Troy in the quarrel about lovely Helen.[1] So they, too, came to an end and died, but

[1] It is plain, therefore, that to Hesiod the Trojan war was a matter of very ancient history.

The "Works and Days" of Hesiod

father Jove ſtablished them apart at the World's end, with goods and government, far away from the immortals; and Saturn reigns over them. They live as happy heroes, free from all care in the Islands of the Bleſt by the deep flowing waters of Oceanus, and three times a year does the bounteous earth yield them her abundant fruits.

Would that it had been my lot not to be of the fifth race 174 but to have been born either before or after; for this is the age of iron, and there is no respite, neither night nor day, from toil, trouble, and death. The gods will lay heavy burdens upon them, and yet even here there will be good mingled with the evil. Jove will take these men, too, when they shall be born hoary-headed. Fathers and children will not be like-minded with one another, nor hoſt with gueſt, nor comrade with comrade; nor will brother befriend brother as in days of yore. When parents grow old their own children will dishonour them, and they will speak harshly to them reproaching them without shame or fear of heaven's anger; they will take the law into their own hands and 187 refuse to repay the coſt of their bringing-up to their aged parents. They will sack one another's cities; a man will get no thanks for being honourable and true to his word, but men will honour rather insolence and evil-doing. Right and Reverence shall not be in their hands; bad men will slander good ones, and will swear to their lies. Grim envy— loud of tongue, delighting in mischief—shall be in the hearts of all poor mortals, while Right and Reverence, clad in robes of white, shall quit this earth and wing their way to Olympus to live among the gods, leaving sin and sorrow to dwell with mortals; and of wrong there shall be no redress.

And now I will speak to kings in a parable, though they 202 know it of their own selves. The hawk spoke to the nightingale as she bore it in her talons high up into the clouds. The poor thing was crying as the claws tore into her flesh and the hawk spoke maſterfully to her saying:

" My good soul what are you screaming for? I have got you and I am much ſtronger than you are. For all your pretty singing you will go where I choose to take you; and I shall eat you or let you go, just as I please. It is only fools who fight force greater than their own; they will get beaten and fare worse to boot." Thus spoke the hawk.

213 Therefore, Perses, hear right and bate your pride. A proud spirit is not for us poor mortals; it goes ill even with a strong man and will sink him when trouble comes upon him. Better take the way on the other side that leads towards righteousness; Right is stronger than Might in the long run, as even a fool may learn to his cost if he tries.

219 For the avenger of false oaths follows soon after a crooked judgement, and Right cries aloud as she is being haled about by those who have taken money for giving unrighteous judgements. She goes weeping about the city and all its guilds, cloaked in darkness and bringing evil on those who have thrust her out and given judgement unrighteously.

225 When men give righteous judgements alike to their own people and to strangers, their city thrives, and the people flourish therein. Peace and fecundity are over their land, and Jove will not visit them with any war. Famine and disaster come not within the gates of those who give righteous judgement, and they need busy themselves with nothing but their feasting. The earth yields them much substance; the tops of their oak trees are loaded with acorns and the trunks are full of bees and honey. Their sheep are heavy with wool; the women bear children who are like their fathers; they abound with good things of every kind, neither need they have anything to do with ships, for the land will yield them harvest.

238 But Jove the son of Saturn will punish those who are proud and high-handed; oftentimes has a whole city suffered for the falsehood and cruelty of one man. The son of Saturn will send down pestilence and famine from heaven and the people shall melt away before them; the women in such a city will be unfruitful, and their wealth shall waste, through the counsels of Jove; sometimes again, he will destroy their host or raze their walls, or bring disaster on their ships at sea.

The "Works and Days" of Hesiod

Therefore, O kings, consider this same righteousness 248 among yourselves; for the gods are near at hand among men to keep an eye on those who harass one another by giving corrupt judgement and fear not the wrath of heaven. There are thirty thousand guardians on the earth set by Jove to keep watch among mortal men; they go about everywhere among men clothed in darkness to take note of good and evil. Moreover there is Jove's virgin daughter, Justice, all glorious and fair to see among the gods that hold Olympus; when any one does her wrong by giving corrupt judgement, she takes a seat beside her father Jove the son of Saturn, and 259 tells him what wicked judges have been doing, that the people may suffer for the sins of their rulers in turning justice awry and harbouring evil in their hearts. Bear these things in mind, O kings with itching palms, and avoid such dealings altogether.

He who wrongs another does wrong also to himself and a wicked plot recoils on him who plots it. For the eye of Jove is all-seeing and all-observing; he sees, and believe me, he does not fail to note, what kind of justice obtains within this city. As things now are it would be better for me to be no longer honest, nor yet for my son, for it is ill to be honest if dishonesty fares better at the hands of justice. But I know that Jove the lord of thunder will not permit this.

Therefore, Perses, consider well; hear justice and refrain 274 from violence altogether, for the son of Saturn has established this law among mankind; he bade the fishes and beasts and winged fowl devour one another, for Right has no place among them; but he gave Right to man, and Right is far better. If a man will give himself to speaking words of truth, Jove will bless him; but if he forswears himself wilfully, bears false witness, and flouts right to his own irreparable hurt, his children after him will be worse than himself; but the offspring of a true man will be better even than he was.

I wish you well, foolish Perses, and therefore do I advise 286 you. Sin you may get by the armful; the way is smooth and it lies close at hand; whereas the immortal gods have set sweat in front of worth; the way is long, steep, and at the outset rugged; but when one has reached the top, what was hard at first will become easy.

293 He is best who thinks for himself and considers what will bring most peace, both now and in the long run. He again is well enough who will be guided by good advice; but good for nothing is he who will neither think nor let another guide him.

298 Be ever mindful, therefore, my good friend Perses, of what I now bid you. Work, that famine may shun you, and good honest Ceres with her fair crown upon her head may love you and fill your garners with store. If a man will not work there is no fit food for him but famine.

303 Hated by gods and men is he who is idle; he is like the stingless drones who do no work, and yet waste what the bees have toiled for. Choose rather to do all things decently and in order that your garners may be loaded with store in season. Work makes men wealthy and rich in flocks, and if you work you will be more in favour with gods and men, for both gods and men hate people who will not work.

311 There is no shame in work; the shame is in sloth. If you work you will soon find idle fellows growing jealous of you; for good repute and power go with wealth. You used to have understanding and should know that work is better if you will only turn your silly mind from hankering after other people's property and work for your living as I bid you.

317 Evil shame attends the needy—[shame which at once so greatly boons and greatly banes us [1]]. Poverty is shamefaced, and Wealth fearless. Gain earned righteously is far better than what is ill-gotten; for even though a man rob riches by force, or compass them with falsehood, as often happens when greed lures men from their better mind and meekness is overborne by might—even in such cases the gods soon

[1] This line is probably interpolated by a copyist from Il. xxiv, 44, 45.

The "Works and Days" of Hesiod

bring such a man down and ruin him, so that his wealth will have lasted but for a little season.

It is all one, whether a man wrongs a suppliant or a stranger or goes up into his brother's bed and lies secretly with his wife, in the way of infamy, or in his fool's heart wrongs orphan children, or if he use harsh words to a parent who is on the threshold of old age, Jove will be angry with him, and in the end will punish him heavily for his evildoing. Therefore, keep your foolish mind utterly from all such deeds.

Offer sacrifice to the immortal gods according to your means, purely and with a clean heart, and burn thigh bones of oxen in their honour. From time to time also propitiate them with drink offerings and incense, both when you go to rest and when the blessed light of day is breaking, that the gods may bear a gracious mind towards you and you may purchase another man's field rather than he yours.

Ask your friend to your feasts, but not your enemy; and ask most often him who lives nearest to you, for if there is something going wrong with you, your neighbours will not wait to gird themselves, but your kinsmen will wait. A bad neighbour is a great plague as a good one is a blessing. It is a creditable thing to have a good neighbour; a man will not lose his cow if he has a good neighbour.

Get just measure from your neighbour when you borrow from him and pay him back amply with the same measure or better if you can, that you may not go lacking should you have need hereafter. Avoid ill-gotten gains; ill-gotten gains are as bad as losses. Be kind to him who is kind to you, and attack him who would attack you. Give to him who will give to you, but not to him who will give you nothing. Unto him that gives shall be given, but no man gives to him who gives nothing. Giving is good and thieving bad, for its wages are death.

Whoso gives willingly, though he give much, is glad and takes pleasure in the giving, but if a man helps himself impudently to but a little, it freezes up the heart; for if you add little to little over and over again, and do so often, the little soon becomes much. The man who keeps on laying by will escape famine, and the store that he has in the house will not worry him; it is better at home than away from home; bear in mind that if it is at home you can get it if you want it, and you will not like wanting it and being unable to get it. Drink freely at the beginning of the cask and at the end of it, but sparingly in the middle; there is no use in sparing when the cask is nearly run out.

370 In dealing with a friend an agreement by word of mouth is enough, but even though he be your own brother see, with a laugh, that there be a witness. Men are ruined alike by trusting and not trusting.

See that no bedizened woman comes prying about your homestead and fooling you with her coaxing tongue. Who trusts women trusts knaves.

376 It is best there should be only one son to inherit his father's property, which will thus grow under his hands. If a man leaves more than one son he should die old.[1] But Jove sometimes vouchsafes great prosperity even to a large family, for the attention of a greater number gives a greater yield.

If, then, you would grow rich do as I shall now bid you and do, and do, and do.

383 Begin your harvest as soon as the Pleiades, children of Atlas, show themselves in the sky and your ploughing when they leave it. They are hidden forty days and forty nights, and year by year they reappear when men begin to sharpen their sickles.

This is the canon of all husbandry alike, whether a man's land is by the sea or in some wooded dell far from the blustering ocean. Strip to sow, strip to plough, and strip to reap, if you would gather the fruits of Ceres in their due season instead of having to beg presently at other people's houses and getting nothing by it—as you lately did to me; but I shall not give you anything more—not another measure. Work,

[1] That the sons may have a strong hand over them till the succession is fully settled. (See Mr. Banks's translation.)

The "Works and Days" of Hesiod

you silly Perses, such works as heaven has ordained for man, lest with your wife and children you have to go about begging piteously among your neighbours and they turn you a deaf ear. Perhaps you may get something for a time or two, but if you trouble them further you may say what you like but you will take nothing by it, and your words will have been all wasted. See to it, then, that you pay your debts and steer clear of hunger.

First of all, get yourself a house, a woman, an ox to plough with—I mean a woman whom you shall have bought not married. One who can mind your cattle. Provide your homestead with all needful implements, or you may have to go begging from some one else and he may refuse you, in which case you must go without it at the proper time and hence lose. Do not put things off till to-morrow or the day after; a man will not fill his barns if he keeps putting things off or doing them half-heartedly; it is care and attention that make things thrive. A man who keeps putting things off will be always in difficulties.

When the fiercest heat of the sun is over, and great Jove sends us his autumnal rains, men feel much lighter in body, for the star Sirius is but a short time over our heads by day, it is mainly by night that he is above the horizon. Wood felled at this season will be least worm-eaten, when the leaves are falling and the trees put out no more shoots. Be sure, therefore, and do all your wood-cutting at this season: for a mortar let the timber be three foot through, and for the pestle three cubits; you will find seven feet to be the most convenient length for an axle, but if you make it eight feet you can cut a beetle for breaking clods from off it. The wheel for a waggon should be three spans across, if the waggon be ten palms long. Bent timber is abundant but when you have hunted up hill and down dale for a piece that will do for the tree of a plough, and found one, bring it home, and let it be of ilex, for this is the stoutest wood for your oxen to plough with when some votary of Minerva[1] has fixed it to the stock

---

[1] I.e., a carpenter or a smith.

and nailed it on to the pole of the plough. But have two ploughs—one made all of a single piece of wood, and the other pieced together,[1] this will be much the best plan, so that if you break one you may yoke your oxen to the other. Bay or elm will make the soundest plough trees. Let the stock of your plough be oak, and the plough-tail of ilex, and get two oxen of some nine years old, for these will be of great strength, and having reached their full prime will be the best to work with, for they will not begin fighting in the middle of a furrow and break your plough, leaving their work half done. As for your plough-man let him be a man of forty, and let him have broken his fast on the half of a quartern loaf—a man who will mind his business and drive a straight furrow, with his heart in his work and not always looking about for some boon companion. Such a man will sow more equally and give you less ground to sow again than a younger man would. The young man will be always thinking about his companions.

Give heed to the sound of the crane when you shall hear its yearly cry sounding in the heavens—it is the signal for you to begin ploughing, and tells you that the rainy season is approaching—a sad hearing for one who has no oxen. At this season feed the cattle that are in your stalls; it is easy enough to say, "Please lend me a waggon and oxen," but it is also easy to refuse and to say, "I have work for my oxen at home." Then the conceited fellow thinks that he can build himself a waggon, but the poor fool does not know how. It takes a hundred pieces of wood to make a waggon, and all these must have been provided and kept in store.

As soon as ever the time for ploughing is at hand bestir yourself with your men to boot, and, wet or dry, plough during the season beginning very early in the morning that your land may teem with increase. Turn the ground over in the spring, and if you give it a second ploughing in summer it will not disappoint you, but sow your fallow land while the

[1] The πηκτὸν ἄροτρον, or plough made of more than one piece of wood is mentioned in Il. x, 353, and xiii, 703.

The "Works and Days" of Hesiod

soil is still light. Fallowing your land will keep the wolf from your door and stay your children from crying for bread.

As soon, moreover, as you grasp the handle of the plough, at the moment when you drive your goad into the backs of your oxen as they strain at the yoke-peg by means of the strap that goes round their necks,[1] pray to Jove of the world below and to chaste Ceres, that her ears of corn may be loaded with ripened grain. Let there be a little lad with a mattock who shall go behind the plough and cover the seed over so as to give more trouble to the birds [2]—for system is the best and want of system the worst of all things. Thus will the ears bow towards the ground with fullness if Jove gives you in the end good increase. Clear the spider's webs from your corn bins, for you will want them, and I doubt not will rejoice when you help yourself from the store that you have garnered; you will get through the winter in good case without having to look to other people, and will be more wanted than wanting.

If you plough in midwinter, you may reap at your leisure for you will take but little; dusty and out of humour you will bind what comes to your hand. You will be able to carry home your whole harvest in a basket, and your neighbours will not think much of you; but Jove is one thing at one time and another at another, and it is hard matter for mortal men to say what he would have. If on the other hand you have been late in ploughing, there is yet a chance that may save you—for if, when the cuckoo begins to delight mankind by singing everywhere in the oak trees, Jove rains for three days without ceasing neither deeper nor less deep than the print of your oxen's hoof, it will prove as well to have ploughed late as early. Take note of everything, and let neither the brightening of spring nor the times when rain is due escape you.

---

[1] Reading μεσάβῳ
[2] We have not been told yet about the sowing of the seed. The ploughman could hardly, I imagine, both plough and sow at the same time.

493   Pass by the seat in the smithy or the lounge in the sun in winter when the cold keeps men from getting to work, for at this season a hardworking man can do much to help things forward; see that the hardships of cruel winter and poverty do not get you in their grip so that your foot swell and your hand shrink. Men who have nothing to do, and whose poverty feeds but on vain hope are apt to harbour evil designs. When a man is sitting in a public lounge, in want and without means of subsistence, the hopes that he will cherish are not good ones. Remind your servants, therefore, while it is yet midsummer, that they should build themselves huts, for it will not be always summer.

  Shun the month Lenaeon, for its days are evil, all of them, and bad for stock; avoid the cruel hoar frosts also which vex the earth when the North wind comes sweeping over the sea from Thrace, the home of horses, till land and forest are in an uproar. Many a lofty oak and sturdy pine does it lay low in the mountain glens, and the vast forest bellows with the sound of its going.

512   The wild beasts shiver and shake with their tails between their legs. Their skin is thick with fur, but the cold wind searches through their shaggy covering; it will pierce the hide of an ox, or the hairy skin of a goat; but the North wind cannot get through a sheep's fleece, for this has had a year to grow in. It will bend an old man double, but it will not touch the tender skin of a maiden who as yet knows naught of love, for she will stay at home in doors with her mother; there she will wash her fair skin, anoint herself with oil, and lie all night in shelter, while the octopus has to live in a house that has no fire, in squalor and gnawing at its own feet for hunger. The sun gives it no light whereby it may pounce out from its hole and feed, for the sun then visits the land and peoples of the dark men, and shines but little upon the

528 Panhellenes. Then do the denizens of the forest, horned and unhorned, grind their teeth as they go about in the thick woods with no other thought than how they may find shelter in warm lairs or rocky caves. They are feeble as an

The "Works and Days" of Hesiod

old man who goes about with a stick, with his back half broken and his eyes fixed upon the ground; that is how they go about, trying to keep out of the snow storm.

Then cover your body well up, as I bid you, with a soft cloak and a shirt that goes down to your heels; let the stuff have much warp and little woof, and wear it that the hairs on your body may bide in peace and not stand up all over you. About your feet bind sandals made of the skin of a butchered ox, let them fit you, and let them be lined with felt. When the winter's cold is at hand, stitch some skins of first-born kids together with threads of ox-hide, that you may have a cloak to your back if it comes on to rain. Have a well-made hat, moreover, to keep your ears dry; for when the wind is North the mornings are bitterly cold; and in the mornings also there comes a mist out of heaven that spreads over rich men's lands and makes the corn grow. This mist has sucked up its moisture from the rivers, and has then been carried by winds high into the air; sometimes it comes down in rain towards evening, and at other times it gets carried away as cloud before the blasts of Thracian Boreas. Finish your work and get home in good time or some black cloud will gather over your head and drench you to the skin; so get out of its way, for this winter month is the hardest of all, being good for neither man nor beast. At this season put your oxen on half rations, but give your men more than their usual allowance, for the length of the nights will help you.[1] Follow this system up to the end of the year, and then divide the rations equally between day and night till Earth our common mother has again brought us her varied fruits.

When Jove shall have completed sixty winter's days from the date of the winter solstice, the star Arcturus leaves the streams of Ocean and begins to show brightly in the twilight. Next after him the swallow, plaintive daughter of Pandion, will rise and show her light to mortals, at the very beginning

---

[1] The sequitur is not obvious—unless the injunction to feed the men servants better be taken as merely parenthetic.

of spring. Begin pruning your vines before she comes, for this will be the best time.

571 When the snail quits the earth and gets up into the plants flying before the Pleiades—this will be no season for hoeing vines: you should then be sharpening your sickles and bid your servants bestir themselves. Let there be no sitting in the shade nor lying a-bed in the morning during harvest time, when the sun is scorching hot; you should then be busy getting your harvest in, and should rise at dawn if you would have plenty, for the third part of the day's work should be got through in the small hours of the morning, for dawn speeds a man on his way and in his work; many a man does she start on a journey, and on the neck of many an ox does she set the yoke.

582 When the artichoke is in blossom and the cicala in her leafy seat pours her shrill song from under her wings in the busy time of summer, then are goats fattest, and wine best; women also are then most wanton, and men most languid, for Sirius scorches them up both brain and body, and their skin is parched with his great heat; at that season seek the shadow of some rock, a flask of Biblian wine, a cake made with the finest flour, milk of goats that are off their milk, the flesh of a heifer that has not been stalled and has not yet calved, or of firstling kids; sit in the shade and drink your wine when you have had enough to eat with your face turned towards the brisk Zephyr. Mix your wine three parts water from some sparkling ever-gushing spring, and let the fourth part be wine.

597 As soon as Orion begins to show tell your servants to begin threshing the goodly gift of Ceres in some breezy place, and on a well-rounded threshing-floor; measure the 600 corn as you put it into your bins. Then when you have gathered your harvest all well and duly within your gates, you should get a bailiff who is without family, and I would have you look out for a serving man who has no children; a female servant with a child at the breast is troublesome; and you should keep a dog—do not grudge him his food—lest

The "Works and Days" of Hesiod

some of those gentry who sleep by day should rob you. Have a store also of hay and of litter that the supply for your oxen and mules may last you the season through. Then when you have done all this bid your servants rest and unyoke your oxen.

When Orion and Sirius shall have reached mid-heaven and Arcturus shall rise with Dawn, then, O Perses, gather your grapes and bring them home. Expose the cask into which you have put the juice of your grapes to the sun for ten days and ten nights and then keep it five days under cover—after which draw the gift of joyous Bacchus off into jars. When the Pleiades and the Hyades and great Orion set, then begin to think about ploughing in due season; and may the year be a good one over the land.

If you are seized with a desire to undertake hazardous voyages, bear in mind that when the Pleiades sink into the vast sea in their flight from mighty Orion, gales of wind are apt to blow from every quarter. Do not keep your ships afloat at that season, but rather attend to your land as I have explained to you. Draw your vessel on to the beach and build stones all round her to break the force of the rainy winds; but take the plug out of her bottom that Jove's rain may not rot her. Stow all the ship's gearing in your house, fold up her sails all orderly, and hang your rudder in the chimney corner; when the right time comes for you to sail draw your ship into the water, and freight her with a suitable cargo that you may return with a profit, as my father and yours did, you silly Perses—sailing the seas to make himself an honest living. He it was who came here with his ship after a long voyage from Cumae in Aeolia, flying not plenty, nor wealth, nor comfort, but the sheer poverty with which Jove is apt to afflict people; and he settled in Ascra, a wretched village near Helicon, bitterly cold in winter, scorchingly hot in summer, and pleasant at no season.

As for you, Perses, attend to all your works in their due order, and especially to those connected with sea-faring. Say what you like in praise of a small ship, but stow your merchandise in a large one—for the larger your freight the larger also will your profit be, if the winds do not blow too hard. Whenever you turn your silly mind towards merchandise, and wish to get out of debt and to avoid the pangs of hunger, I will tell you all about the roaring sea, though I am not learned in the matter either of ships or navigation; indeed, I have never been on the sea at all save once when I went over to Euboea from Aulis, where the Achaeans waited a whole winter when they were getting their forces together from all Hellas to make war on Troy, the land of fair women. I crossed from Aulis to the games in honour of mighty Amphidamas, and to Chalcis, for his sons had made it known that there would be many prizes; and I was awarded a tripod with two handles as a prize for a hymn. I made an offering of this tripod to the Muses of Mt. Helicon, at the place where they first inspired me. This is all the experience of ships that I have ever had, but I can tell you Jove's mind concerning them, for the muses have endowed me with an infinite command of song.

663 The best time for making a voyage is during the fifty days that follow upon the solstice when summer is drawing to a close. You will not wreck your ship at that season, nor will the sea drown your men, unless Neptune lord of the earthquake sets himself to wreck you, or Jove king of the immortals compasses your destruction, for the issues of good or evil are in their hands. At that season the winds are steady and the sea safe; you can therefore draw your ship into the water in confidence, relying upon the winds, and get your cargo duly within her, but come home again as fast as you can; do not wait for the new wine, nor for the autumn rain and the beginning of winter with the great gales that the South wind raises when it begins to blow after heavy rain in autumn and makes the sea dangerous.

678 There is also a time in spring when men make voyages; as soon as the buds begin to show on the twigs of a fig tree about as large as the print of a crow's foot the sea is fit for sailing, but a voyage at this season is dangerous—I do not

advise it, I do not approve of it; for the voyage will be a snatched one, and you will hardly escape trouble of some sort. Nevertheless men are foolish enough to go voyages even then, for money is the life and soul of us poor mortals, but drowning is a horrible death. I bid you, therefore, think well over all that I have been saying to you. And again, do not put all your substance on to a single ship, leave the greater part behind, and put the smaller half on board. It is a sad thing for a man to meet with a mishap on the high seas; [and it is a sad thing if you have overloaded your waggon so that the axle breaks and your load is damaged][1] use moderation in all things, and let everything be done in its due season.

Marry when you are of an age to do so, that is to say when you are not far short of thirty nor much beyond it. That is the right age at which to marry. Let the woman have been full grown four years, and get married in the fifth. Marry a maid, that you may get her into good ways, give the preference to one who lives near you,[2] and look well about you, or your neighbours will chuckle over your marriage. A good wife is the best thing a man can have; and a bad one—one who is always fishing for invitations to dinner—is the worst. No matter how good a man may be she will singe him without even having a torch to set him alight with, and she will age him before his time.

Be sure and shun heaven's anger. Do not put your friend on a level with your brother, but if you do, see that you do him no injury. Do not tell lies merely for the sake of talking; if your friend without provocation says or does anything that you do not like, give him back twice as good as he gave; if after this he would be friends with you and make amends, accept it. Men who are always changing their friends are never any good. Do not look one thing and think another.

---

[1] The lines enclosed in square brackets are suspected. It is possible that they were interpolated by Perses.
[2] The Italians have a proverb: "Chi lontano va ammogliare sarà ingannato o verrà ingannare."

715   Do not let people say that you have many guests, nor yet that you have none; nor again that you keep bad company, nor speak ill of honest people. Never be so cruel as to reproach a man with his poverty, for poverty is as the gods who live for ever may choose to send it. There is no greater treasure than that of being a man of few words, and temperate language is the truest kind of eloquence. If you speak evil you will hear worse back again. Do not be disagreeable when you go to a dinner where the guests have paid so much a head all round. Such dinners are at once the most pleasant and the least expensive.[1] Never make a drink-offering in the morning to Jove nor to any other of the gods with unwashen hands; they will not listen to you and will spurn your prayers if you do.

727   Do not stand upright and make water towards the sun; and from the time he sets until he rises again be sure you never make water as you go along, without stopping, neither if you are on a road or off one, nor bare yourself when you pass water at all—for the nights belong to the blessed gods; a god-fearing and well-disposed person will pass his water squatting or he will go up against the wall of the yard. Do not expose your private parts near the fire
735 indoors when you are defiled with semen—avoid this. And do not get children when you have just come from a funeral, but rather on your return from a feast in honour of the gods.

  Never cross a river on foot without first looking upon the fair stream and praying, and also washing your hands in the water. If a man crosses a river sinfully and with unwashen hands, the gods will be angry with him and punish him.

  Do not pare your nails at a feast in honour of the gods.[2]

744   Never when men are drinking, place the jug from which the cup-bearer fills the guests' cups above the mixing bowl—this is a particularly unlucky thing to do. When you are

---

[1] Or perhaps the meaning is: "You will gain most and lose least by making yourself agreeable."

[2] Literally "do not cut the dead from the quick on your five-branched [limb]."

332

The "Works and Days" of Hesiod

building a house do not leave it unfinished lest the cawing crow should settle on it and crow there. Neither wash nor eat from vessels that have not yet been used for sacrifice, for this, too, is unlucky.

When a child is twelve years old do not let him be idle, 750 this is not well, for it will make him unmanly—nor yet when he is only twelve months, the one is as bad as the other. Never let a man wash himself in a woman's bath; the penalty for this is one that will last for some time. If you chance to see sacrifices in the act of being burned, do not mock at rites that you cannot understand, or heaven will be angry with you.

Never make water into the channel of a flowing stream, 757 nor into its source; be specially careful to avoid this; nor yet void your ordure into it, for this is by no means well. Do as I have told you, and avoid getting a bad name. Bad repute is a burden light to lift, but hard either to carry or to put down. When everybody says a thing one can never quite get rid of it, for Rumour, too, is among the gods.

Note well the days that Jove vouchsafes us, and tell your 765 servants that the thirtieth day of the month is the best for surveying work and for dealing out rations—it being the day on which the people hold their court of justice.

The following are the days more especially appointed by 769 the will of Jove: first of all, there is the first of the month and the fourth, and the seventh, which is a holy day, for it is the birthday of Apollo, the son of Leto. The eighth and ninth, as we get on into the month, are two good days for all kinds of work; so are the eleventh and twelfth, both of them; the first for shearing sheep and cutting ripe corn, but the twelfth is much better than the eleventh, for on that day the spider hangs in the air and spins her web on a long summer's day, and the ant heaps up her hoard. On this day a woman should set up her loom and begin work.

Never sow on the thirteenth day of the first half of the 780 month, but for setting plants this is the best. The sixteenth day is very unfavourable for plants, but it is a good day for a man to be born on; it is not, however, a good day for a woman to be either born or married on. Nor again is the sixth of the month a good day for a girl to be born on, but it is favourable for cutting kids or lambs, and putting up a fold for your sheep. It is a good day for a man to be born on, and it likes sarcasm, lies, deceitful words, and soft sayings spoken in secret.

790 Cut boars and bulls on the eighth day of the month, and mules on the twelfth. On the great twentieth, that is to say on the longest day, beget for yourself a son who shall prove wise—for if begotten on that day he will be of excellent judgement. The tenth also is a good day for a boy to be born on, and the fourteenth for a girl. On this day pat your sheep, cattle, dog, and mules with your hand so as to tame them. Be sure and avoid all worries on the fourth day whether of the second half of the month, or of the first,[1] for it is a very perfect day.

800 On the fourth day of the month marry and bring your wife home after having consulted the omens that are most favourable for this matter. But avoid the fifths of all the months; these days are very bad ones, for on that day they say that the Erinyes attended at the birth of Orcus,[2] who was born of strife to be the bane of those who perjure themselves. On the seventeenth of the month let men watch well and throw the corn on to the threshing floor. Let the woodcutter cut wood for furniture, and much timber suitable for shipbuilding.[3] Begin shipbuilding on the fourth day.

810 The middle ninth day of a month[4] gets better towards twilight, but the first ninth is an altogether unexceptionable day; it is good either for planting or for being born on, whether for boy or girl and it is not unlucky for anything at all.

---

[1] *I.e.*, either on the nineteenth day of a month, or on the fourth day. Or else on the twenty-fourth and fourth days, according as the month is here held to consist of three decades, or two periods of fifteen days.
[2] Reading ΓΕΙΝΟΜΕΝΟΝ.   [3] Reading ἄρμενα.
[4] *I.e.*, the nineteenth.

The "Works and Days" of Hesiod

Few people know that the twenty-ninth day is the best 814 for broaching a cask, yoking oxen, mules, or horses, and also for launching a ship, but it has a reputation for untruthfulness. Broach a cask on the fourth day of a month, but the best day of all is the fourteenth. Few, again, know that the twenty-fourth day of the month is best in the morning, but grows worse towards evening.

The foregoing are the days which are of great importance 822 to mankind; those that lie between them are harmless and bring neither good nor ill. One man praises one day and another another, but few know anything certain about them. A day sometimes proves to be a stepmother, and sometimes a mother; blest indeed is he who knows all these things and heeds them, discerning omens and avoiding transgressions so as to be guiltless in the eye of heaven.